To the past and future children

of the movement.

CLIK
CLIK
CLIK CLIK

CLIK
CLIK
CLIK
CLIK

BIRMINGHAM, ALABAMA.

now, i just, i dunno--

you nervous, Carole?

maybe a bit-- it's my first time on clarinet

playing at the game tomorrow--

LADIES

i'm just worried about messin' up in front of all those people--

like Jerry?

hey, I'm nervous too--

BOOM!

--today's my first day as USHER--

4

Y'ALL BETTER HURRY ALONG, NOW.

SUNDAY SCHOOL'S NEARLY OVER, AND THE MAIN SERVICE'LL BE STARTIN' SOON.

yes, ma'am.

CLIK
CLIK
CLIK
CLIK
CLIK

hee hee

shh!

CLIK
CLIK CLIK TIK
CLIK TIK

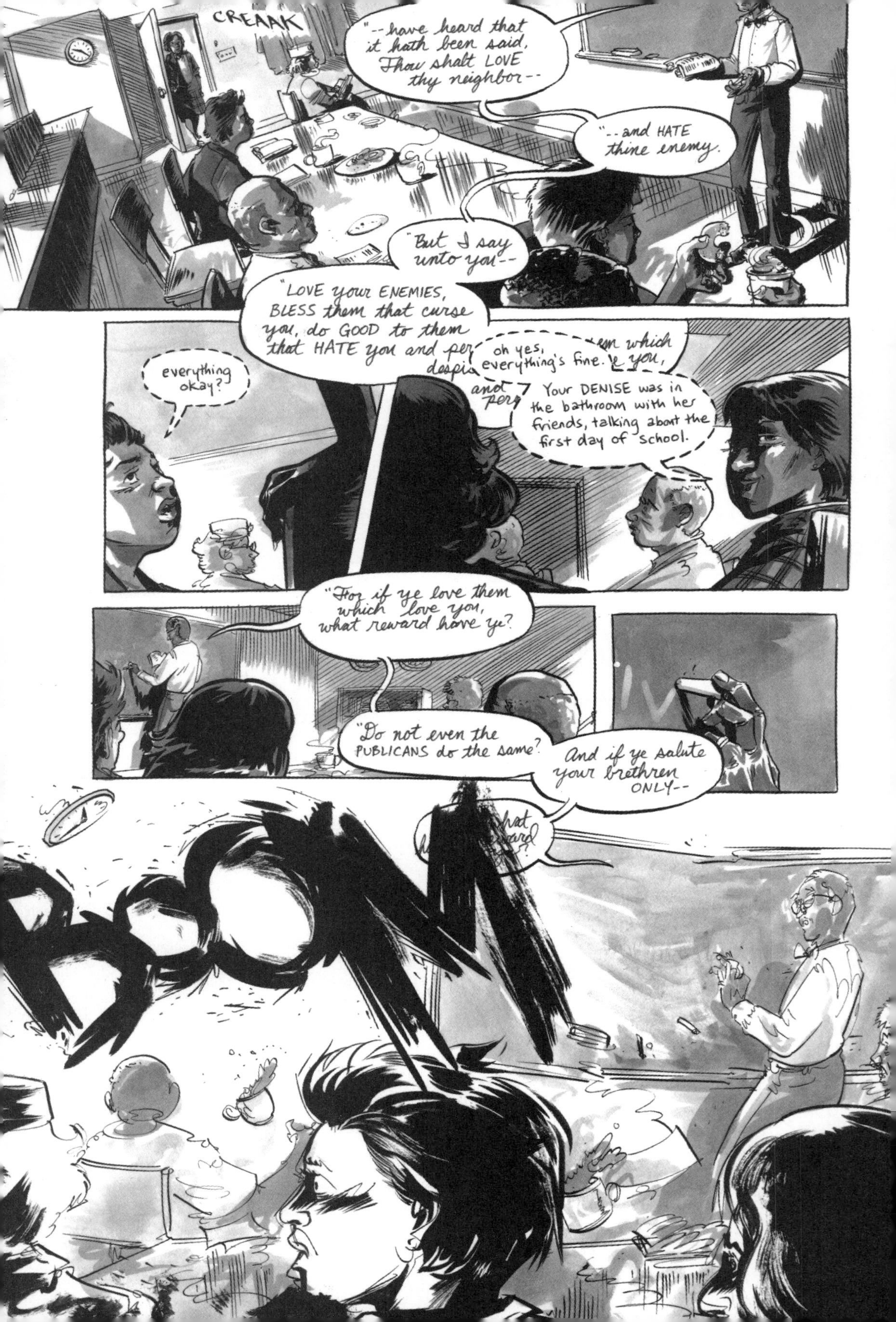
CREAAK
"--have heard that it hath been said, Thou shalt LOVE thy neighbor--
"--and HATE thine enemy.
"But I say unto you--
"LOVE your ENEMIES, BLESS them that curse you, do GOOD to them that HATE you and per
everything okay?
oh yes, everything's fine.
Your DENISE was in the bathroom with her friends, talking about the first day of school.
"For if ye love them which love you, what reward have ye?
"Do not even the PUBLICANS do the same?
And if ye salute your brethren ONLY--

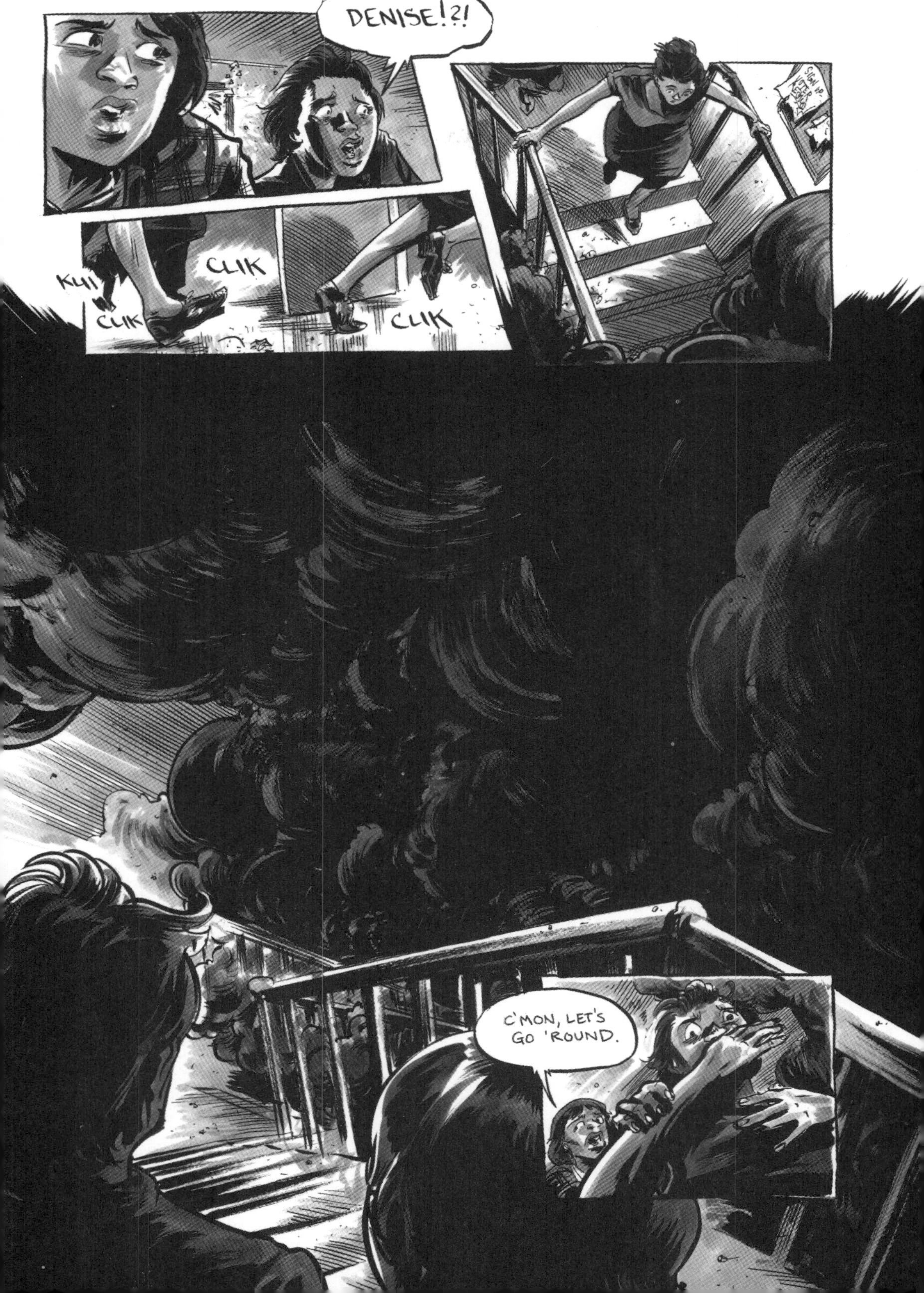
DENISE!?!
CLIK
CLIK
CLIK
C'MON, LET'S GO 'ROUND.

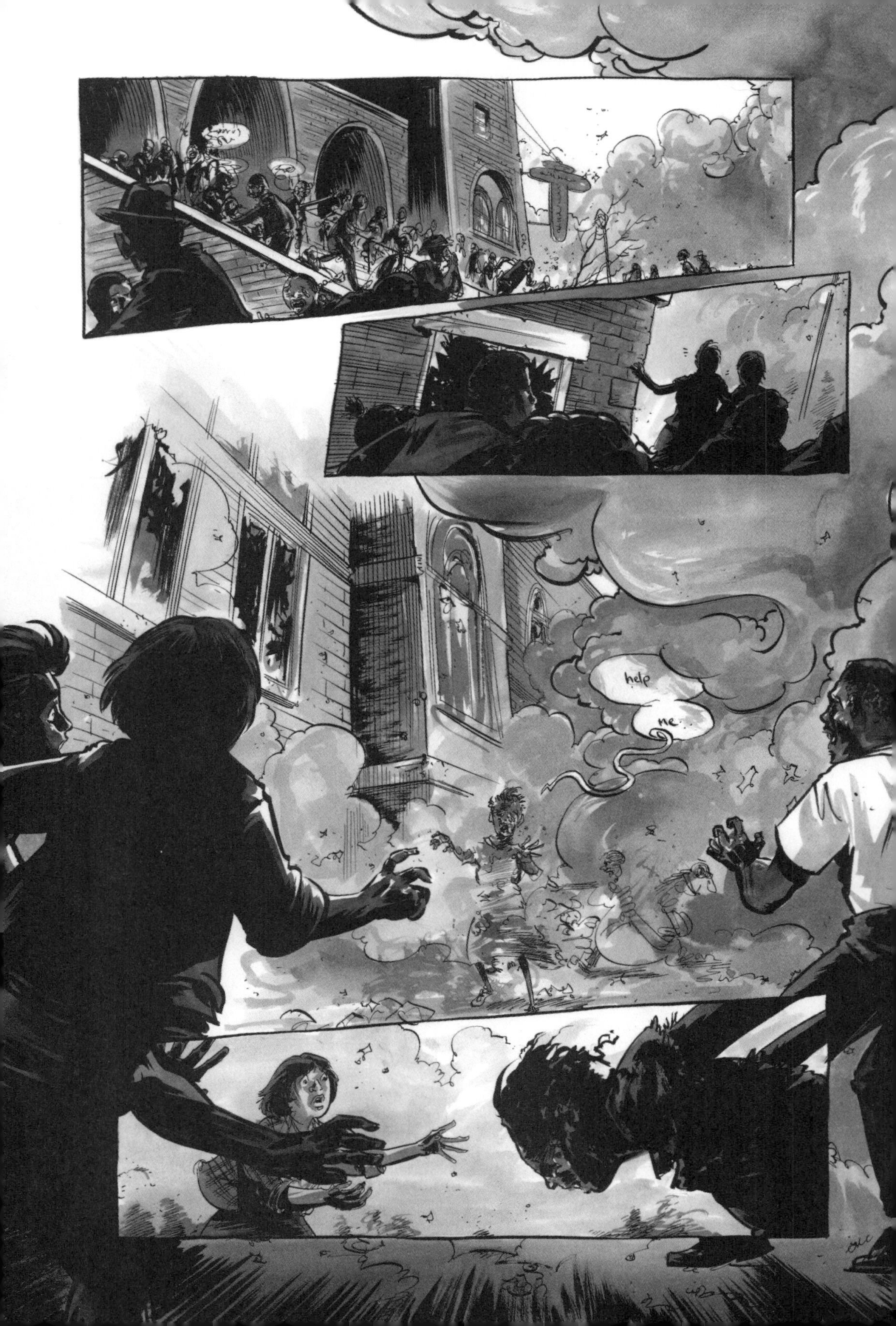
help
me

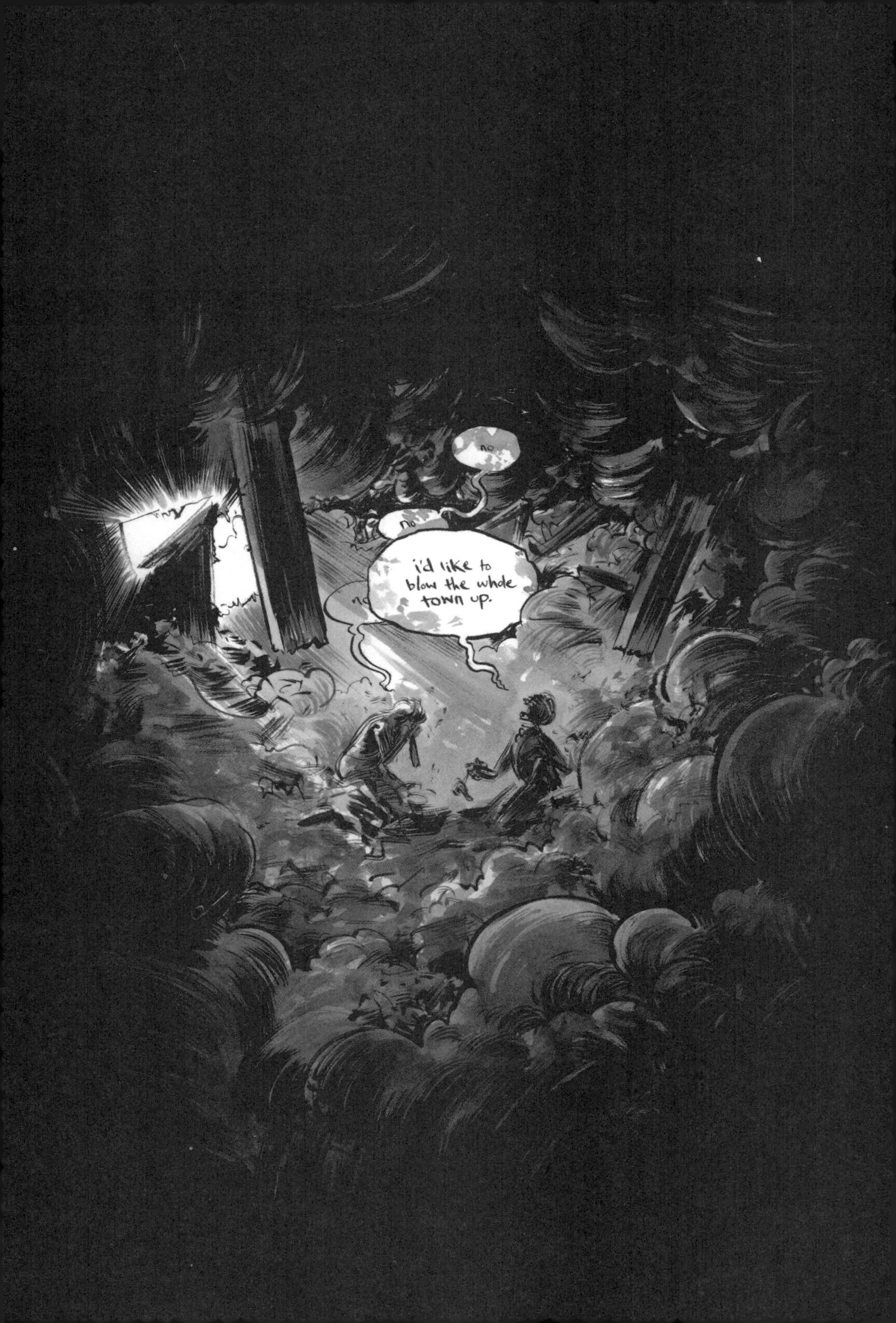

no
no
no
i'd like to blow the whole town up.

PIKE COUNTY, ALABAMA.

♪ He breaks the power of cancell'd sin, ♪ He sets the prisoner free; ♪ His blood can make the foulest

RRRRIIIIIII''NNNGGGGG

clear ...WE INTERRUPT THIS BROADCAST FOR A BREAKING NEWS BULLETIN! THERE HAS BEEN A BOMBING AT THE SIXTEENTH STREET BAPTIST CHURCH IN BIRMINGHAM--

RRRRIIIINNNNG

RRIIIIIINNGG

HELLO?

--Yes, just a minute.

HELLO!?

LEWIS?! IT'S FORMAN-- DID YOU HEAR?!

YES, JUST NOW.

AT THIS TIME WE HAVE NO INFORMATIO ABOUT CASUALTIES...

YOU NEED TO GET TO BIRMINGHAM RIGHT AWAY.

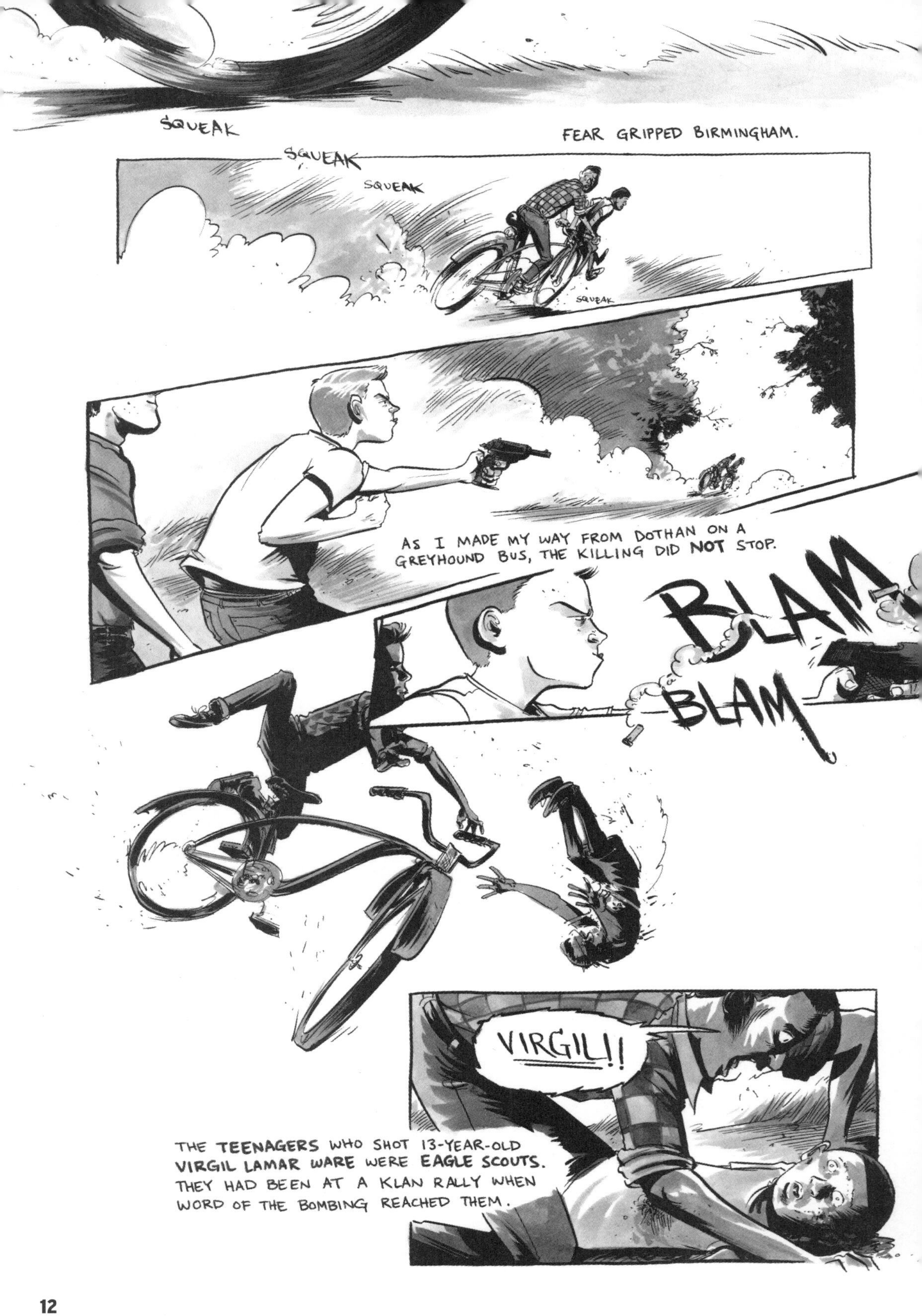
SQUEAK
FEAR GRIPPED BIRMINGHAM.
SQUEAK
SQUEAK
SQUEAK
AS I MADE MY WAY FROM DOTHAN ON A GREYHOUND BUS, THE KILLING DID **NOT** STOP.
BLAM
BLAM
VIRGIL!!
THE **TEENAGERS** WHO SHOT 13-YEAR-OLD **VIRGIL LAMAR WARE** WERE **EAGLE SCOUTS**. THEY HAD BEEN AT A KLAN RALLY WHEN WORD OF THE BOMBING REACHED THEM.

OTHER WHITE TEENAGERS DROVE THROUGH TOWN **CELEBRATING** THE DEATHS OF THOSE FOUR LITTLE GIRLS.

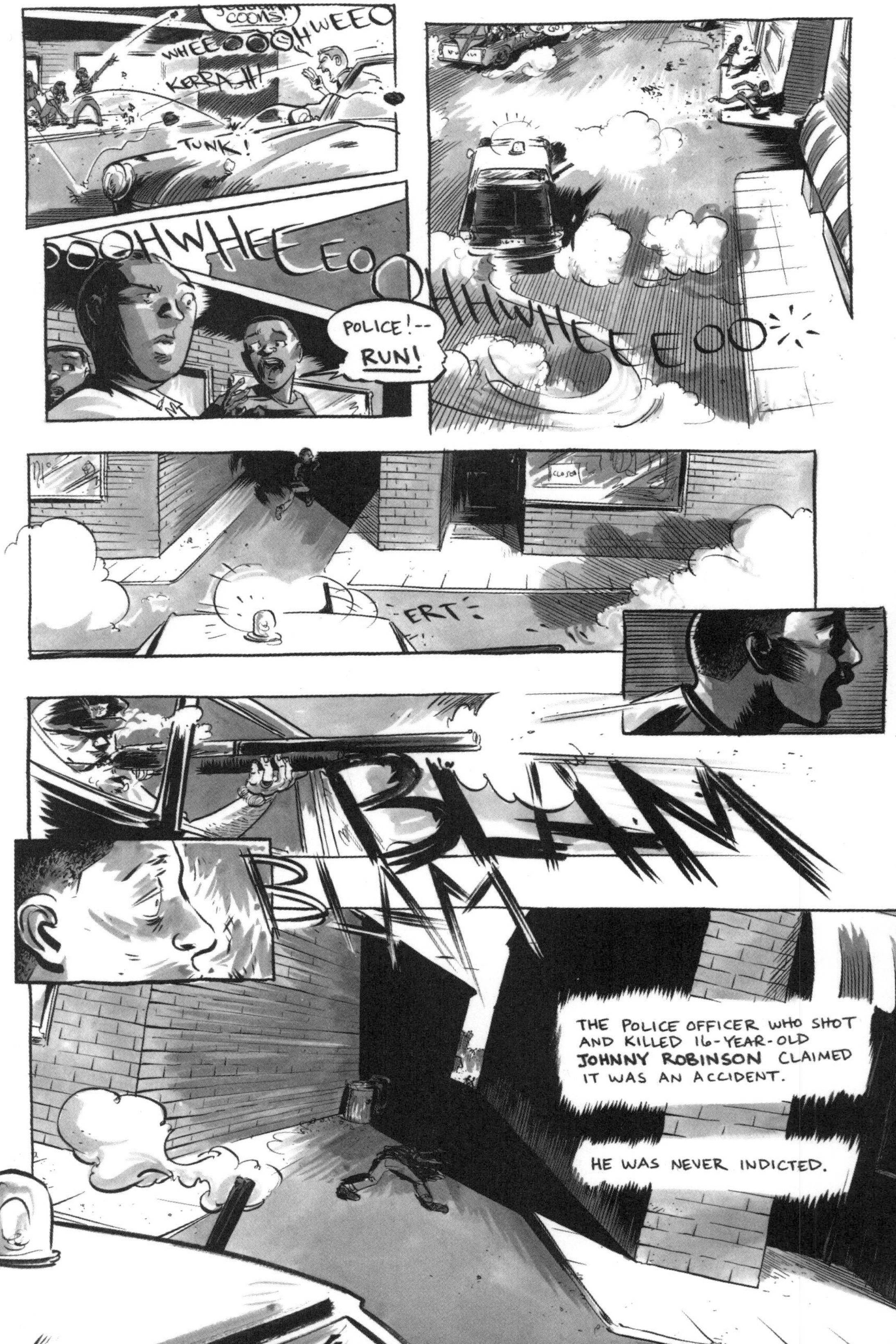
COONS!
WHEEOOOOHWEEO
KERRASH!
TUNK!
OOOHWHEEEOOHHWHEEEOO
POLICE!-- RUN!
ERT
BLAM
BLAM
THE POLICE OFFICER WHO SHOT AND KILLED 16-YEAR-OLD JOHNNY ROBINSON CLAIMED IT WAS AN ACCIDENT.
HE WAS NEVER INDICTED.

I ARRIVED AT THE SAME BIRMINGHAM BUS TERMINAL WHERE WE HAD SPENT THE NIGHT UNDER SIEGE DURING THE **FREEDOM RIDE.**

JULIAN BOND, SNCC'S COMMUNICATIONS DIRECTOR, HAD ALREADY ARRIVED FROM ATLANTA,

AND WE WENT TO THE CHURCH TOGETHER.

KRUNCH

16TH STREET BAPTIST CHURCH WAS A HEADQUARTERS OF THE MOVEMENT IN BIRMINGHAM...

BUT THIS SUNDAY WAS ITS ANNUAL "YOUTH DAY," AND IT HAD BEEN PACKED WITH YOUNG PEOPLE.

ONCE THE SMOKE CLEARED, TWENTY-ONE CHILDREN LAY INJURED.

FOUR YOUNG GIRLS-- ADDIE MAE COLLINS, CAROLE ROBERTSON, CYNTHIA WESLEY, AND DENISE McNAIR--

WERE DEAD.

FOUR LITTLE CHILDREN MURDERED IN THE HOUSE OF THE LORD--

HOW COULD OUR QUEST FOR HUMAN DIGNITY SPAWN SUCH EVIL?

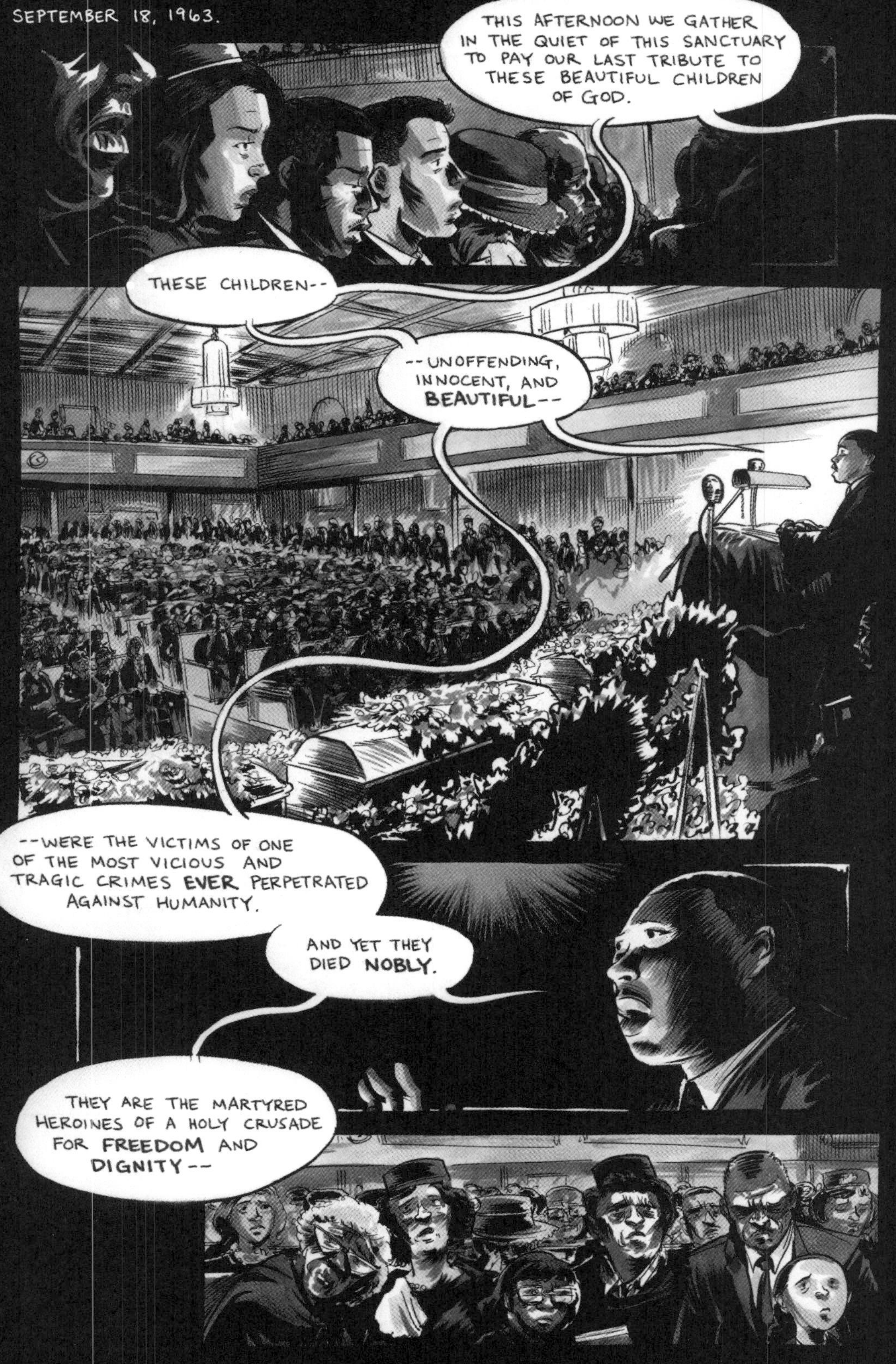
SEPTEMBER 18, 1963.
THIS AFTERNOON WE GATHER IN THE QUIET OF THIS SANCTUARY TO PAY OUR LAST TRIBUTE TO THESE BEAUTIFUL CHILDREN OF GOD.
THESE CHILDREN--
--UNOFFENDING, INNOCENT, AND BEAUTIFUL--
--WERE THE VICTIMS OF ONE OF THE MOST VICIOUS AND TRAGIC CRIMES EVER PERPETRATED AGAINST HUMANITY.
AND YET THEY DIED NOBLY.
THEY ARE THE MARTYRED HEROINES OF A HOLY CRUSADE FOR FREEDOM AND DIGNITY--

--AND SO THIS AFTERNOON, IN A REAL SENSE THEY HAVE SOMETHING TO SAY TO EACH OF US IN THEIR DEATHS.

THEY SAY TO US THAT WE MUST BE CONCERNED NOT MERELY ABOUT **WHO** MURDERED THEM, BUT ABOUT THE **SYSTEM**, THE WAY OF LIFE, THE PHILOSOPHY WHICH PRODUCED THE MURDERERS.

WE ALL KNEW WHAT DR. KING MEANT. GOVERNOR **GEORGE WALLACE** HAD STARTED HIS TERM DECLARING "**SEGREGATION FOREVER**," AND TWO WEEKS BEFORE THE BOMBING, HE WAS QUOTED IN THE PAPER SAYING, "WHAT THIS COUNTRY NEEDS IS A FEW FIRST-CLASS **FUNERALS**."

UNLESS WE COULD GIVE **ALL** ITS CITIZENS A POLITICAL VOICE, ALABAMA WOULD CONTINUE TO ELECT PEOPLE LIKE WALLACE.

DIANE NASH AND I MET WITH DR. KING TO PRESENT A **PLAN**.

SHE AND JAMES BEVEL WERE NOW MARRIED AND RAISING A LITTLE GIRL OF THEIR OWN. NEWS OF THE BOMBING HAD SHAKEN THEM UP SO BADLY THAT SHE CAME TO BIRMINGHAM TO PROPOSE AN ALL-OUT **REVOLUTION**.

DR. KING, WHEN CHILDREN ARE **MURDERED**...

WE CAN TELL PEOPLE NOT TO FIGHT **ONLY** IF WE OFFER THEM A WAY BY WHICH **JUSTICE** CAN BE SERVED WITHOUT VIOLENCE.

SOME IN **SCLC** HAD TALKED ABOUT MARCHING TO MONTGOMERY TO PLACE A FUNERAL WREATH ON THE ALABAMA STATE HOUSE,

BUT DIANE'S PLAN WENT **FAR** BEYOND.

HER "**ACTION IN MONTGOMERY**" WOULD RECRUIT A NONVIOLENT "ARMY" OF THOUSANDS OF YOUNG PEOPLE TO POUR INTO THE CAPITAL CITY--

CUTTING OFF ROADS, TRAINS, AIRPORTS, PHONE LINES, ELECTRICITY, AND LOCAL BUSINESSES UNTIL THE STATE GOVERNMENT WAS COMPLETELY **SHUT DOWN**.

THERE WERE TWO OBJECTIVES:

FORCE **GOVERNOR WALLACE** OUT OF OFFICE,

AND ALLOW **EVERY** ADULT IN ALABAMA TO **VOTE**.

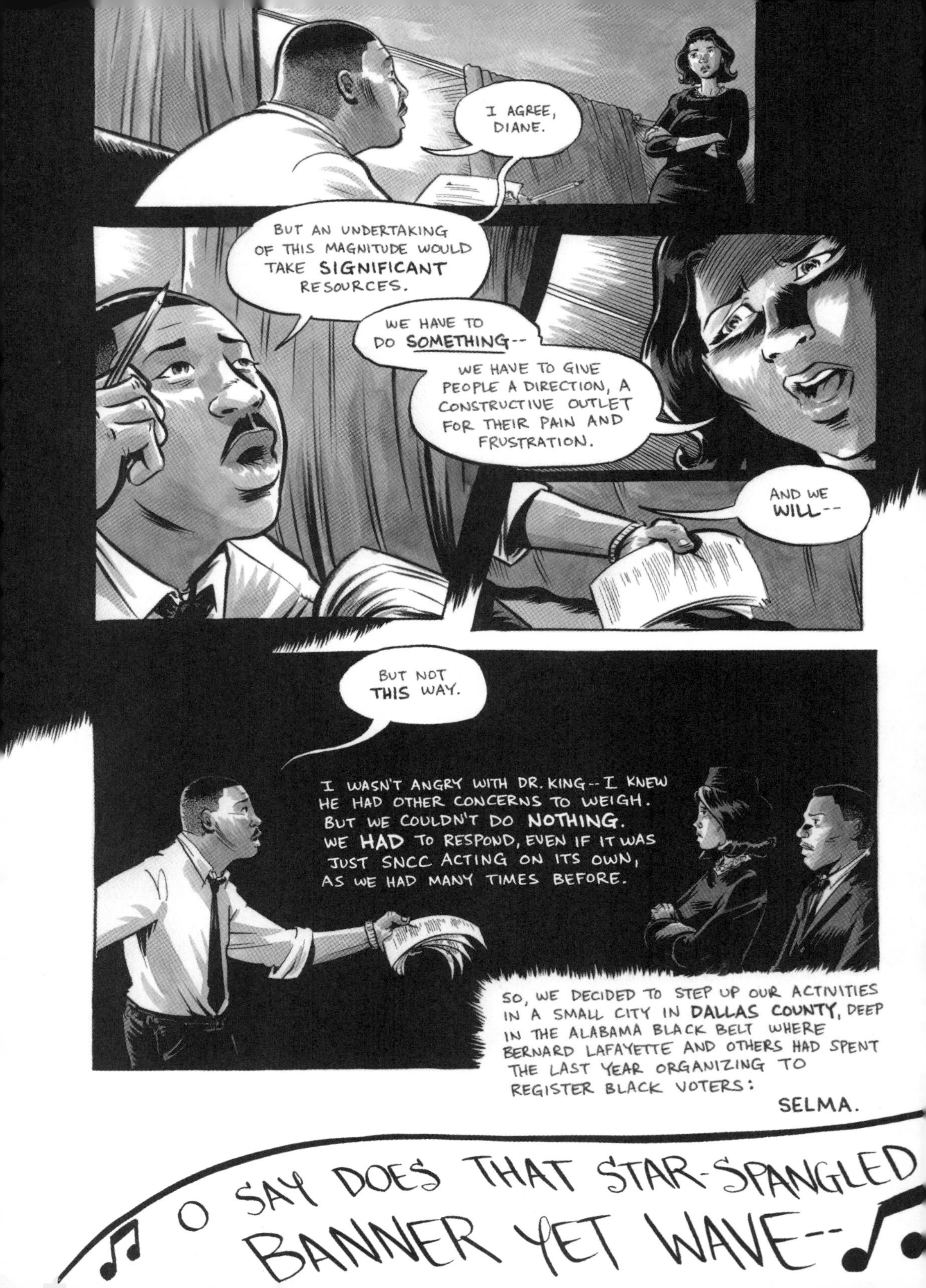
I AGREE, DIANE.
BUT AN UNDERTAKING OF THIS MAGNITUDE WOULD TAKE SIGNIFICANT RESOURCES.
WE HAVE TO DO SOMETHING--
WE HAVE TO GIVE PEOPLE A DIRECTION, A CONSTRUCTIVE OUTLET FOR THEIR PAIN AND FRUSTRATION.
AND WE WILL--
BUT NOT THIS WAY.
I WASN'T ANGRY WITH DR. KING--I KNEW HE HAD OTHER CONCERNS TO WEIGH. BUT WE COULDN'T DO NOTHING. WE HAD TO RESPOND, EVEN IF IT WAS JUST SNCC ACTING ON ITS OWN, AS WE HAD MANY TIMES BEFORE.
SO, WE DECIDED TO STEP UP OUR ACTIVITIES IN A SMALL CITY IN DALLAS COUNTY, DEEP IN THE ALABAMA BLACK BELT WHERE BERNARD LAFAYETTE AND OTHERS HAD SPENT THE LAST YEAR ORGANIZING TO REGISTER BLACK VOTERS:
SELMA.
O SAY DOES THAT STAR-SPANGLED BANNER YET WAVE--

JANUARY 20, 2009.

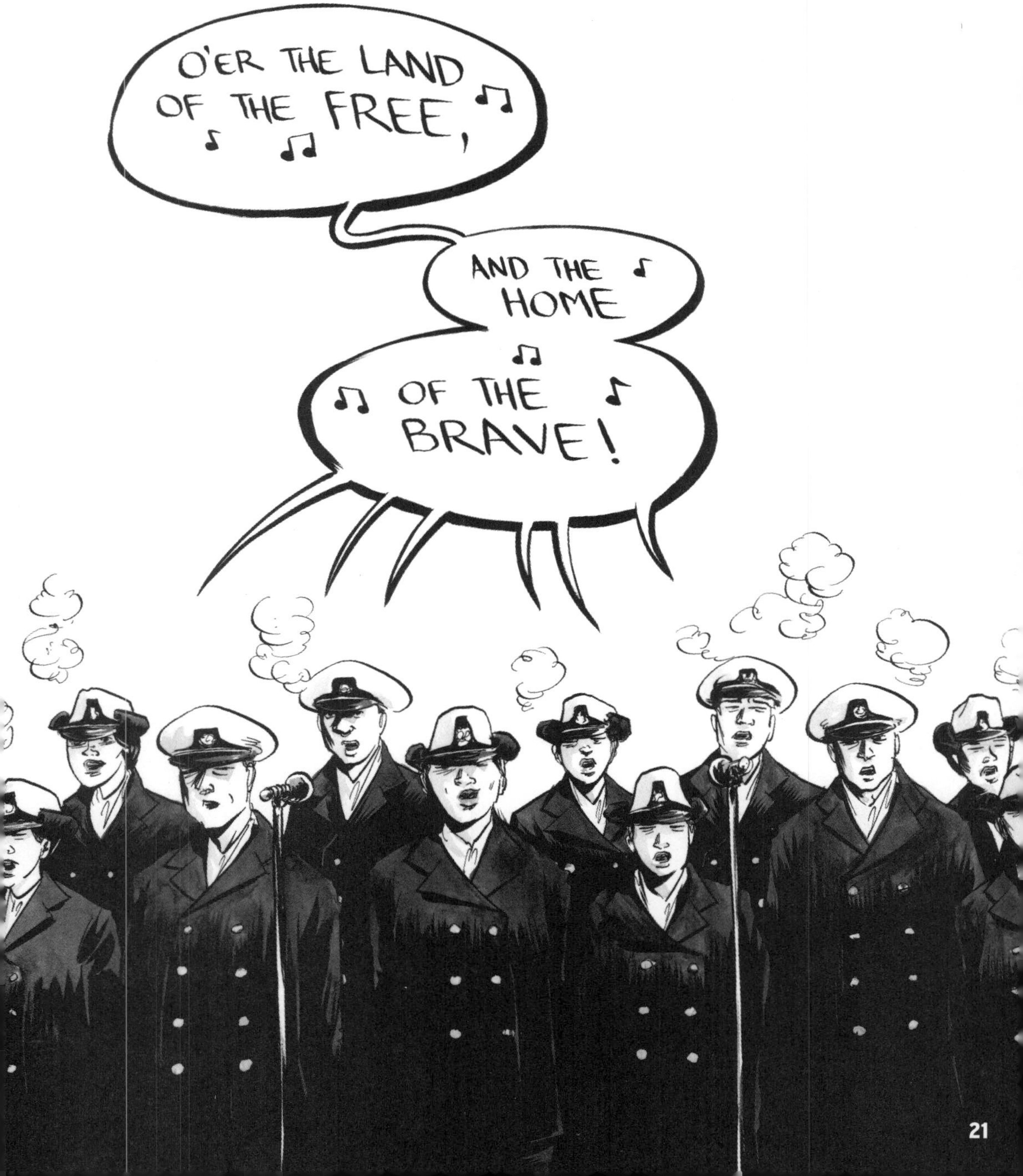
O'ER THE LAND OF THE FREE,
AND THE HOME
OF THE BRAVE!

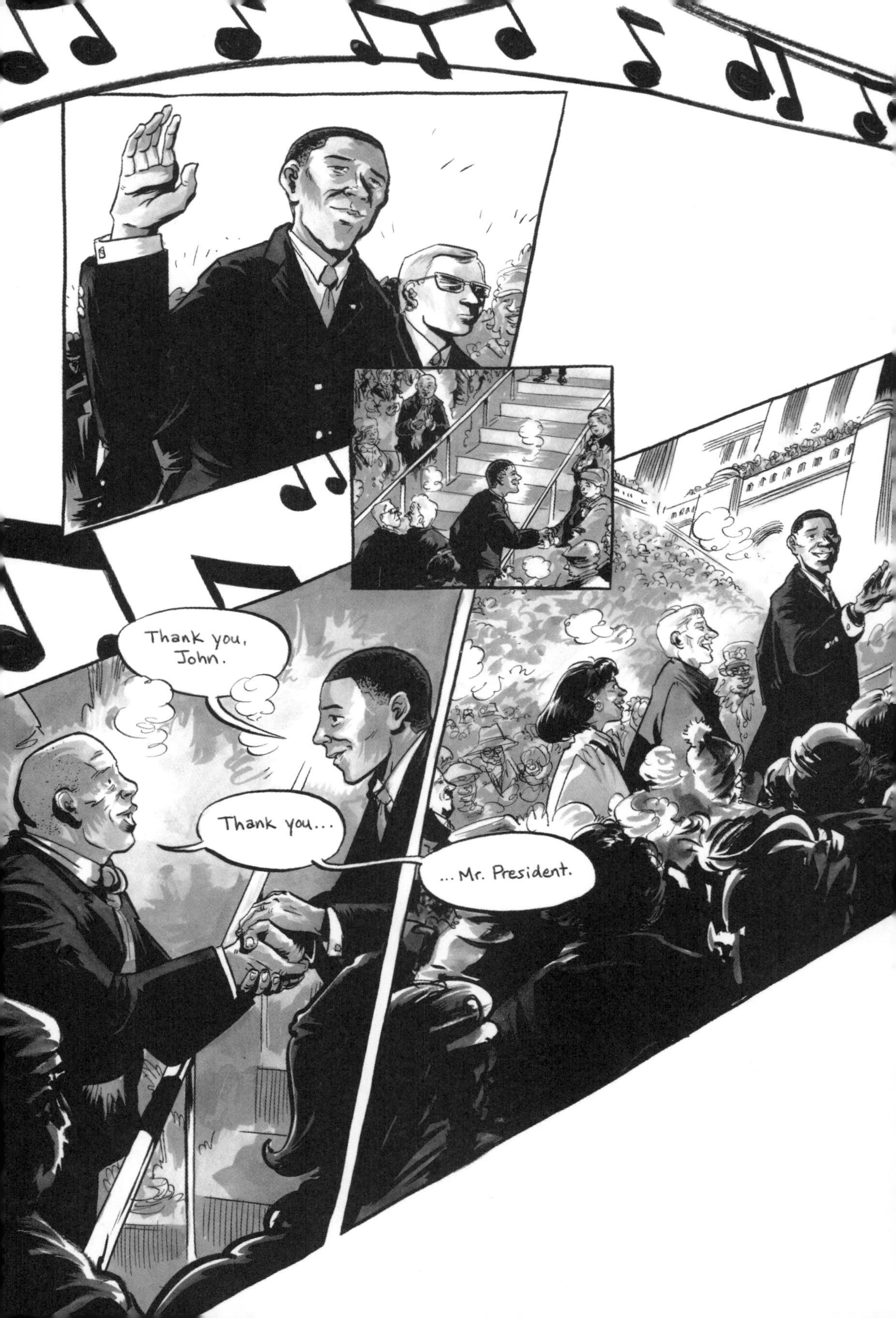
Thank you, John.
Thank you...
...Mr. President.

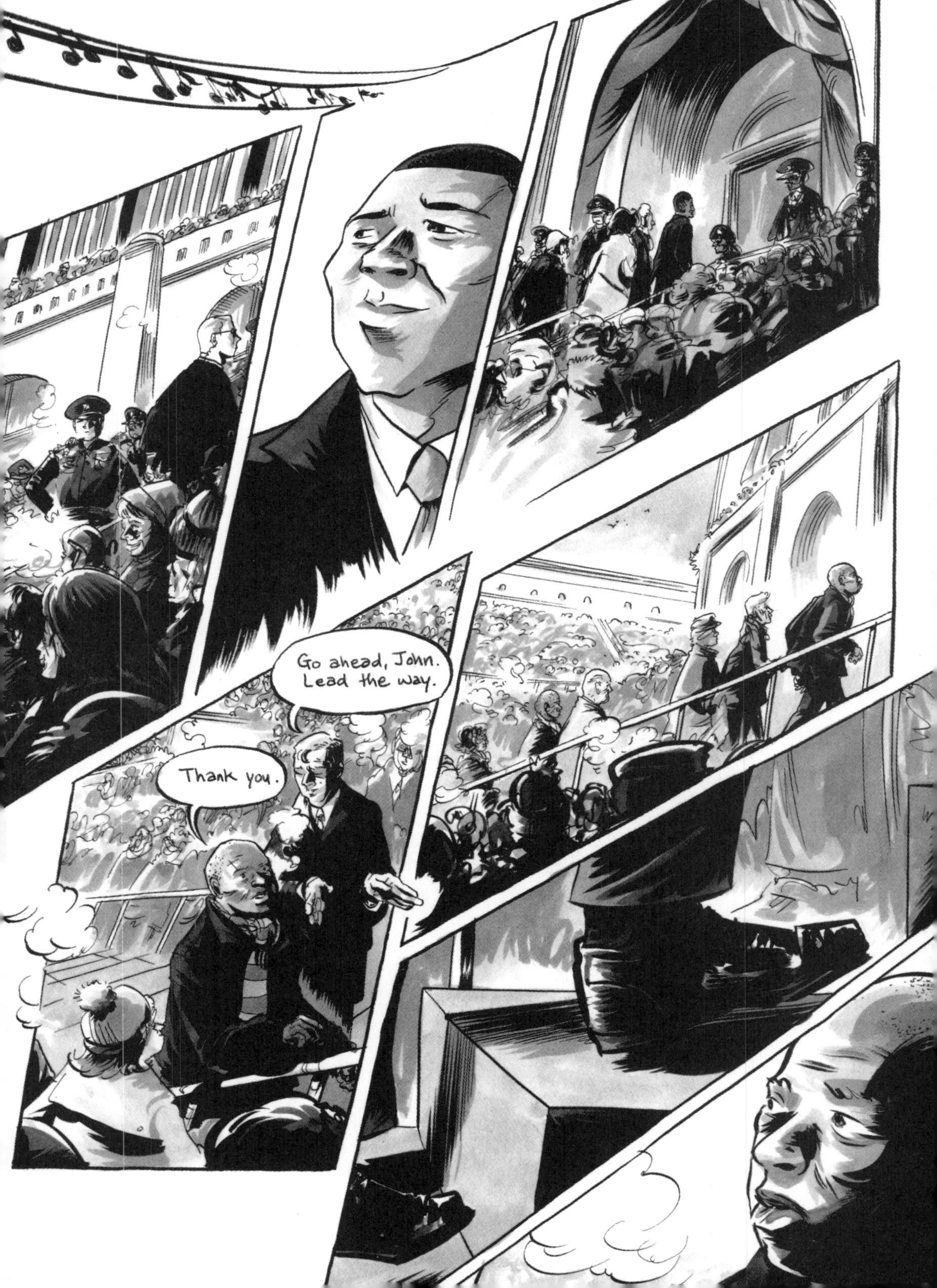
Go ahead, John. Lead the way.
Thank you.

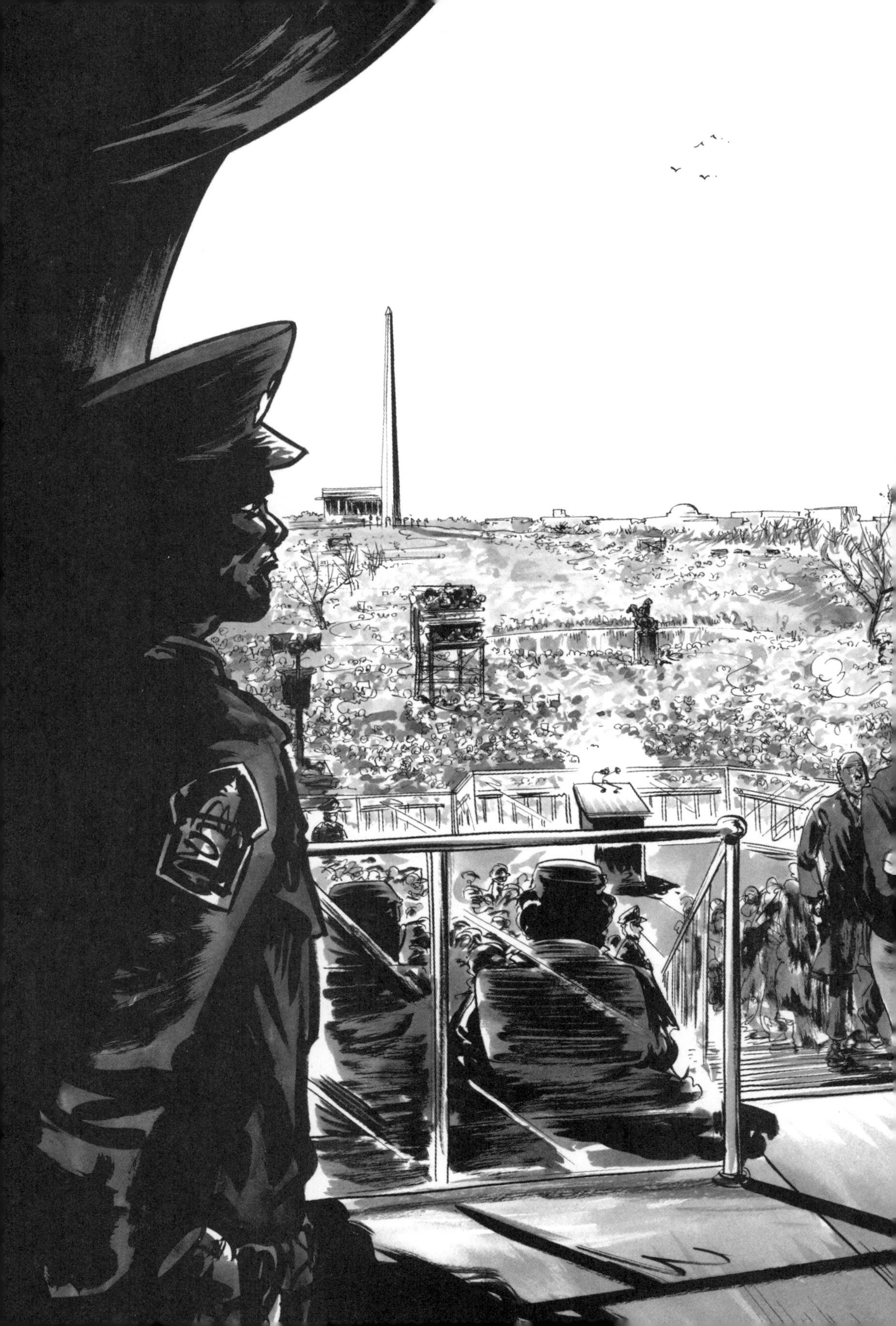

MARCH: BOOK THREE

WRITTEN BY JOHN LEWIS & ANDREW AYDIN
ART BY NATE POWELL

JIM CLARK WAS THE SHERIFF OF DALLAS COUNTY.
HE WAS MEAN, VIOLENT, AND EASILY PROVOKED.

HE WAS MADE ALL THE MORE DANGEROUS BY THE
SUNDRY GANG OF WHITE MEN HE **DEPUTIZED** FOR
THE SOLE PURPOSE OF DOING WHATEVER IT TOOK
TO STOP BLACK PEOPLE FROM VOTING.

FROM POOR LABORERS TO WEALTHY LANDOWNERS,
SHERIFF CLARK AND HIS "POSSE" OFTEN CARRIED
CATTLE PRODS-- AND THEY DID **NOT** USE THEM ON COWS.

WHEN **BULL CONNOR** PUT OUT A CALL FOR
REINFORCEMENTS DURING DR. KING'S CAMPAIGN IN
BIRMINGHAM EARLIER THAT YEAR, DALLAS COUNTY
ANSWERED WITH SHERIFF CLARK LEADING MORE
THAN **TWO HUNDRED** POSSEMEN TO HELP.

THERE WAS NO DOUBT THAT
A MOVE ON SELMA WOULD BE
MET WITH VIOLENCE.

SEPTEMBER 23, 1963.

THE DAY AFTER THE BOMBING, 63 PROTESTERS HAD BEEN ARRESTED IN SELMA, INCLUDING SEVERAL WHO WERE BEATEN BY THE POLICE.

SHERIFF CLARK, AND AL LINGO OF THE ALABAMA STATE TROOPERS, LED THE BRUTAL RESPONSE, WHICH PROVOKED LOCAL TEENAGERS TO PICKET THE NEXT DAY IN FRONT OF THE COUNTY COURTHOUSE--

IT WAS THE FIRST TIME ANYONE IN SELMA HAD EVER DARED TO CHALLENGE SHERIFF CLARK ON HIS OWN DOORSTEP.

THE PICKETERS WERE ARRESTED--

--BUT NOW A MOVEMENT WAS AFOOT.

NIGHTLY MASS MEETINGS BEGAN.

LOCAL BLACK LEADERS REQUESTED THAT MILITARY PERSONNEL FROM NEARBY CRAIG AIR FORCE BASE NO LONGER BE ALLOWED TO TAKE LEAVE IN SELMA, SINCE THE CITY WAS **DEFYING** FEDERAL LAW BY ENFORCING SEGREGATION.

THE REQUEST WAS IGNORED.

AS CHAIRMAN OF **SNCC**, I SENT A TELEGRAM TO DEFENSE SECRETARY ROBERT MCNAMARA DESCRIBING WHAT WAS HAPPENING.

THE DEFENSE SECRETARY'S OFFICE RESPONDED BY SAYING THE BASE COMMANDER "MAY NOT INTERVENE IN BEHALF OF PERSONS NOT UNDER HIS COMMAND."

WITH THAT CURT DISMISSAL, I DECIDED IT WAS TIME TO JOIN THE PEOPLE IN SELMA.

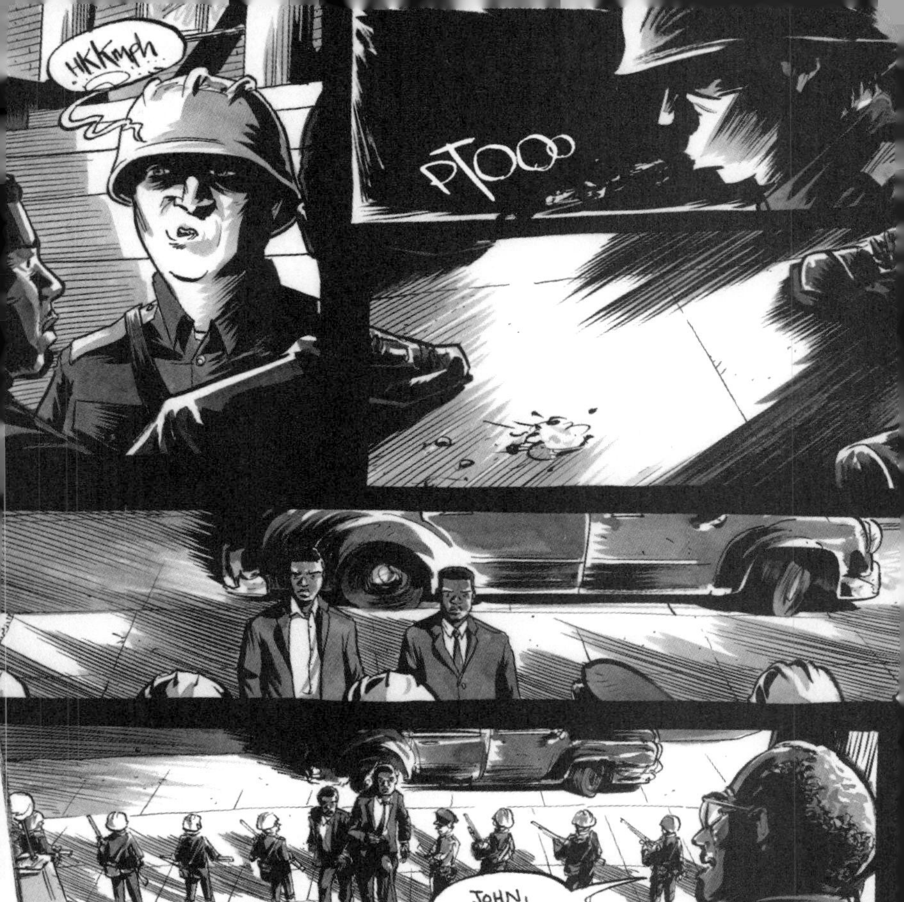
HKKmph
PTOOO
JOHN, JIM--
GLAD YOU MADE IT.
ME TOO. HAS THE MEETING STARTED?
YES, THEY'RE READY FOR YOU.

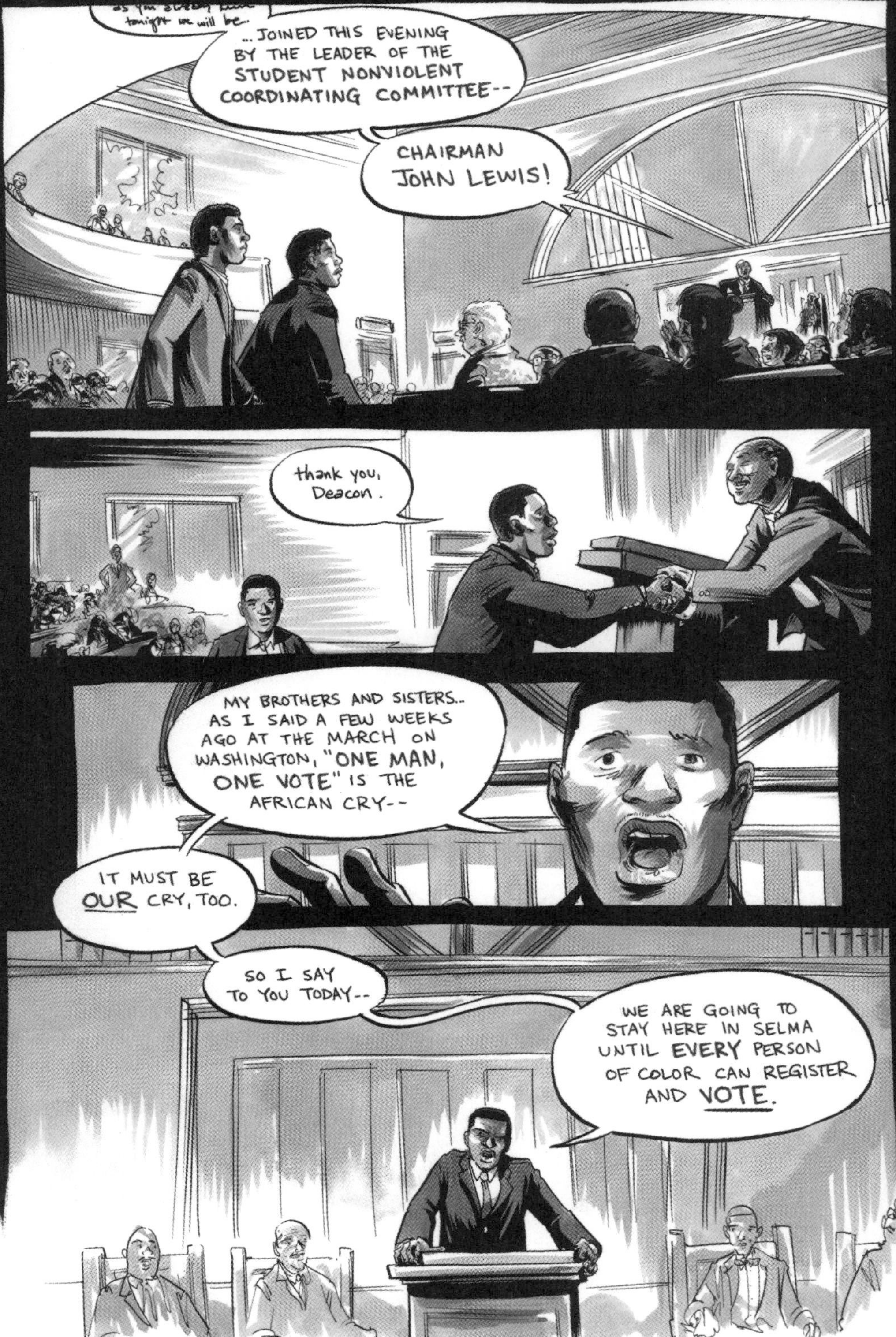
tonight we will be.
...JOINED THIS EVENING BY THE LEADER OF THE STUDENT NONVIOLENT COORDINATING COMMITTEE--
CHAIRMAN JOHN LEWIS!
thank you, Deacon.
MY BROTHERS AND SISTERS.. AS I SAID A FEW WEEKS AGO AT THE MARCH ON WASHINGTON, "ONE MAN, ONE VOTE" IS THE AFRICAN CRY--
IT MUST BE OUR CRY, TOO.
SO I SAY TO YOU TODAY--
WE ARE GOING TO STAY HERE IN SELMA UNTIL EVERY PERSON OF COLOR CAN REGISTER AND VOTE.

IN SELMA -- AND THROUGHOUT MOST OF THE SOUTH AT THAT TIME-- IT WAS ALMOST **IMPOSSIBLE** FOR AFRICAN-AMERICANS TO REGISTER TO VOTE.

IN DALLAS COUNTY, ONLY **2.1%** OF AFRICAN-AMERICANS OF VOTING AGE WERE REGISTERED.

I'd like to register to vote.

Sure, lemme get the forms for you.

I'd like to register to vote, please.

≋ahem≋ uh, I see.

wait here.

THERE WERE MANY DIFFERENT WAYS TO **STOP** PEOPLE FROM VOTING.

Here you go-- Let me know if you have any questions.

IN SOME PLACES AFRICAN-AMERICANS WERE ASKED TO COUNT THE NUMBER OF JELLY BEANS IN A JAR, OR THE NUMBER OF BUBBLES IN A BAR OF SOAP.

THE REGISTRAR OF VOTERS HELD **ALL** OF THE POWER, AND COULD DECIDE TO WAIVE, OR STRICTLY ENFORCE, **ANY** OF THE RULES, AT **ANY** TIME, FOR **ANY** REASON.

good catch!

oops, you forgot one.

...form, and also your li test. It is in three pa Questions in the la section should b answered in th form of an essay.

THIS INCLUDED **LITERACY TESTS**, OFTEN **ONLY** GIVEN TO BLACK APPLICANTS.

Here you go.

Thanks-- have a great day.

REGISTRAR OF VOTERS

TAP TAP

THEY WERE FILLED WITH QUESTIONS MEANT TO TRIP UP EVEN THE SMARTEST PERSON-- BUT **NOT** EVERYONE HAD TO TAKE THEM.

REGISTRAR OF VOTERS

You're **TAKIN'** too long-- you **FAIL**, nigger.

get outta here.

KRUMPLE

EVEN IF A BLACK CITIZEN WERE **ABLE** TO REGISTER, THEIR NAME WOULD BE PRINTED IN THE LOCAL PAPER-- MAKING THEM A **TARGET**. THE WHITE CITIZENS COUNCIL COULD PRESSURE THEIR EMPLOYER TO FIRE THEM. THEIR HOUSE COULD BE BURNED DOWN BY THE KKK. OR **WORSE**.

THE NEXT DEMONSTRATION IN FRONT OF
THE DALLAS COUNTY COURTHOUSE
RESULTED IN **30** ARRESTS...

...SO WE RESPONDED WITH
AN EVEN **LARGER** PROTEST.

DALLAS COUNTY
COURTHOUSE

GIVE US
THE VOTE

ONE MAN
ONE VOTE

I PARTICIPATED, ALONG WITH A GROUP
OF STUDENTS FROM SELMA UNIVERSITY.

ONE MAN,
ONE
VOTE

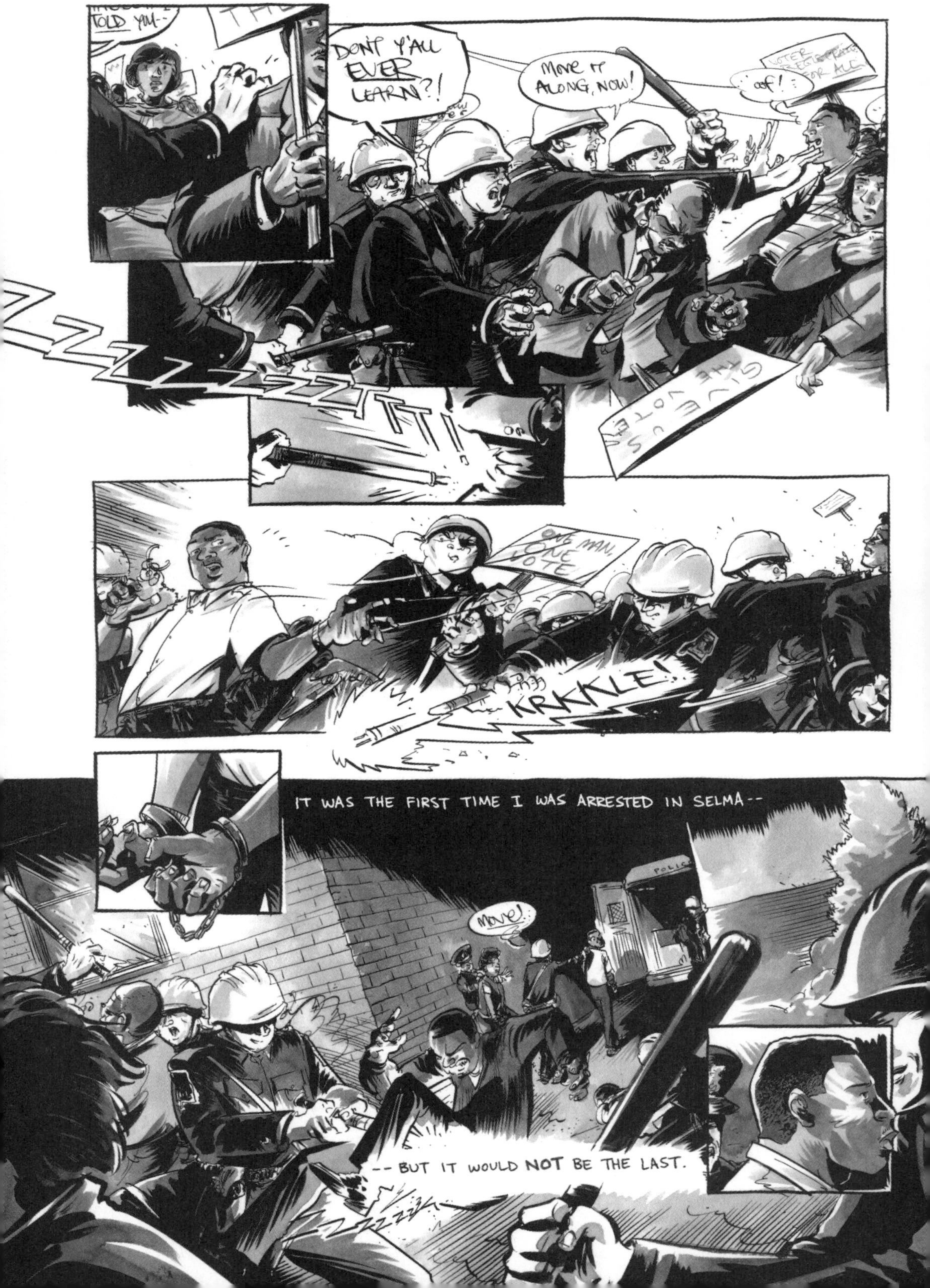
TOLD YOU--
DON'T Y'ALL EVER LEARN?!
Move it ALONG, NOW!
oof!
GIVE US THE VOTE
ONE MAN, ONE VOTE
KRAKKLE!
IT WAS THE FIRST TIME I WAS ARRESTED IN SELMA--
Move!
--BUT IT WOULD NOT BE THE LAST.

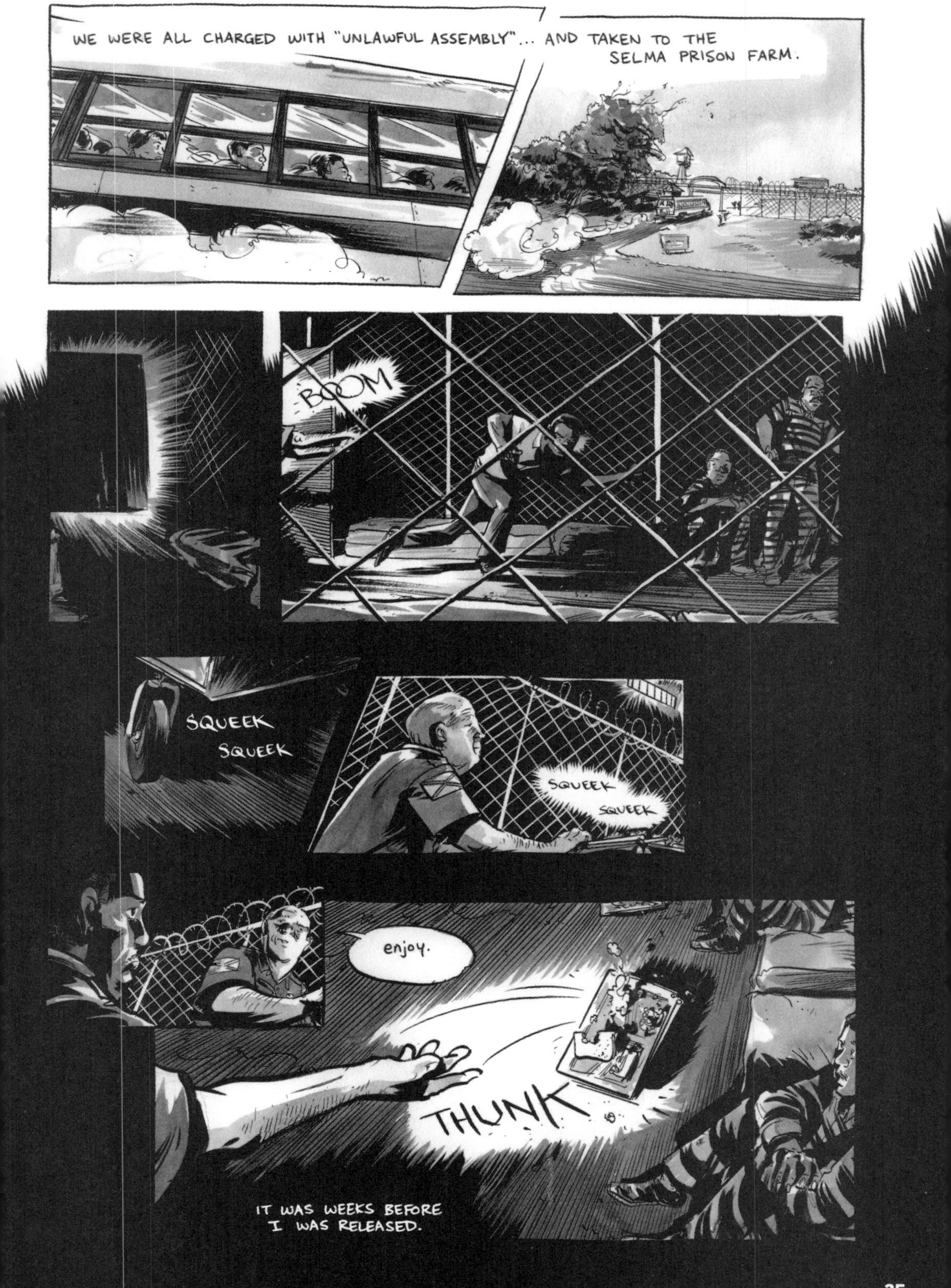

WE WERE ALL CHARGED WITH "UNLAWFUL ASSEMBLY"... AND TAKEN TO THE SELMA PRISON FARM.
BOOM
SQUEEK
SQUEEK
SQUEEK
SQUEEK
enjoy.
THUNK
IT WAS WEEKS BEFORE I WAS RELEASED.

IN DALLAS COUNTY, YOU COULD ONLY REGISTER TO VOTE ON THE FIRST AND THIRD MONDAYS OF THE MONTH. SO WHILE I WAS IN JAIL, SNCC DECIDED TO USE THE NEXT VOTER REGISTRATION DAY TO STAGE ITS LARGEST MOBILIZATION YET.

THE EFFORT QUICKLY FOUND A NAME:

FREEDOM DAY.

THE FEDERAL GOVERNMENT IS **NOT** DOING WHAT IT IS SUPPOSED TO DO.

EVEN RENOWNED AUTHOR JAMES BALDWIN CAME WITH HIS BROTHER TO SUPPORT THOSE IN LINE.

IT WAS HOT, BUT NO ONE WAS ALLOWED TO LEAVE THE LINE FOR WATER OR TO USE THE BATHROOM.

EVEN IF THEY COULD, THE "COLORED" BATHROOMS HAD BEEN **LOCKED.**

AT NOON, THE REGISTRAR OF VOTERS LEFT FOR A TWO-HOUR LUNCH BREAK.

VROOM

BY THAT TIME, ONLY TWELVE PEOPLE HAD BEEN ADMITTED TO SEE THE REGISTRAR.

FIFTEEN MINUTES LATER, THE ALABAMA STATE TROOPERS ARRIVED.

VRMmmm! VRRRMMM! VRRRMMm

ERRRT!

SCREEEEE

THUP

THUD THUD

FPASH

MAJOR JOE SMELLEY WAS THE TROOPER IN CHARGE THAT DAY.

IF ANY OF Y'ALL LEAVES THAT LINE FOR ANY REASON -- IF YOU HAVE TO GO TO THE BATHROOM, OR YOU'RE THIRSTY -- ANY REASON WHATSOEVER--

YOU'RE NOT COMING BACK, Y'HEAR?!

AND YOU AGITATORS!! YOU'RE NOT ALLOWED TO BRING 'EM ANYTHING--

NO FOOD! NO WATER!

IT BECAME A BATTLE OF WILLS.

AFTER A FEW MORE HOURS,

PRASH!

SOME FOLKS STANDING IN LINE WERE LOOKING LIKE THEY MIGHT COLLAPSE.

SHERIFF CLARK--

FINALLY, JIM FORMAN AND AMELIA BOYNTON, A LOCAL BUSINESSWOMAN WHO HAD BEEN ORGANIZING REGISTRATION EFFORTS HERE FOR **DECADES**, MADE AN APPEAL.

SHERIFF CLARK, THESE PEOPLE COULD **DIE**-- LET US BRING THEM SOME WATER.

SOME HAVEN'T HAD ANYTHING TO DRINK IN FIVE OR SIX **HOURS**.

SHERIFF CLARK, IT DOESN'T SEEM LIKE A VERY CHRISTIAN THING TO LET PEOPLE DROP DEAD ON YOUR COURTHOUSE STEPS.

IF THEY'RE SO THIRSTY, THEN THEY CAN GET OUTTA LINE AND GET SOMETHING TO DRINK. AIN'T **NOBODY** STOPPING 'EM. BUT IF I SEE ANY OF YOU NIGGERS TRYING TO BRING 'EM ANYTHING--

--IF I SEE YOU SO MUCH AS **TALKING** TO 'EM, I'LL ARREST YOU FOR... for...

... FOR MOLESTIN' PEOPLE TRYING TO REGISTER TO VOTE.

TWO SNCC FIELD SECRETARIES, AVERY WILLIAMS AND CHICO NEBLETT, COULDN'T WAIT ANY LONGER.

THUD

THWACK

FPASH!

STILL,

THE LINE HELD AND NO ONE LEFT.

TO US, MAKING IT THROUGH THE ENTIRE DAY
WITHOUT A MASS ARREST WAS PROGRESS.
THOUGH ONLY A FEW PEOPLE WERE ABLE
TO SEE THE REGISTRAR, WE FELT
IT WAS A **VICTORY**.

AFTER I WAS RELEASED FROM THE SELMA PRISON FARM, MY DUTIES AS CHAIRMAN OF SNCC TOOK ME AWAY FROM SELMA TO ALL PARTS OF THE COUNTRY.

I WAS GIVING SPEECHES, BUT I WAS ALSO RAISING MONEY.

MY BROTHERS AND SISTERS, ALL OF US MUST GET IN THE REVOLUTION.

AFTER THE MARCH ON WASHINGTON, A SUBSTANTIAL AMOUNT OF MONEY WAS MADE AVAILABLE TO DIFFERENT GROUPS WITHIN THE MOVEMENT--

BUT ROY WILKINS IN PARTICULAR SAW TO IT THAT THE FORMULA FOR DISTRIBUTING THESE FUNDS WOULD SEND THE MOST TO ORGANIZATIONS THAT ALREADY HAD MONEY, LIKE HIS NAACP.

WE MUST GET IN THE STREETS OF EVERY CITY, EVERY VILLAGE, EVERY TOWN OF THIS NATION...

SNCC HAD ALREADY BEEN GROWING APART FROM THE MAINSTREAM OF THE MOVEMENT. WE WERE YOUNGER AND, BY THEIR ACCOUNTS, MORE RADICAL.

BUT THE AMOUNT OF FUNDING WE RECEIVED WAS A SMALL FRACTION OF WHAT THE OTHER GROUPS RECEIVED, AND IT ONLY SERVED TO WIDEN THE D I V I D E.

...UNTIL TRUE FREEDOM COMES TO EVERY HUMAN BEING.

BUT WITHIN SNCC THERE WAS ALWAYS A DISTRUST OF MONEY, AND THE STRINGS THAT WERE OFTEN ATTACHED. IF IT CAME DOWN TO MONEY OR OUR INDEPENDENCE...

WE MUST SEEK MORE THAN CIVIL RIGHTS: WE MUST SEEK LOVE, PEACE, AND TRUE BROTHERHOOD.

... WELL, WE COULD ALWAYS MAKE DO WITHOUT MUCH MONEY.

MEANWHILE, DIANE'S IDEA FOR AN ALL-OUT ASSAULT DID **NOT** FADE AWAY. IT BEGAN TO TAKE SHAPE IN ANOTHER FORM, AND IN ANOTHER STATE:

MISSISSIPPI.

IT WAS LED BY **BOB MOSES**, WHO HAD SPENT THE LAST THREE YEARS IN THE STATE ORGANIZING SNCC CHAPTERS. HE WAS ALSO HEAD OF THE **COUNCIL OF FEDERATED ORGANIZATIONS (COFO)**, A COALITION OF **SNCC, SCLC, CORE,** AND **NAACP** ACTIVISTS FOR COORDINATING VOTING RIGHTS EFFORTS.

MOSES WAS BECOMING INCREASINGLY WELL-KNOWN IN THE MOVEMENT. SMART AND GENTLE, HE AVOIDED THE SPOTLIGHT PARTLY AS A PERSONAL PHILOSOPHY--

--AND PARTLY BECAUSE BEING TOO WELL-KNOWN IN MISSISSIPPI COULD BE **DEADLY.**

HE HAD A GRADUATE DEGREE FROM HARVARD, BUT LIKE MANY OF US, BOB STARTED WEARING **OVERALLS** TO SHOW SOLIDARITY WITH THE FARMERS AND RURAL FOLKS WE WERE WORKING WITH.

WITH **AL LOWENSTEIN**, A WHITE ACTIVIST AND FORMER DEAN AT STANFORD UNIVERSITY, MOSES CONCEIVED OF A "**MOCK ELECTION**" TO TAKE PLACE IN MISSISSIPPI AT THE **SAME TIME** AS THE **ACTUAL** STATE-WIDE ELECTIONS.

FREEDOM VOTE

LOWENSTEIN HAD COMPARED THE CONDITIONS
IN MISSISSIPPI TO THOSE IN **SOUTH AFRICA**
UNDER **APARTHEID**, SO HE AND BOB MOSES
MODELED THEIR IDEA AFTER A SIMILAR
EFFORT BY SOUTH AFRICAN ACTIVISTS.

AS SNCC ORGANIZED THE EFFORT,
WE GAVE IT A NAME:

FREEDOM VOTE.

THE PLAN WAS TO STAGE OUR **OWN** ELECTION,
WITH OUR **OWN** CANDIDATES. THIS WOULD GIVE
BLACK WOMEN AND MEN A SENSE OF WHAT IT
WAS LIKE TO ACTUALLY VOTE, **AND** DRAMATIZE
THE **EXCLUSION** OF AFRICAN-AMERICANS
FROM THE ELECTORAL PROCESS.

AT THE END OF OCTOBER,

I WENT TO MISSISSIPPI TO HELP WITH FINAL PREPARATIONS FOR THE FREEDOM VOTE, AND TO SPEAK THROUGHOUT THE STATE,

ENCOURAGING PEOPLE TO PARTICIPATE.

JACKSON

IT WAS MY FIRST TIME IN JACKSON SINCE THE FREEDOM RIDE.

MEN'S RESTROOM

MEN'S RESTROOM

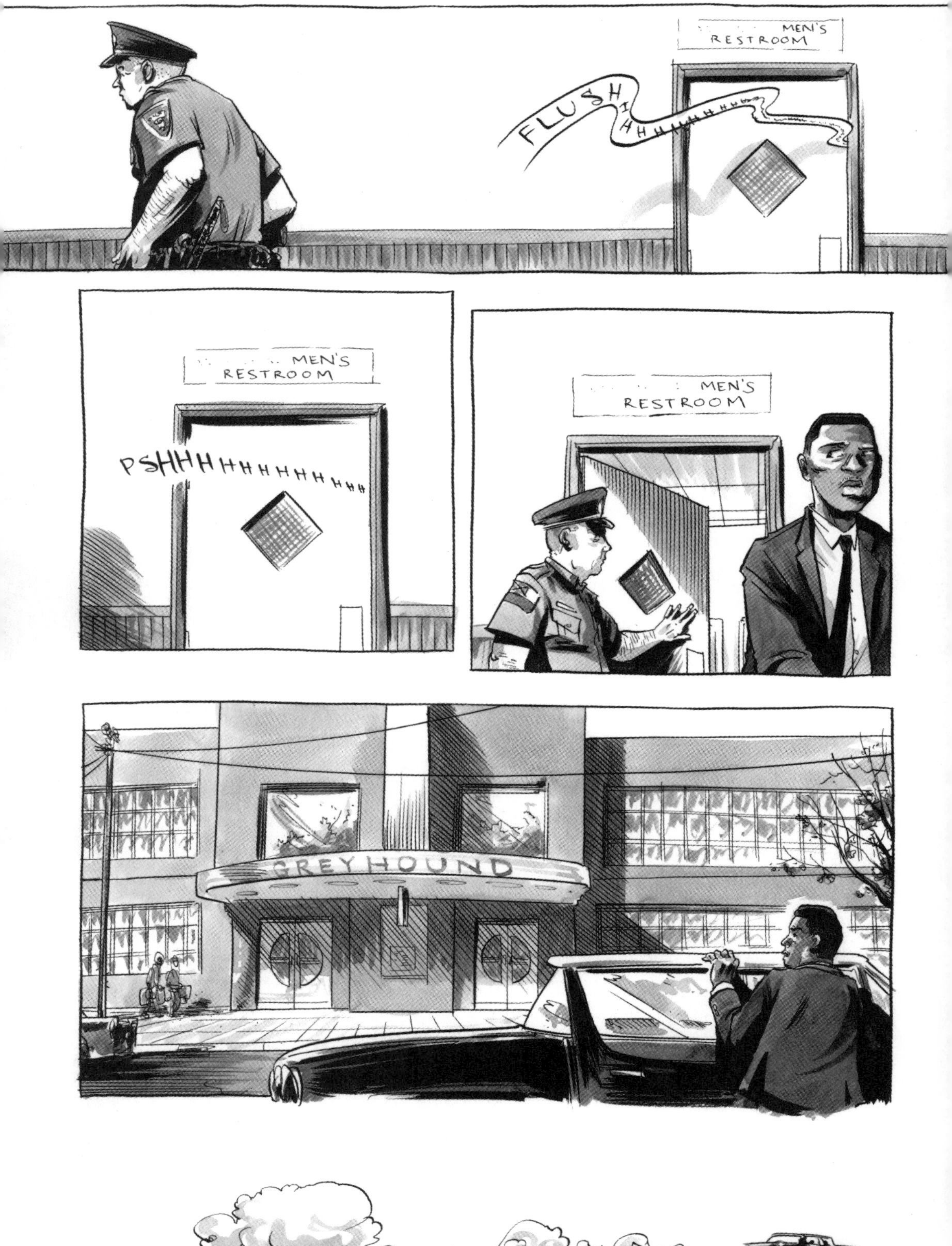
MEN'S RESTROOM
FLUSHHHHHHHHHHHH
MEN'S RESTROOM
PSHHHHHHHHHHHHH
MEN'S RESTROOM
GREYHOUND

NO PERSON REPRESENTED MORE TO WHAT SNCC WAS ATTEMPTING TO ACCOMPLISH IN MISSISSIPPI THAN A WOMAN NAMED **FANNIE LOU HAMER.**

SHE HEARD JAMES BEVEL SPEAK IN 1962, AND WAS SO MOVED THAT SHE WENT TO THE COURTHOUSE IN INDIANOLA TO ATTEMPT TO REGISTER TO **VOTE.**

WHEN WORD GOT AROUND ABOUT WHAT SHE TRIED TO DO, SHE WAS **FIRED** FROM HER JOB, **ARRESTED,** AND SEVERELY **BEATEN.**

AFTERWARDS SHE JOINED SNCC AND BECAME ONE OF THE HARDEST-WORKING, MOST DEDICATED ACTIVISTS I HAVE **EVER** KNOWN.

IN MANY WAYS, FANNIE LOU HAMER BECAME THE **SOUL** OF THE MISSISSIPPI MOVEMENT.

AS THE FREEDOM VOTE NEARED AND HER ROLE IN THE MOVEMENT GREW, SO DID THE VIOLENCE.

JOHN LEWIS, IS THAT YOU?!

HOW YOU DOING, MS. HAMER?

THE ONLY THING THEY CAN DO TO ME IS KILL ME--

AND IT SEEMS LIKE THEY'VE BEEN TRYING TO DO THAT JUST A LITTLE BIT AT A TIME SINCE I COULD REMEMBER.

OVER THE YEARS, MS. HAMER ENDURED REPEATED ARRESTS, THREATS TO HER FAMILY, AND A BEATING BY A POLICE OFFICER SO BRUTAL THAT IT CAUSED HER TO LIMP FOR THE REST OF HER LIFE. BUT THAT DID **NOT** STOP HER.

NOW JOHN LEWIS, LET ME TELL YOU, IF YOU'RE GOING TO COME TO MISSISSIPPI...

... YOU CAN'T COME HERE AND STAY FOR ONE DAY OR ONE NIGHT. YOU'VE GOTTA STAY FOR THE LONG HAUL.

BY THE TIME THE FREEDOM VOTE BEGAN, SNCC HAD HUNDREDS OF BALLOT BOXES ACROSS THE STATE. IT WAS A MARVEL OF GRASSROOTS ORGANIZING-- THEY WERE IN BEAUTY PARLORS AND BARBER SHOPS, IN CHURCHES AND MEETING HALLS, IN GROCERY STORES AND ON ROADSIDE TABLES.

I KNOW MISSISSIPPI, AND YOU'D BETTER BE READY TO MOVE IN.

WHEN ALL WAS SAID AND DONE, MORE THAN **90,000** BLACK VOTERS-- WHO WERE BEING SYSTEMATICALLY EXCLUDED FROM FEDERAL, STATE, AND LOCAL ELECTIONS-- PARTICIPATED IN THE FREEDOM VOTE.

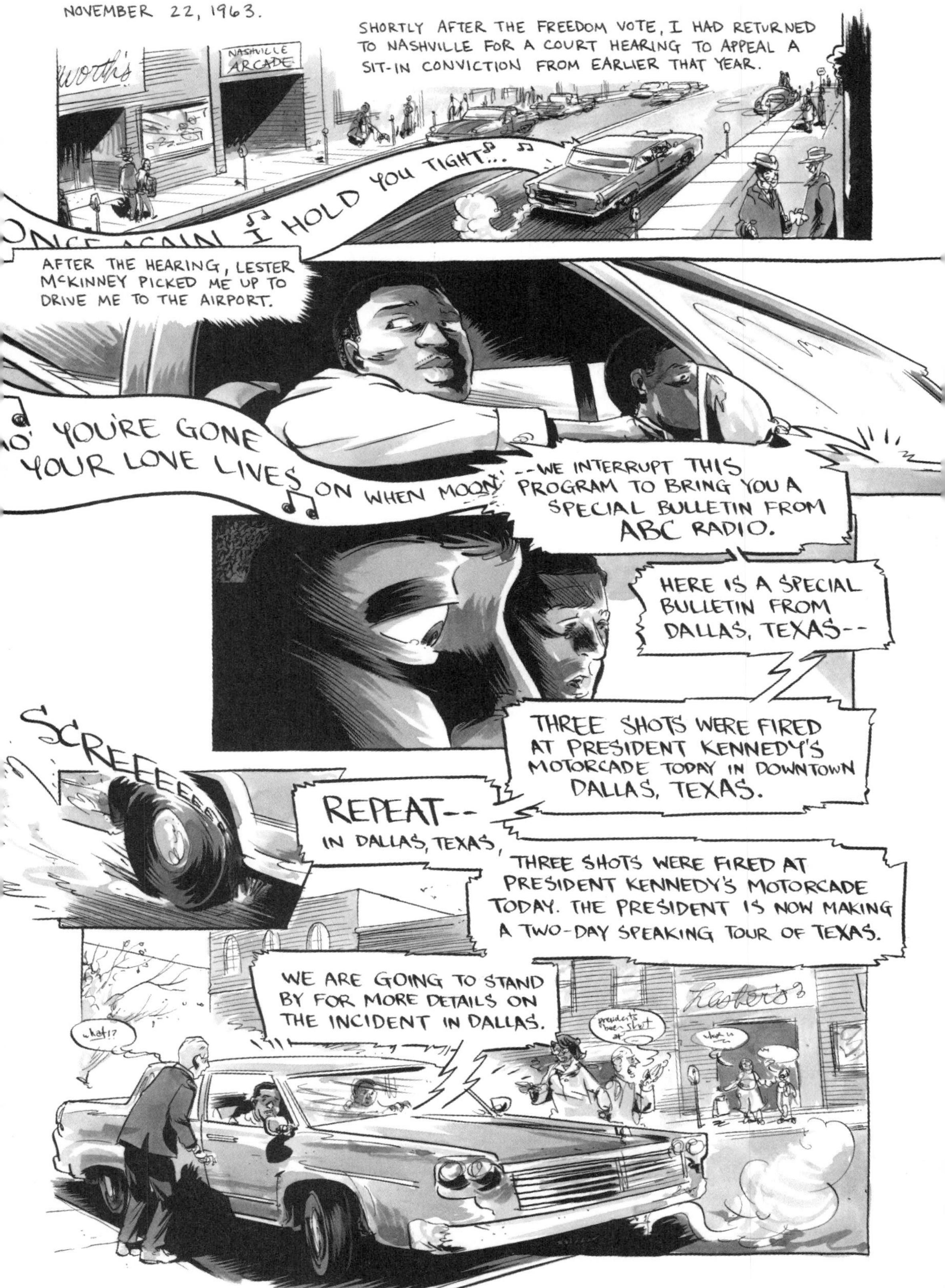
NOVEMBER 22, 1963.
SHORTLY AFTER THE FREEDOM VOTE, I HAD RETURNED TO NASHVILLE FOR A COURT HEARING TO APPEAL A SIT-IN CONVICTION FROM EARLIER THAT YEAR.
NASHVILLE ARCADE
ONCE AGAIN I HOLD YOU TIGHT...
AFTER THE HEARING, LESTER M^cKINNEY PICKED ME UP TO DRIVE ME TO THE AIRPORT.
THO' YOU'RE GONE YOUR LOVE LIVES ON WHEN MOON
--WE INTERRUPT THIS PROGRAM TO BRING YOU A SPECIAL BULLETIN FROM ABC RADIO.
HERE IS A SPECIAL BULLETIN FROM DALLAS, TEXAS--
THREE SHOTS WERE FIRED AT PRESIDENT KENNEDY'S MOTORCADE TODAY IN DOWNTOWN DALLAS, TEXAS.
SCREEEEEEEE
REPEAT-- IN DALLAS, TEXAS,
THREE SHOTS WERE FIRED AT PRESIDENT KENNEDY'S MOTORCADE TODAY. THE PRESIDENT IS NOW MAKING A TWO-DAY SPEAKING TOUR OF TEXAS.
WE ARE GOING TO STAND BY FOR MORE DETAILS ON THE INCIDENT IN DALLAS.
what!?
presidents been shot

I DIDN'T KNOW WHAT TO DO.

I HAD A SPEECH TO GIVE THAT EVENING IN DETROIT,

BUT ALL I WANTED WAS TO GO **HOME** TO ATLANTA.

I WENT AHEAD TO DETROIT.

hang in there, brother.

APPARENT GUNSHOT--

--HERE IS A FLASH FROM THE ASSOCIATED PRESS IN DALLAS--

--TWO PRIESTS WHO WERE WITH MR. KENNEDY SAY HE IS DEAD OF BULLET WOUNDS...

THE SPEECH I GAVE THAT NIGHT BECAME A **EULOGY** FOR OUR SLAIN PRESIDENT.

WHEN I GOT HOME TO ATLANTA AFTER
MY TRIP, I SPENT THE DAY ALONE IN
MY APARTMENT, WATCHING PRESIDENT
KENNEDY'S FUNERAL.

I KEPT THINKING ABOUT MEDGAR EVERS AND THE
LITTLE GIRLS IN BIRMINGHAM. NOW, THE PRESIDENT
WHO REPRESENTED SO MUCH **HOPE** FOR SO MANY
PEOPLE HAD BEEN MURDERED.

FOR SO MANY MONTHS I'D KEPT MY EMOTIONS
BOTTLED UP TO BE STRONG FOR THOSE COUNTING
ON ME TO LEAD,

BUT THERE I WAS,

ALONE

IN THE
DARK

WITH
IT
ALL.

WITHIN SNCC, PRESIDENT KENNEDY'S DEATH BROUGHT OUR DEEPEST FEARS TO THE FOREFRONT.

--I AM SAD THAT KENNEDY WAS KILLED. WE MOURN FOR HIM.

WILL THEY THINK THAT LIBERALISM IS DEAD WHEN THE MAN IS DEAD?

BUT I'M **MORE** CONCERNED ABOUT OUR FIELD STAFF. A LOT OF THEM HAVE TO BE THINKING THAT, IF THE **PRESIDENT** CAN BE KILLED, THEN **THEY** DON'T STAND A CHANCE. THEY CAN BE MURDERED AT ANY TIME.

THIS COULD PROVOKE A CRACKDOWN ON THE SO-CALLED "RADICAL" ORGANIZATIONS. YOU **KNOW** THAT'S GOING TO INCLUDE SNCC--

ANYONE WHO'S LEFT OF CENTER WILL BE SUBJECT TO A **PURGE.**

WE DON'T KNOW THAT.

PRESIDENT KENNEDY'S DEATH COULD BRING PEOPLE **TOGETHER.** IT COULD SERVE AS A UNIFYING MOMENT.

PRESIDENT LYNDON BAINES JOHNSON DELIVERED HIS FIRST SPEECH AS COMMANDER-IN-CHIEF TO A JOINT SESSION OF CONGRESS LAST NIGHT.

NO MEMORIAL OR EULOGY COULD MORE ELOQUENTLY HONOR PRESIDENT KENNEDY'S MEMORY THAN THE EARLIEST POSSIBLE PASSAGE OF THE **CIVIL RIGHTS BILL** FOR WHICH HE FOUGHT.

I WAS ENCOURAGED TO HEAR THE NEW PRESIDENT PUBLICLY COMMIT HIMSELF TO THE CAUSE OF CIVIL RIGHTS LEGISLATION--

BUT WE HAD NO IDEA HOW **DEEP** HIS COMMITMENT MIGHT RUN.

AT A **COFO** MEETING IN MISSISSIPPI, HEIGHTENED
TENSION BETWEEN BLACK AND WHITE SNCC VOLUNTEERS
LINGERED FROM THE FREEDOM VOTE -- EVEN AS
BOB MOSES SOUGHT TO BRING **MORE** WHITE VOLUNTEERS
TO THE STATE TO BUILD A LARGER SUMMER EFFORT.

IF WE'RE TRYING TO
BREAK DOWN THIS BARRIER
OF SEGREGATION, WE CAN'T
SEGREGATE **OURSELVES.**

THERE HAD BEEN SEVERAL COMPLAINTS ABOUT WHITE VOLUNTEERS TRYING
TO **TAKE OVER.** IT ALSO LEFT A NUMBER OF PEOPLE SORE THAT THE
PRESS HAD FOCUSED MUCH OF THEIR ATTENTION ON THE **WHITE** WORKERS,
OFTEN IDENTIFIED BY NAME, SHOWN WORKING ALONGSIDE NAMELESS BLACKS.

WE CANNOT DO
THIS ALONE.

THE **ONLY** WAY THIS
CAN WORK IS TO HAVE WHITE
PEOPLE WORKING **ALONGSIDE** YOU,
SO THEN IT CHANGES THE WHOLE
COMPLEXION OF WHAT YOU'RE
DOING. SO IT ISN'T NEGRO
FIGHTING WHITE--

--IT'S A QUESTION OF
RATIONAL PEOPLE AGAINST
IRRATIONAL PEOPLE.

BUT WE HAVE
TO LEAD
SOMETHING!

WE'RE LOSING THE
ONE THING WHERE
THE NEGRO CAN
STAND **FIRST.**

I ALWAYS THOUGHT
THE ONE THING WE CAN
DO FOR THIS COUNTRY THAT
NO ONE ELSE CAN DO
IS BE **ABOVE** THE
RACE ISSUE.

PRESIDENT JOHNSON MOVED QUICKLY ON HIS PROMISE TO PASS A CIVIL RIGHTS BILL. UNFORTUNATELY, THAT MEANT PRESSURING MANY CIVIL RIGHTS GROUPS, SNCC INCLUDED, TO **HALT** OUR PROTESTS AND DEMONSTRATIONS--

HE FELT OUR ACTIONS WERE MAKING IT HARDER FOR HIM TO WIN VOTES IN CONGRESS.

WE **STRONGLY DISAGREED.**

I'LL ADMIT, I HAD SOME PRECONCEIVED NOTIONS ABOUT PRESIDENT JOHNSON.

HE WAS A **SOUTHERNER**-- A TEXAN-- WHICH MADE ME SUSPICIOUS.

AND HE HAD **BLOCKED** HIS SHARE OF CIVIL RIGHTS LEGISLATION DURING HIS TIME AS A CONGRESSMAN.

BUT I FELT I HAD TO GIVE HIM A CHANCE. I HOPED THAT THE COMING CAMPAIGN IN MISSISSIPPI MIGHT HELP PUSH HIM THE RIGHT WAY -- MAYBE EVEN SHAPE HIS ATTITUDES LIKE I FELT WE HAD BEGUN TO DO WITH THE KENNEDY BROTHERS.

MANY IN SNCC DID **NOT** SHARE MY HOPE.

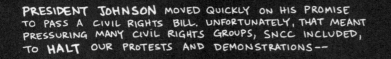

DING!

DESPITE THE JOHNSON ADMINISTRATION'S PLEAS,
WE DID **NOT** STOP OUR DEMONSTRATIONS.

DING!

IN **ATLANTA**, INTEGRATION OF RESTAURANTS
AND LUNCH COUNTERS HAD BEEN SLOW.
WE TARGETED A RESTAURANT CALLED THE "TODDLE HOUSE,"
OWNED BY THE DOBBS CORPORATION.

WHAT DO YOU
THINK YOU'RE DOING?

WE ARE HOPING
TO HAVE
SOMETHING
TO EAT.

EACH OF THE PARTICIPANTS THAT DAY, MYSELF INCLUDED,
HAD PURCHASED **ONE SHARE** OF THE DOBBS CORPORATION.

WELL, I'M CALLING
THE POLICE.

Sssssss

WHAT SORT OF SENSE DID IT MAKE IF WE COULD **OWN** PART
OF A COMPANY, BUT NOT BE **SERVED** BY IT?

= DING =

AFTER WE WERE ARRESTED,

SNCC CHAPTERS ALL OVER THE COUNTRY TARGETED ESTABLISHMENTS OPERATED BY THE DOBBS CORPORATION. THE PROTESTS TEMPORARILY **SHUT DOWN** MORE THAN A DOZEN OF THEIR BUSINESSES, AND WE ANNOUNCED PLANS TO ATTEND THEIR ANNUAL SHAREHOLDER MEETING.

OUR CAMPAIGN **WORKED**-- WITHIN A FEW MONTHS, THE DOBBS CORPORATION INTEGRATED **ALL** OF THEIR ESTABLISHMENTS, INCLUDING THOSE IN ATLANTA.

DECEMBER 31, 1963.

I WAS RELEASED FROM JAIL IN TIME TO ATTEND THE LAST SNCC EXECUTIVE COMMITTEE MEETING OF THE YEAR.

WE HAD A WIDE-RANGING DISCUSSION, BUT THE ONE WEIGHING MOST HEAVILY ON OUR ORGANIZATION WAS HOW TO PROCEED WITH THE MISSISSIPPI FREEDOM PROJECT.

THE INITIATIVE FOR THIS PROJECT COMES FROM THE FREEDOM VOTE, WHICH BROUGHT MANY WHITE STUDENTS TO THE STATE TO VOLUNTEER. THERE ARE A NUMBER OF PROBLEMS TO CONSIDER--

THE DEVELOPMENT OF NEGRO LEADERSHIP, POSSIBLE VIOLENCE, THE ABILITIES OF OUR PRESENT STAFF TO DIRECT THEM...

DISCUSSIONS AT THE COFO MEETING LAST MONTH WERE HEATED, AND IT WAS DECIDED TO LIMIT THE NUMBER OF WHITE STUDENTS IN MISSISSIPPI THIS SUMMER TO <u>100</u>.

GROUPS ARE OBVIOUSLY ORGANIZING TO COME DOWN. SNCC HAS TO DECIDE WHETHER TO HAVE A PROJECT, WHAT IT WILL DO, AND HOW MANY WILL BE INVOLVED.

THERE ARE ESSENTIALLY TWO PROPOSALS.

ONE-- PUSHED BY AL LOWENSTEIN--

POUR IN THOUSANDS OF STUDENTS AND FORCE A SHOWDOWN BETWEEN LOCAL AND FEDERAL GOVERNMENTS.

TWO-- DEVELOP A SIX-WEEK INTENSIVE LITERACY EDUCATION PROGRAM, PROPOSED BY DR. JOHN BLYTH, AND WORK OUT JUST HOW MANY STUDENTS COULD BE USED IN THESE "FREEDOM SCHOOLS".

I BELIEVE WE SHOULD DO EVERYTHING WE CAN IN MISSISSIPPI THIS SUMMER-- WE SHOULD DO THE SMALLER INTENSIVE PROGRAMS AND SATURATE THE STATE WITH VOLUNTEERS.

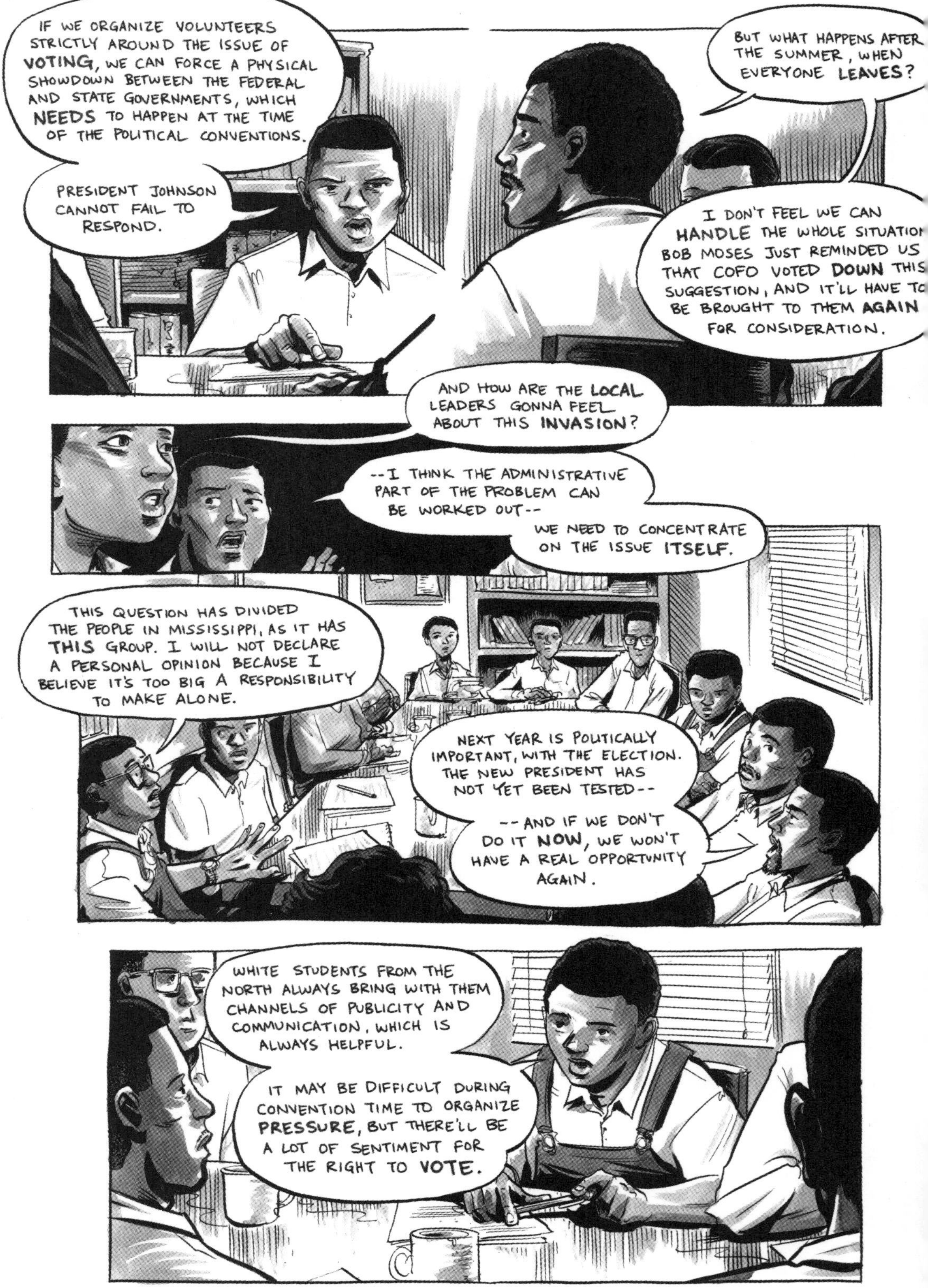
IF WE ORGANIZE VOLUNTEERS STRICTLY AROUND THE ISSUE OF VOTING, WE CAN FORCE A PHYSICAL SHOWDOWN BETWEEN THE FEDERAL AND STATE GOVERNMENTS, WHICH NEEDS TO HAPPEN AT THE TIME OF THE POLITICAL CONVENTIONS.
PRESIDENT JOHNSON CANNOT FAIL TO RESPOND.
BUT WHAT HAPPENS AFTER THE SUMMER, WHEN EVERYONE LEAVES?
I DON'T FEEL WE CAN HANDLE THE WHOLE SITUATION. BOB MOSES JUST REMINDED US THAT COFO VOTED DOWN THIS SUGGESTION, AND IT'LL HAVE TO BE BROUGHT TO THEM AGAIN FOR CONSIDERATION.
AND HOW ARE THE LOCAL LEADERS GONNA FEEL ABOUT THIS INVASION?
--I THINK THE ADMINISTRATIVE PART OF THE PROBLEM CAN BE WORKED OUT--
WE NEED TO CONCENTRATE ON THE ISSUE ITSELF.
THIS QUESTION HAS DIVIDED THE PEOPLE IN MISSISSIPPI, AS IT HAS THIS GROUP. I WILL NOT DECLARE A PERSONAL OPINION BECAUSE I BELIEVE IT'S TOO BIG A RESPONSIBILITY TO MAKE ALONE.
NEXT YEAR IS POLITICALLY IMPORTANT, WITH THE ELECTION. THE NEW PRESIDENT HAS NOT YET BEEN TESTED--
--AND IF WE DON'T DO IT NOW, WE WON'T HAVE A REAL OPPORTUNITY AGAIN.
WHITE STUDENTS FROM THE NORTH ALWAYS BRING WITH THEM CHANNELS OF PUBLICITY AND COMMUNICATION, WHICH IS ALWAYS HELPFUL.
IT MAY BE DIFFICULT DURING CONVENTION TIME TO ORGANIZE PRESSURE, BUT THERE'LL BE A LOT OF SENTIMENT FOR THE RIGHT TO VOTE.

IF WE DECIDE TO DO THIS, WE HAVE TO BEGIN BY TRAINING A GROUP OF 20 NOW, AS SUB-SECTION LEADERS FOR THE LARGER ONE.

PEOPLE WILL HAVE TO UNDERSTAND THAT THEY WILL OPERATE AS A **UNIT**, COMING TO THE SUPPORT OF SOMEONE IN TROUBLE, ACROSS THE STATE.

THEY **MUST** PREPARE TO GET ARRESTED.

WHAT ABOUT THE EFFECT ON THE **WHOLE** OF SNCC?

ARE WE WILLING TO RISK DISINTEGRATION OF OUR TOTAL OPERATION IN SUCH A CONFRONTATION?

I MOVE THAT THE COMMITTEE VOTE TO ADOPT THE FOLLOWING MOTION:

"DURING THE PRESIDENTIAL ELECTION YEAR OF 1964, SNCC INTENDS TO OBTAIN THE RIGHT FOR **ALL** CITIZENS OF MISSISSIPPI TO VOTE, USING AS MANY PEOPLE AS NECESSARY TO OBTAIN THAT END."

THE MOTION PASSED UNANIMOUSLY.

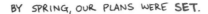

BY SPRING, OUR PLANS WERE **SET**.

WE DECIDED TO ANNOUNCE OUR INTENTIONS AT THE **AMERICAN SOCIETY OF NEWSPAPER EDITORS** CONVENTION. IT WAS OUR CHANCE TO MAKE OUR CASE TO THE NEWS MEDIA, WHOSE COVERAGE WOULD BE ESSENTIAL.

Hi, John. It's good to see you again.

Hello, Mr. Attorney General. It's good to see you too, sir.

IT WAS THE FIRST TIME I'D SEEN ROBERT KENNEDY SINCE HIS BROTHER'S DEATH.

I WAS JOINED BY **WHITNEY YOUNG, ROY WILKINS, AND JAMES FARMER,** WHOSE ORGANIZATIONS WERE SUPPORTING THE SUMMER PROJECT.

ANY PERSON WHO, IN ANY WAY, INTERFERES WITH THE RIGHT OF A NEGRO TO VOTE IN MISSISSIPPI COMMITS A **CRIME** AGAINST THE FEDERAL GOVERNMENT.

HE COMMITS AS MUCH OF A CRIME AS DOES THE GUNMAN WHO WALKS INTO A BANK AND **ROBS** IT.

TITLE 18, SECTION 594 OF THE UNITED STATES CODE MAKES IT A CRIME TO INTERFERE WITH THE RIGHT TO VOTE--

THAT LAW HAS BEEN ON THE BOOKS SINCE 1948, BUT NOBODY HAS EVER BEEN PROSECUTED UNDER IT.

I DOUBT IF THERE IS A POLICEMAN OF ANY SORT IN MISSISSIPPI WHO HAS NOT BROKEN THAT LAW SEVERAL TIMES SINCE 1948,

BUT NOT ONE OF THEM HAS BEEN ARRESTED AND PROSECUTED FOR IT.

THE FEDERAL GOVERNMENT-- THE PRESENT ADMINISTRATION, AT ANY RATE-- HAS NOT HELPED THE MOVEMENT WITH THE APPOINTMENT OF FEDERAL JUDGES.

FOR EXAMPLE, FEDERAL JUDGE HAROLD COX OF MISSISSIPPI, WHO WAS APPOINTED IN 1961, CALLED NEGRO APPLICANTS

a bunch of niggers.

AND SAID THEY WERE ACTING LIKE

a bunch of chimpanzees.

AND SO I SAY, THE STRUGGLE IS JUST BEGINNING.

THIS SUMMER, HOWEVER, WE ARE AGAIN PRESENTING THE FEDERAL GOVERNMENT WITH AN OPPORTUNITY TO ACT.

WITH THE COOPERATION OF OTHER CIVIL RIGHTS GROUPS, UNDER THE BANNER OF THE COUNCIL OF FEDERATED ORGANIZATIONS, WE PLAN TO INSTALL SOME ONE THOUSAND SUMMER WORKERS IN MISSISSIPPI.

61

THEY WILL TEACH IN THE **FREEDOM SCHOOLS**, STAFF COMMUNITY CENTERS,

REGISTER AS MANY AS **400,000** NEGROES ON MOCK POLLING LISTS,

AND WILL DO THE OFTEN-DANGEROUS WORK OF VOTER REGISTRATION.

THERE ARE FOUR CONGRESSIONAL CANDIDATES IN MISSISSIPPI TODAY WHO ARE NEGROES.

IF THEY **LOSE**,

THEY PLAN TO **CHALLENGE** THE RIGHT OF **WHITE** MISSISSIPPIANS TO CHOOSE WHO SHALL REPRESENT THE STATE IN CONGRESS.

THERE WILL BE CHALLENGES AT THE **DEMOCRATIC CONVENTION** IN AUGUST, AND WE WILL SEE WHETHER THE COUNTRY IS READY AND PREPARED TO ALLOW **FULL** REPRESENTATION IN CONGRESS.

THE FEDERAL GOVERNMENT'S CHALLENGE WILL COME EARLIER.

IT WILL COME AS IT IS COMING **NOW**, AND HAS BEEN,

IN THE **BLACK BELT** AREAS OF THE DEEP SOUTH.

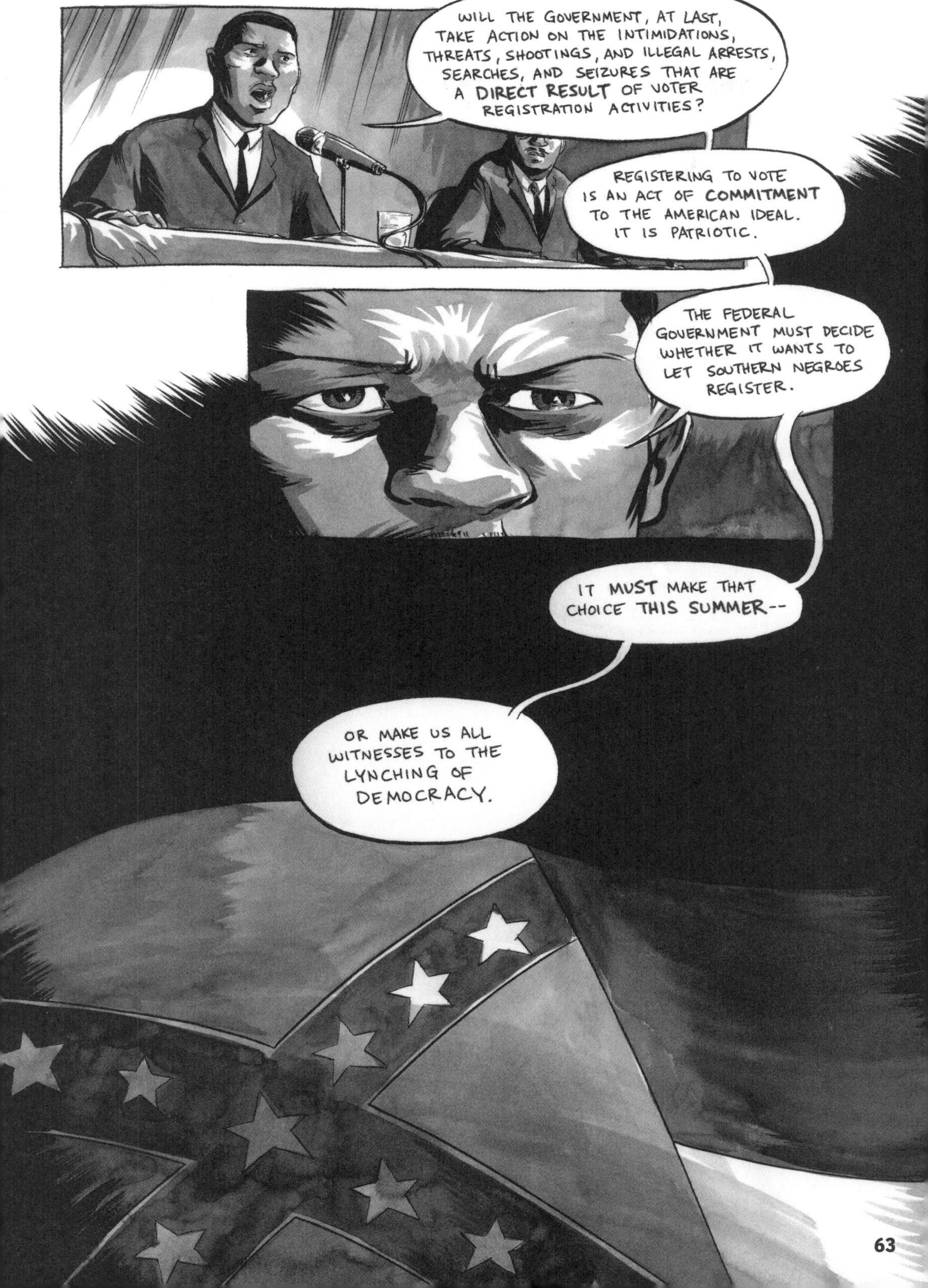
WILL THE GOVERNMENT, AT LAST, TAKE ACTION ON THE INTIMIDATIONS, THREATS, SHOOTINGS, AND ILLEGAL ARRESTS, SEARCHES, AND SEIZURES THAT ARE A DIRECT RESULT OF VOTER REGISTRATION ACTIVITIES?
REGISTERING TO VOTE IS AN ACT OF COMMITMENT TO THE AMERICAN IDEAL. IT IS PATRIOTIC.
THE FEDERAL GOVERNMENT MUST DECIDE WHETHER IT WANTS TO LET SOUTHERN NEGROES REGISTER.
IT MUST MAKE THAT CHOICE THIS SUMMER--
OR MAKE US ALL WITNESSES TO THE LYNCHING OF DEMOCRACY.

EVEN AS I GAVE MY SPEECH, THE STATE OF MISSISSIPPI WAS PREPARING.

THEY SAW OUR PLANS AS AN INVASION, AN **ATTACK** ON THEIR WAY OF LIFE.

GOVERNOR PAUL JOHNSON **DOUBLED** THE NUMBER OF STATE PATROLMEN ON DUTY, AND JACKSON MAYOR ALLEN THOMPSON DOUBLED THE SIZE OF HIS POLICE FORCE BY **DEPUTIZING** DOZENS OF WHITE MEN.

WEAPONS OF ALL SORTS WERE STOCKPILED TO **ARM** THEM.

MAYOR THOMPSON EVEN HAD AN ARMORED PERSONNEL CARRIER THAT COULD TRANSPORT TWELVE MEN-- IT BECAME KNOWN AS "**THOMPSON'S TANK.**"

THIS IS **IT**-- **THEY** AREN'T BLUFFING, AND **WE** AREN'T BLUFFING. WE'RE GONNA BE READY FOR THEM...

THEY WON'T HAVE A <u>CHANCE</u>.

ON APRIL 26, THE MISSISSIPPI FREEDOM DEMOCRATIC PARTY (MFDP) WAS OFFICIALLY CREATED.

THE FREEDOM VOTE HAD BEEN A MOCK ELECTION, BUT THE MISSISSIPPI SUMMER PROJECT, OR **FREEDOM SUMMER**, WAS ABOUT GOING AFTER **REAL** VOTES.

THROUGH OUR NEWLY CREATED INSURGENT POLITICAL PARTY, WE INTENDED TO CHALLENGE THE STATE'S **SEGREGATION-BASED** DEMOCRATIC PARTY AND ITS WHITES-ONLY DELEGATION FOR THEIR SEATS AT THE DEMOCRATIC CONVENTION IN ATLANTIC CITY, NEW JERSEY.

THE PLAN WAS TO **PARTICIPATE** IN THE PRECINCT, COUNTY, AND STATE CONVENTIONS OF MISSISSIPPI'S DEMOCRATIC PARTY. BY GOING THROUGH THE PROPER PROCEDURES, **MFDP** WOULD THEN HAVE LEGAL GROUNDS TO CHALLENGE THE PARTY'S CLAIM TO ITS SEATS AT THE **NATIONAL** CONVENTION.

FREEDOM DEMOCRATIC PARTY

IN A SINGLE NIGHT, THE KLAN BURNED CROSSES IN 64 OF THE STATE'S 82 COUNTIES AS A WARNING.

LOCAL WHITE PEOPLE WHO DESPISED WHAT WE WERE DOING DIDN'T BOTHER HIDING IT, FROM THE PRESS OR ANYBODY ELSE.

We killed two-month-old Indian babies to take this country, and now they want us to give it away to the nigguhs.

YOU'RE GOING TO BE CLASSIFIED INTO TWO GROUPS IN MISSISSIPPI:

NIGGERS, AND NIGGER-LOVERS.

JUNE 13, 1964.

OXFORD, OHIO -- MISSISSIPPI SUMMER PROJECT TRAINING CAMP

AND THEY'RE TOUGHER ON NIGGER-LOVERS.

MORE THAN 300 STUDENTS SHOWED UP FOR THE FIRST WEEKEND OF TRAINING.

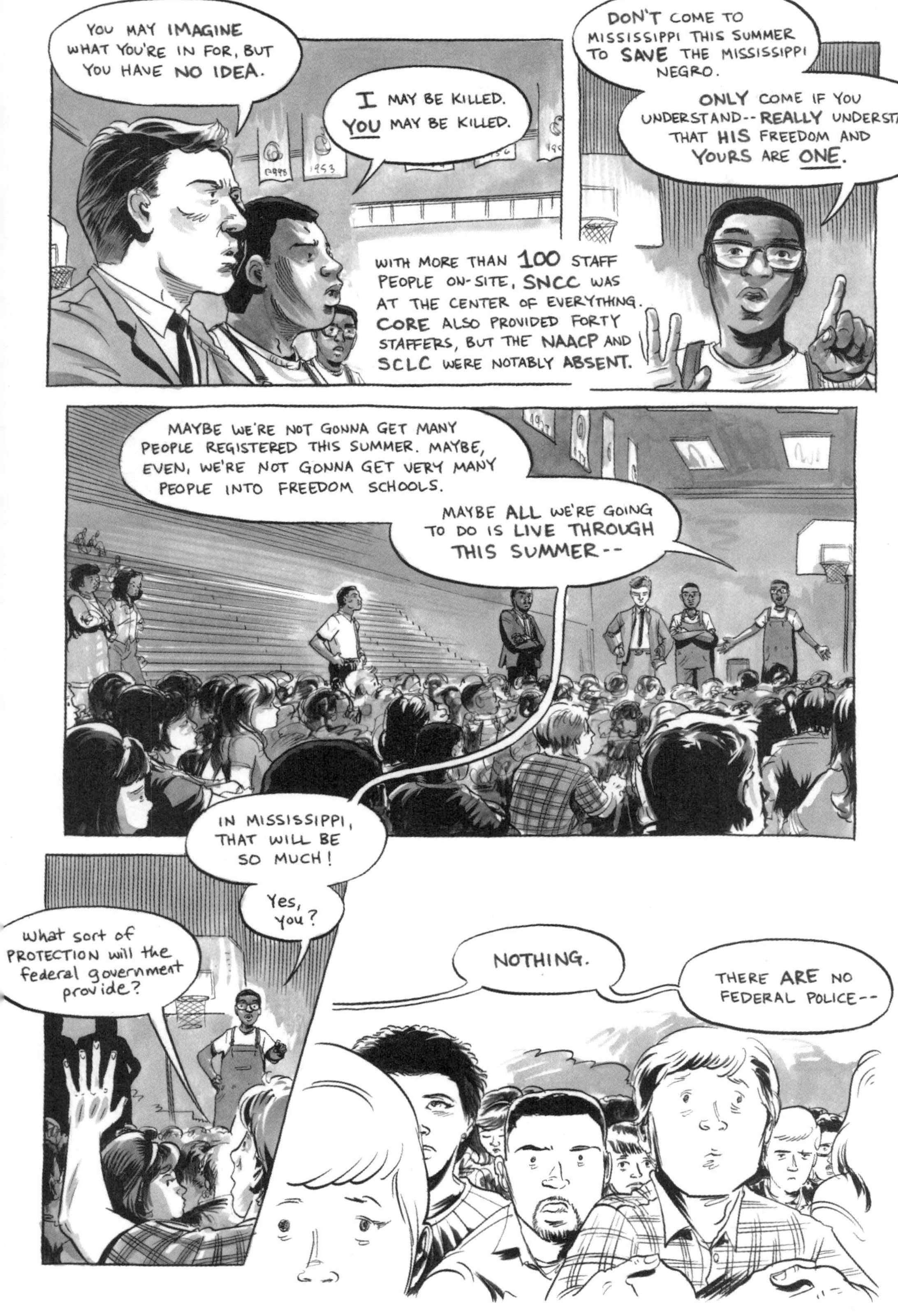
YOU MAY IMAGINE WHAT YOU'RE IN FOR, BUT YOU HAVE NO IDEA.
I MAY BE KILLED. YOU MAY BE KILLED.
WITH MORE THAN 100 STAFF PEOPLE ON-SITE, SNCC WAS AT THE CENTER OF EVERYTHING. CORE ALSO PROVIDED FORTY STAFFERS, BUT THE NAACP AND SCLC WERE NOTABLY ABSENT.
DON'T COME TO MISSISSIPPI THIS SUMMER TO SAVE THE MISSISSIPPI NEGRO.
ONLY COME IF YOU UNDERSTAND--REALLY UNDERSTAND--THAT HIS FREEDOM AND YOURS ARE ONE.
MAYBE WE'RE NOT GONNA GET MANY PEOPLE REGISTERED THIS SUMMER. MAYBE, EVEN, WE'RE NOT GONNA GET VERY MANY PEOPLE INTO FREEDOM SCHOOLS.
MAYBE ALL WE'RE GOING TO DO IS LIVE THROUGH THIS SUMMER--
IN MISSISSIPPI, THAT WILL BE SO MUCH!
Yes, you?
What sort of PROTECTION will the federal government provide?
NOTHING.
THERE ARE NO FEDERAL POLICE--

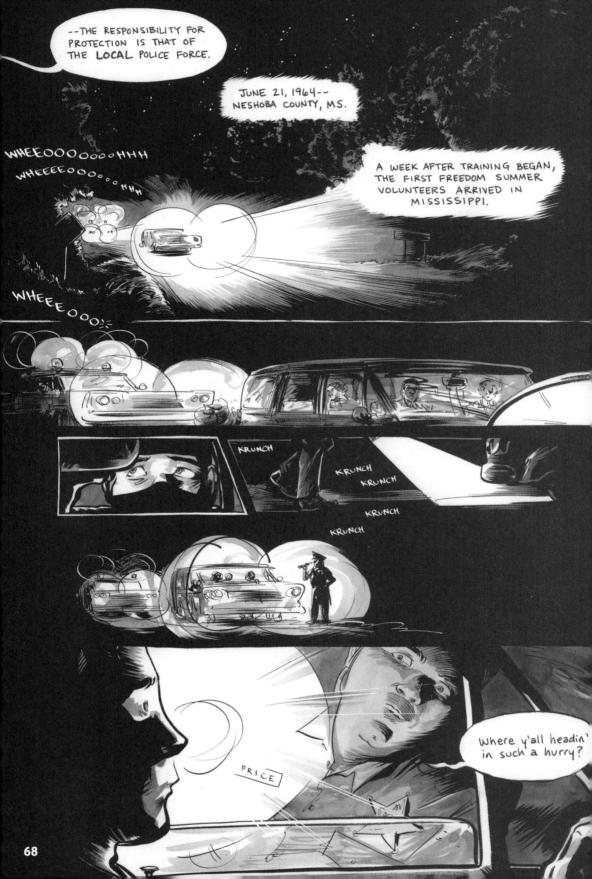

RIINNG
RIINNNNNGGG
RIIIINNNG

Hello..?

JOHN?

WE HAVE A PROBLEM--

THREE OF OUR VOLUNTEERS HAVEN'T CHECKED IN.

John?

you hear me, John?

I COULDN'T BELIEVE IT. NOT YET.

WE HADN'T EVEN GOTTEN STARTED.

MOST EVERYONE IN SNCC KNEW **MICKEY SCHWERNER**. HE WAS A HARD WORKER FROM BROOKLYN WHO HAD GONE WITH HIS WIFE, **RITA**, TO WORK AS **CORE** FIELD SECRETARIES IN NESHOBA COUNTY. LOCAL KLANSMEN CALLED HIM "THE JEW BOY WITH THE BEARD."

ANDY GOODMAN WAS A NEWCOMER. I HAD MET HIM DURING ONE OF THE TRAINING SESSIONS IN OHIO. A TWENTY-ONE YEAR OLD STUDENT AT QUEENS COLLEGE MAJORING IN ANTHROPOLOGY, ANDY WAS THE YOUNGEST OF THE THREE.

I NEVER MET **JAMES CHANEY**. A **CORE** FIELD SECRETARY AND NATIVE MISSISSIPPIAN, HE WAS A PLASTERER BY TRADE. AND HE WAS BLACK, WHICH MIGHT HAVE BEEN WHAT DREW THE ATTENTION OF DEPUTY SHERIFF PRICE.

WORD OF THE THREE MISSING CIVIL RIGHTS WORKERS
QUICKLY REACHED THE STAFFERS AND VOLUNTEERS
STILL TRAINING IN OHIO.

THEY WERE IN SHOCK.

HAS ANYONE READ TOLKIEN'S
FELLOWSHIP OF THE RING?

IT HAS A LOT TO SAY
ABOUT GOOD AND EVIL.

TIRED AND DISTRAUGHT,
BOB MOSES SPOKE TO THE
NEXT WAVE OF VOLUNTEERS
ONE LAST TIME BEFORE THEY
SET OUT FOR MISSISSIPPI.

=sigh=

the kids
are dead.

WHEN WE HEARD THE NEWS AT THE BEGINNING, I KNEW THEY WERE DEAD.

WHEN WE HEARD THEY'D BEEN ARRESTED, I KNEW THERE HAD BEEN A FRAME-UP.

WE DIDN'T SAY THIS EARLIER BECAUSE OF RITA-- BECAUSE SHE WAS REALLY HOLDING OUT FOR EVERY HOPE.

There may be more deaths.

I JUSTIFY MYSELF BECAUSE I'M TAKING RISKS MYSELF, AND I'M NOT ASKING PEOPLE TO DO THINGS I'M NOT WILLING TO DO.

AND THE OTHER THING IS, PEOPLE WERE BEING KILLED ALREADY-- THE NEGROES OF MISSISSIPPI-- AND I FEEL, ANYWAY, RESPONSIBLE FOR THEIR DEATHS.

HERBERT LEE... KILLED. LOUIS ALLEN... KILLED. FIVE OTHERS THIS YEAR.

IN SOME WAY, YOU HAVE TO COME TO GRIPS WITH THAT, KNOW WHAT IT MEANS.

IF YOU'RE GOING TO DO ANYTHING ABOUT IT, OTHER PEOPLE ARE GOING TO BE KILLED.

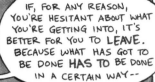

IN OUR COUNTRY WE HAVE SOME REAL **EVIL**, AND THE ATTEMPT TO DO SOMETHING ABOUT IT INVOLVES ENORMOUS EFFORT...

..AND THEREFORE, TREMENDOUS RISKS.

IF, FOR ANY REASON, YOU'RE HESITANT ABOUT WHAT YOU'RE GETTING INTO, IT'S BETTER FOR YOU TO **LEAVE**. BECAUSE WHAT HAS GOT TO BE DONE **HAS TO BE DONE** IN A CERTAIN WAY--

--OR OTHERWISE IT **WON'T** GET DONE.

♪ they say that freedom is a constant struggle ♫

♪ they say that freedom is a constant struggle-- ♫

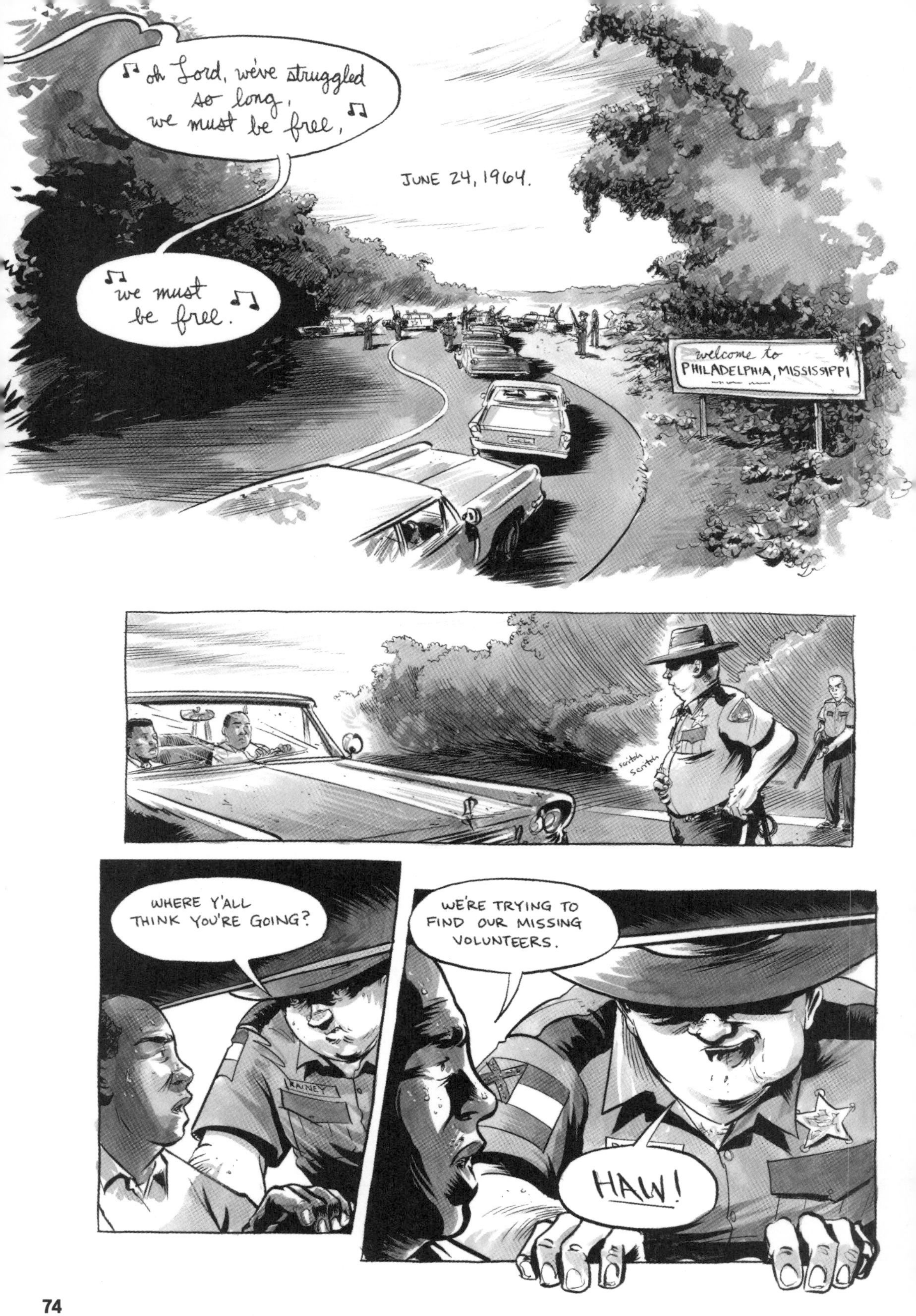
♫ oh Lord, we've struggled so long, we must be free, ♫
♫ we must be free. ♫
JUNE 24, 1964.
welcome to
PHILADELPHIA, MISSISSIPPI
WHERE Y'ALL THINK YOU'RE GOING?
WE'RE TRYING TO FIND OUR MISSING VOLUNTEERS.
HAW!

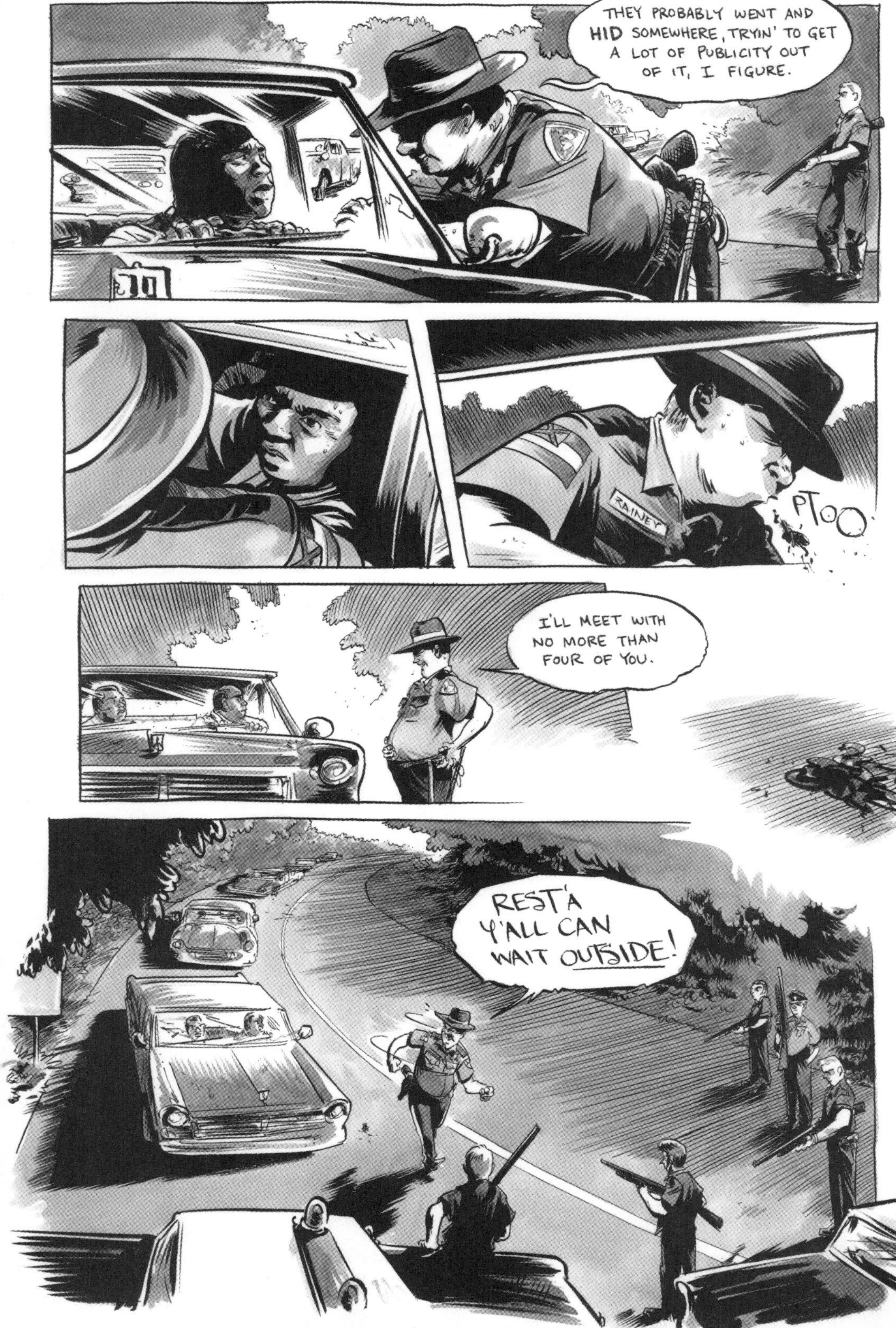
THEY PROBABLY WENT AND HID SOMEWHERE, TRYIN' TO GET A LOT OF PUBLICITY OUT OF IT, I FIGURE.
RAINEY
PTOO
I'LL MEET WITH NO MORE THAN FOUR OF YOU.
REST'A Y'ALL CAN WAIT OUTSIDE!

WHAT WE KNEW AT THAT POINT WAS THAT **MICHAEL SCHWERNER**, **ANDREW GOODMAN**, AND **JAMES CHANEY** HAD BEEN DRIVING BACK FROM INVESTIGATING A BURNED-DOWN CHURCH--

--ONE WE'D BEEN USING AS A **FREEDOM SCHOOL**--

--WHEN THEY WERE ARRESTED FOR SPEEDING AND TAKEN TO JAIL.

NESHOBA COUNTY DEPUTY SHERIFF **CECIL PRICE** ACKNOWLEDGED HE HAD ARRESTED THREE MEN AND TAKEN THEM TO THE PHILADELPHIA CITY JAIL.

ACCORDING TO HIM, THEY WERE RELEASED LATE THAT EVENING AND TOLD TO "LEAVE THE COUNTY."

THE BURNED-OUT SHELL OF THE **CORE** STATION WAGON THEY'D BEEN USING WAS PULLED FROM THE WATERS OF BOGUE CHITTO CREEK,

BUT NO BODIES WERE FOUND.

WELL...

...WHAT CAN WE HELP YOU BOYS WITH?

RAINE

WE DEMAND TO SEE THE CHURCH THAT WAS BURNED, MT. ZION.

YOU'LL NEED A SEARCH WARRANT. IT'S PRIVATE PROPERTY.

THEN LET US SEE THE CAR-- THAT'S **CORE** PROPERTY.

THAT WOULD BE IMPOSSIBLE--

YOU MIGHT DESTROY EVIDENCE.

SPLOOP

So you admit there has been a _crime_.

--IF THERE HAS BEEN A CRIME!

THOSE BOYS MAY HAVE DECIDED TO GO UP NORTH OR SOMEPLACE, AND HAVE A SHORT VACATION.

THEY'LL PROBABLY BE COMING BACK SHORTLY.

LET US HELP WITH THE SEARCH, THEN.

WE HAVE MANY VOLUNTEERS WHO ARE READY TO HELP.

No, no, it's private property...

there's water moccasins--

that would be trespassing.

we don't want anything to happen to you down there.

BY THE TIME THE MEETING ENDED, I HAD NO DOUBT THAT THEY KNEW WHAT HAPPENED.

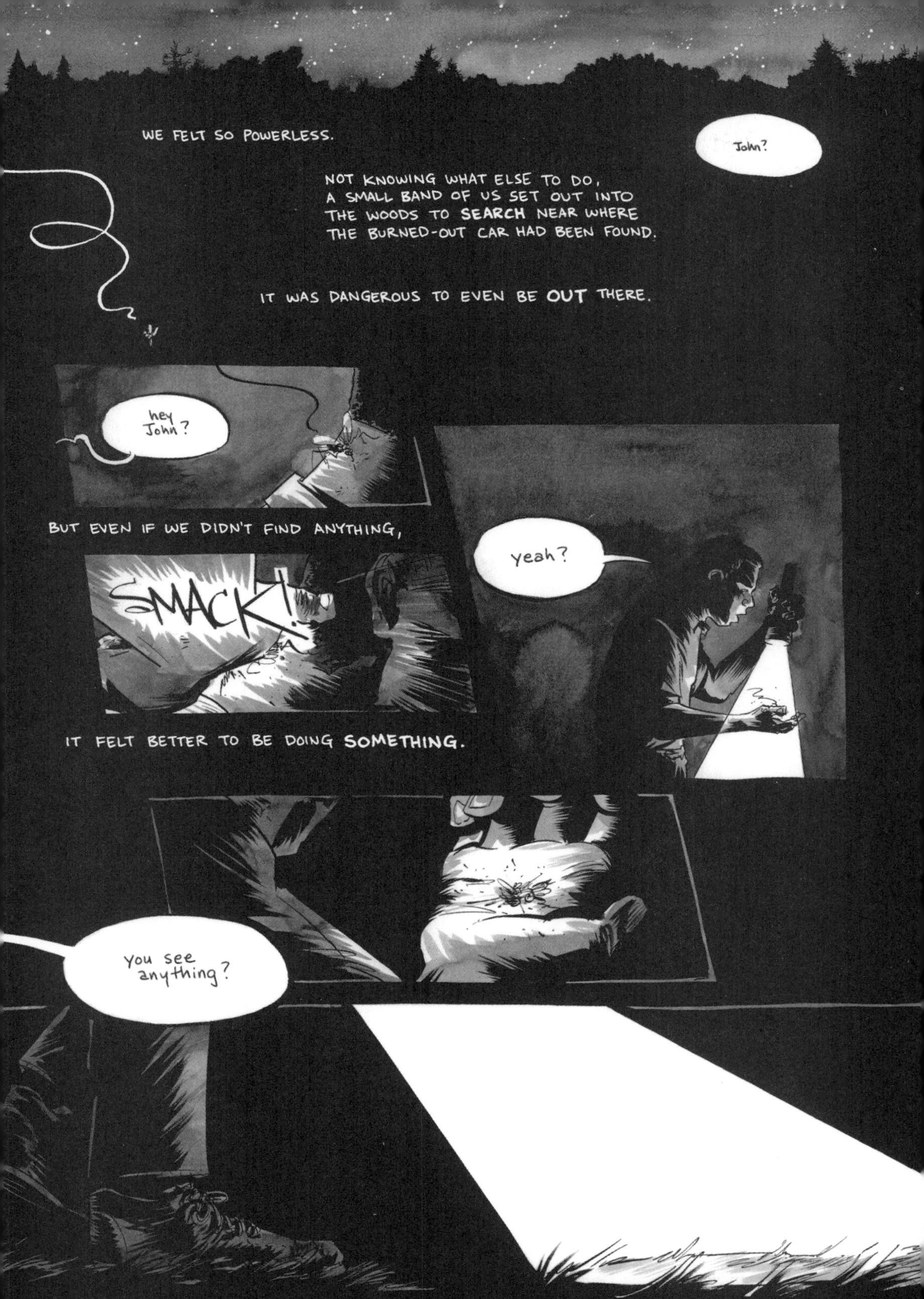
WE FELT SO POWERLESS.
John?
NOT KNOWING WHAT ELSE TO DO, A SMALL BAND OF US SET OUT INTO THE WOODS TO SEARCH NEAR WHERE THE BURNED-OUT CAR HAD BEEN FOUND.
IT WAS DANGEROUS TO EVEN BE OUT THERE.
hey John?
BUT EVEN IF WE DIDN'T FIND ANYTHING,
SMACK!
yeah?
IT FELT BETTER TO BE DOING SOMETHING.
you see anything?

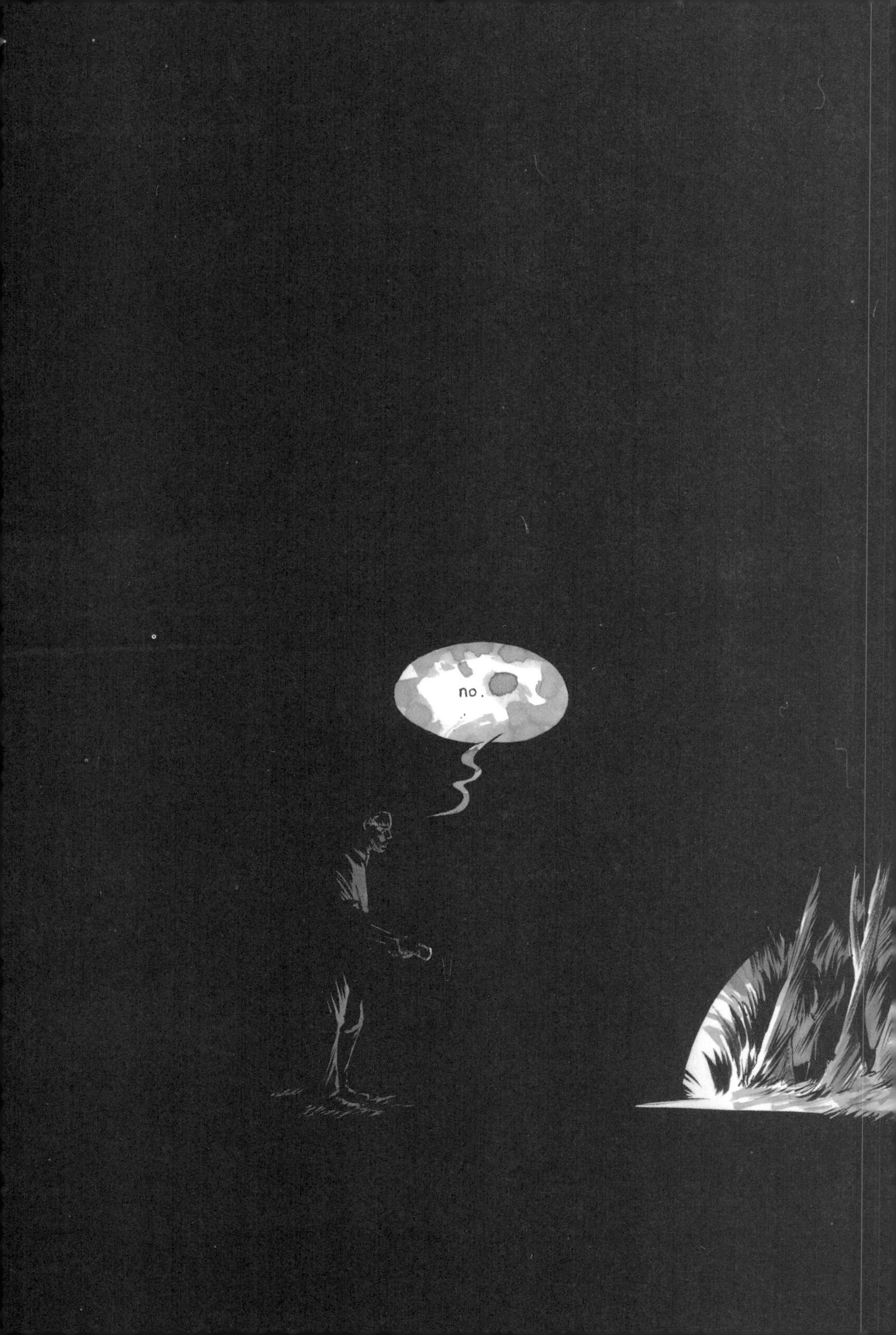
no.

THEIR DISAPPEARANCE WAS THE LEAD NEWS STORY ON TELEVISION AND IN NEWSPAPERS THAT ENTIRE WEEK.

YOU'VE GOT YESTERDAY'S REPORT?

...YES. It's not pretty.

≡sigh≡ OKAY, GIVE ME THE GUTS OF IT.

IT QUICKLY BECAME CLEAR THAT WE WERE RIGHT TO BELIEVE THE COUNTRY WOULD RESPOND DIFFERENTLY ONCE YOUNG **WHITE** PEOPLE STARTED DYING ALONGSIDE THE COUNTLESS BLACK ACTIVISTS WHO SIMPLY DISAPPEARED WITHOUT A TRACE--

--BUT THAT DIDN'T STOP THE VIOLENCE WE FACED.

RULEVILLE-- JUNE 24ᵗʰ, 2AM--

A CAR DRIVEN BY WHITES CIRCLED NOISILY AROUND THE NEGRO COMMUNITY FOR ABOUT TWO HOURS, HURLING BOTTLES AT CARS AND INTO HOMES.

SEVEN INCIDENTS WERE REPORTED TO THE POLICE, BUT THEY **NEVER** ARRIVED ON THE SCENE.

WE MADE A DIRECT APPEAL TO PRESIDENT JOHNSON AND ATTORNEY GENERAL ROBERT KENNEDY FOR INTERVENTION.

CANTON, JUNE 24ᵗʰ-- A CAR FREQUENTLY USED BY **CORE** WORKERS WAS STRUCK BY A **BULLET** AT ABOUT 9:15 PM, APPROXIMATELY TWO MILES OUTSIDE JACKSON, ON THE ROAD TO CANTON.

PRESIDENT JOHNSON RESPONDED BY ORDERING DEFENSE SECRETARY McNAMARA TO SEND **200** ACTIVE DUTY NAVY SAILORS. ATTORNEY GENERAL KENNEDY ORDERED THE FBI TO SEND **150** AGENTS--

--BUT THE SAILORS AND FBI AGENTS WERE ONLY SENT TO MISSISSIPPI TO SEARCH FOR THE MISSING CIVIL RIGHTS WORKERS, NOT TO PROTECT US.

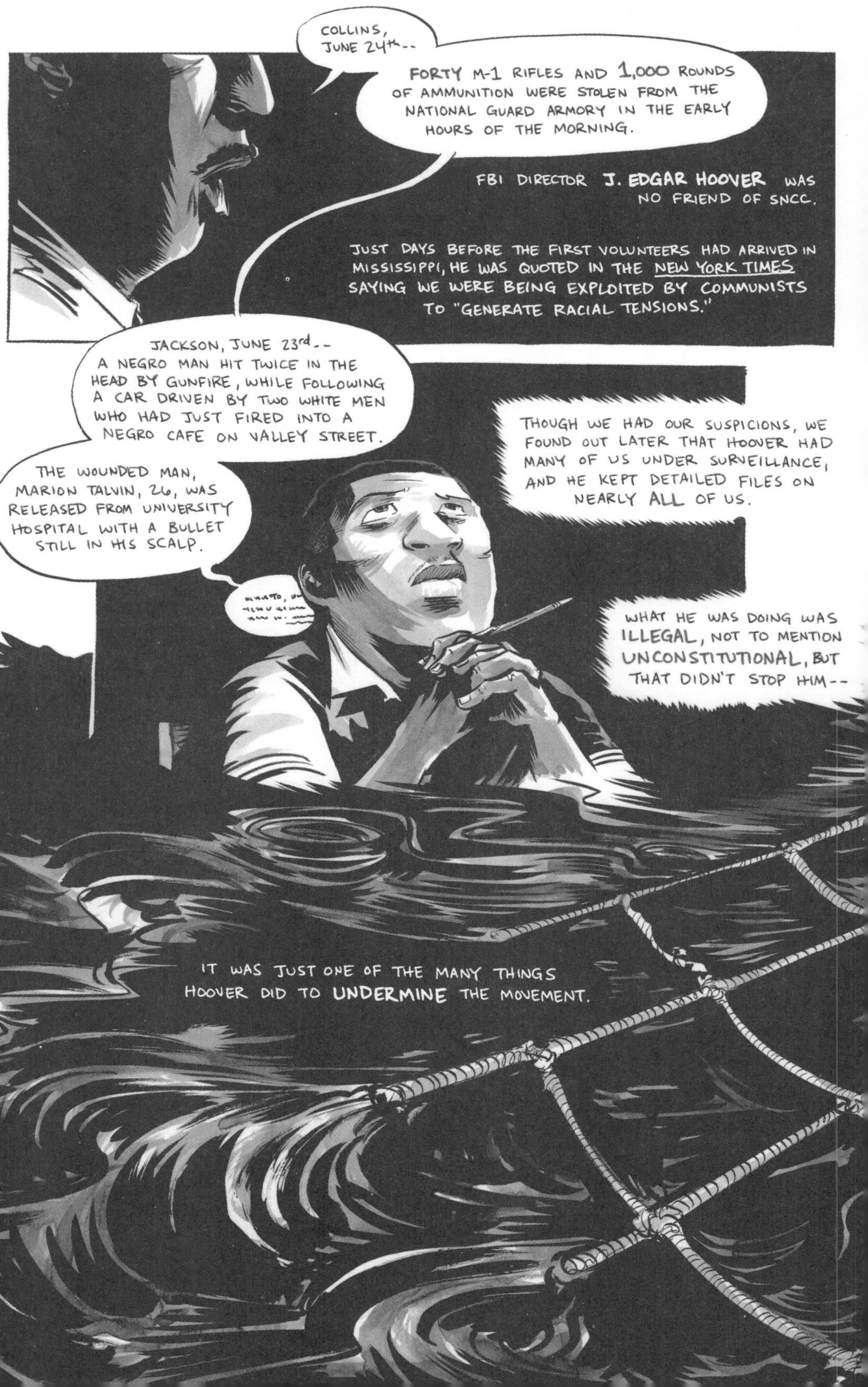
COLLINS, JUNE 24th--
FORTY M-1 RIFLES AND 1,000 ROUNDS OF AMMUNITION WERE STOLEN FROM THE NATIONAL GUARD ARMORY IN THE EARLY HOURS OF THE MORNING.
FBI DIRECTOR J. EDGAR HOOVER WAS NO FRIEND OF SNCC.
JUST DAYS BEFORE THE FIRST VOLUNTEERS HAD ARRIVED IN MISSISSIPPI, HE WAS QUOTED IN THE NEW YORK TIMES SAYING WE WERE BEING EXPLOITED BY COMMUNISTS TO "GENERATE RACIAL TENSIONS."
JACKSON, JUNE 23rd-- A NEGRO MAN HIT TWICE IN THE HEAD BY GUNFIRE, WHILE FOLLOWING A CAR DRIVEN BY TWO WHITE MEN WHO HAD JUST FIRED INTO A NEGRO CAFE ON VALLEY STREET.
THE WOUNDED MAN, MARION TALVIN, 26, WAS RELEASED FROM UNIVERSITY HOSPITAL WITH A BULLET STILL IN HIS SCALP.
THOUGH WE HAD OUR SUSPICIONS, WE FOUND OUT LATER THAT HOOVER HAD MANY OF US UNDER SURVEILLANCE, AND HE KEPT DETAILED FILES ON NEARLY ALL OF US.
WHAT HE WAS DOING WAS ILLEGAL, NOT TO MENTION UNCONSTITUTIONAL, BUT THAT DIDN'T STOP HIM--
IT WAS JUST ONE OF THE MANY THINGS HOOVER DID TO UNDERMINE THE MOVEMENT.

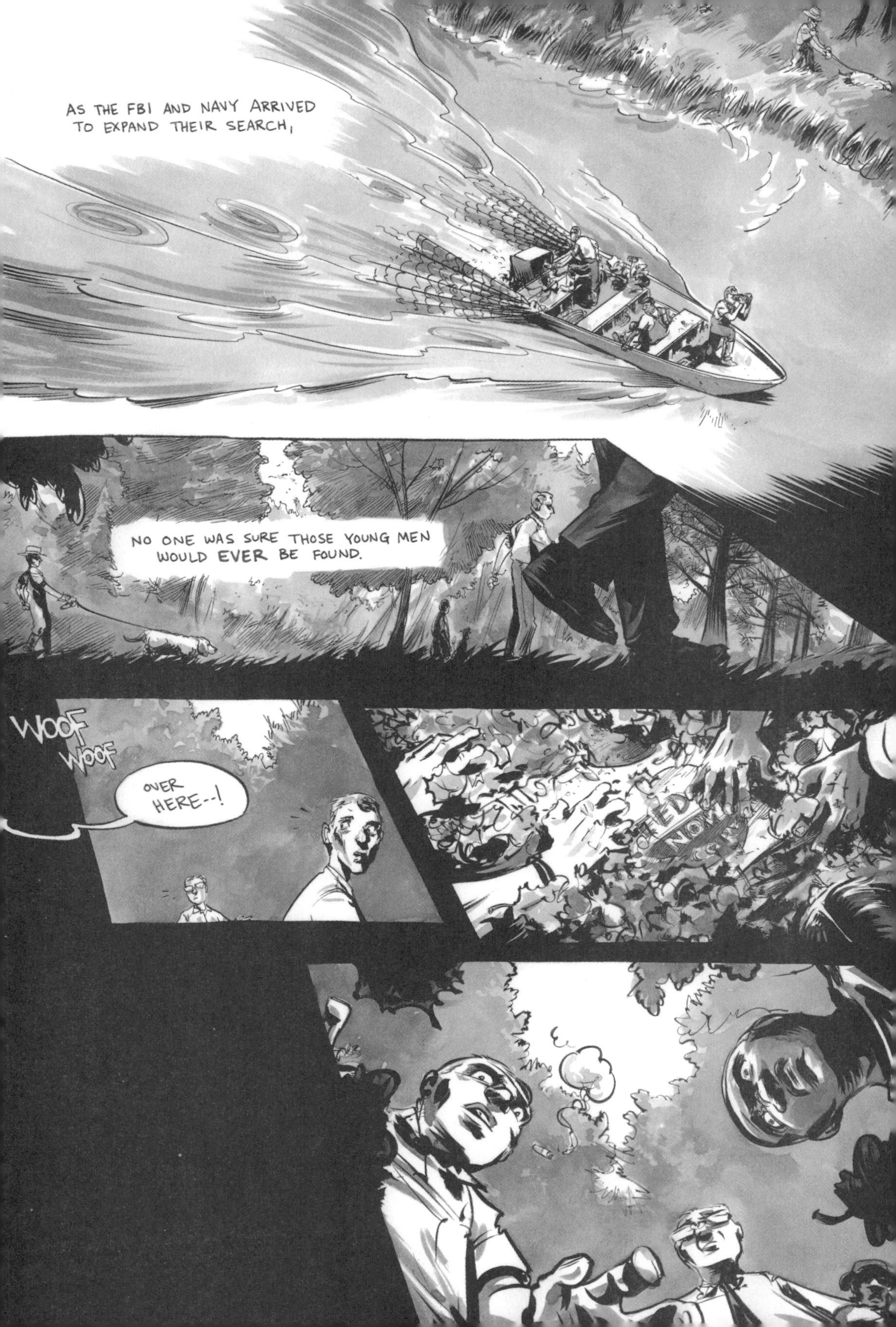
AS THE FBI AND NAVY ARRIVED TO EXPAND THEIR SEARCH,
NO ONE WAS SURE THOSE YOUNG MEN WOULD EVER BE FOUND.
WOOF WOOF
OVER HERE--!

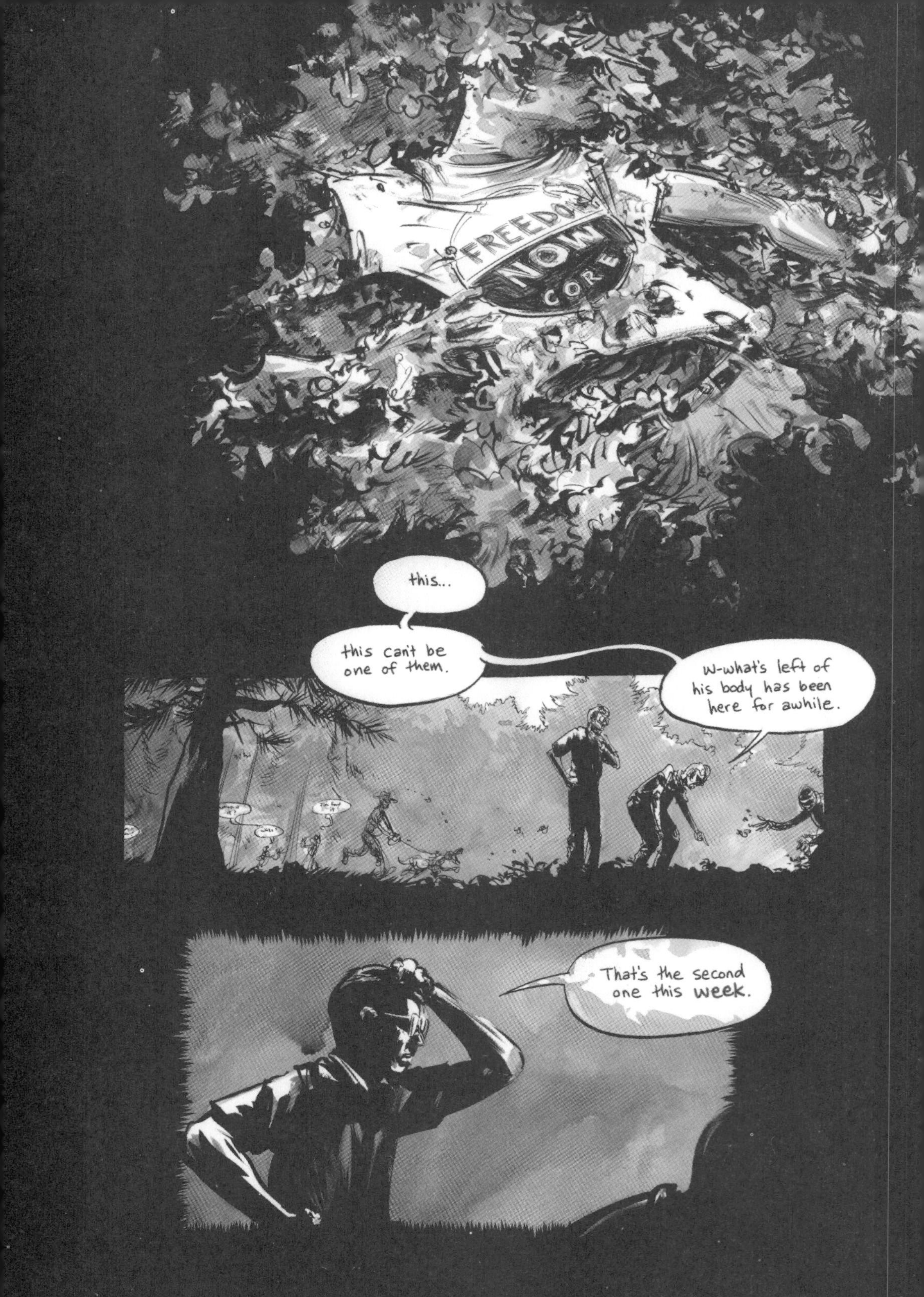
FREEDOM NOW CORE
this...
this can't be one of them.
w-what's left of his body has been here for awhile.
That's the second one this week.

ON JULY 2, THE **CIVIL RIGHTS ACT OF 1964** WAS SIGNED INTO LAW.

ON PAPER, PRESIDENT JOHNSON HAD MADE GOOD ON HIS PROMISE TO GET A STRONG BILL THROUGH THE CONGRESS--

IT BANNED **DISCRIMINATION** IN PLACES OF PUBLIC ACCOMMODATION.

IT FORBADE DISCRIMINATION IN **HIRING** PRACTICES BY BUSINESSES WITH MORE THAN **100** EMPLOYEES.

IT ENDED **SEGREGATION** IN PUBLIC SCHOOLS, LIBRARIES, AND PARKS.

BUT-- AS I HAD SAID AT THE MARCH ON WASHINGTON-- IT DID **NOT** BAN "LITERACY TESTS" AND OTHER VOTING RESTRICTIONS.

I WAS INVITED TO ATTEND THE SIGNING CEREMONY, BUT I DECIDED TO STAY IN THE **SOUTH.** I FELT THAT WAS WHERE I **BELONGED.**

THE NEWS FROM WASHINGTON SEEMED SO FAR AWAY--

WE WERE IN THE MIDDLE OF A <u>WAR.</u>

THE THREE CIVIL RIGHTS WORKERS WERE STILL MISSING, AND THE REAL TEST OF THE CIVIL RIGHTS ACT-- **ENFORCEMENT--** WAS YET TO COME.

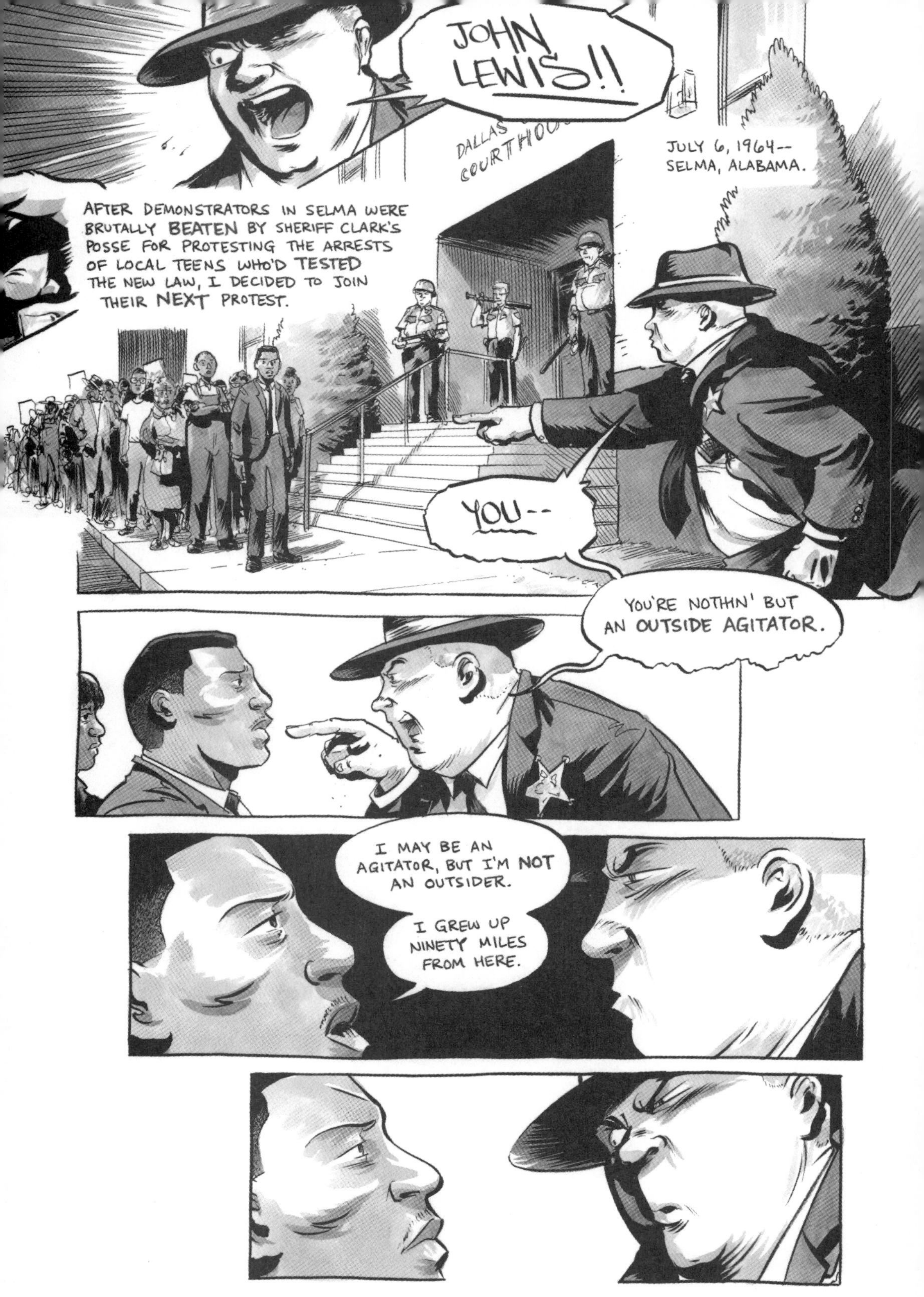
JOHN LEWIS!!
DALLAS COURTHOU
JULY 6, 1964-- SELMA, ALABAMA.
AFTER DEMONSTRATORS IN SELMA WERE BRUTALLY BEATEN BY SHERIFF CLARK'S POSSE FOR PROTESTING THE ARRESTS OF LOCAL TEENS WHO'D TESTED THE NEW LAW, I DECIDED TO JOIN THEIR NEXT PROTEST.
YOU--
YOU'RE NOTHIN' BUT AN OUTSIDE AGITATOR.
I MAY BE AN AGITATOR, BUT I'M NOT AN OUTSIDER.
I GREW UP NINETY MILES FROM HERE.

OUR ARRESTS LED TO AN **INJUNCTION** BY AN ALABAMA CIRCUIT JUDGE NAMED **JAMES HARE**, FORBIDDING GATHERINGS OF MORE THAN **THREE PEOPLE** IN THE CITY OF SELMA.

IT SPECIFICALLY NAMED **47** PEOPLE-- INCLUDING ME-- AND **15** ORGANIZATIONS, INCLUDING **SNCC**. OUR ATTORNEYS SPENT THE REST OF 1964 TRYING UNSUCCESSFULLY TO GET IT LIFTED.

IT **STOPPED** THE SELMA MOVEMENT IN ITS TRACKS.

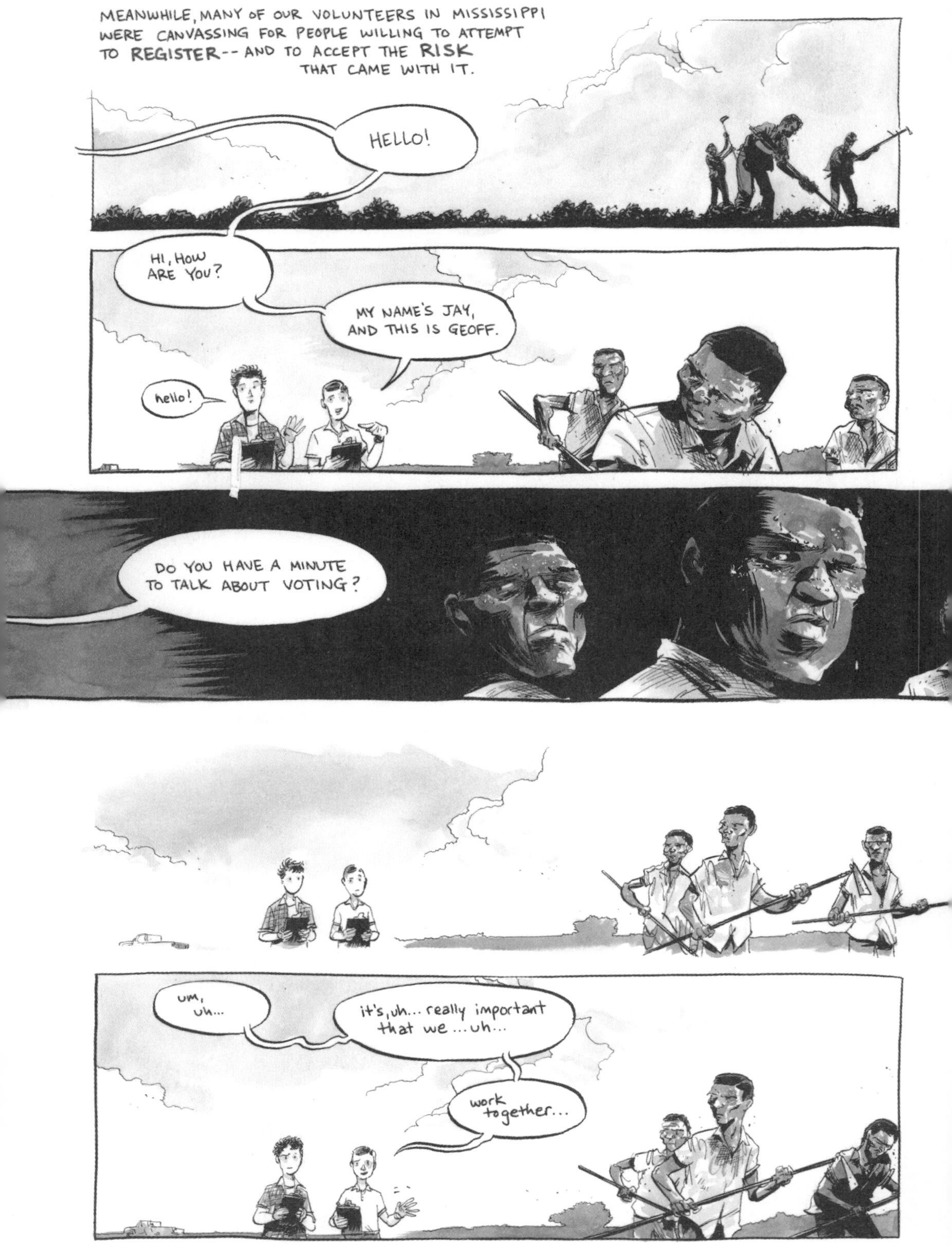
MEANWHILE, MANY OF OUR VOLUNTEERS IN MISSISSIPPI WERE CANVASSING FOR PEOPLE WILLING TO ATTEMPT TO REGISTER-- AND TO ACCEPT THE RISK THAT CAME WITH IT.
HELLO!
HI, HOW ARE YOU?
MY NAME'S JAY, AND THIS IS GEOFF.
hello!
DO YOU HAVE A MINUTE TO TALK ABOUT VOTING?
um, uh...
it's, uh... really important that we ... uh...
work together...

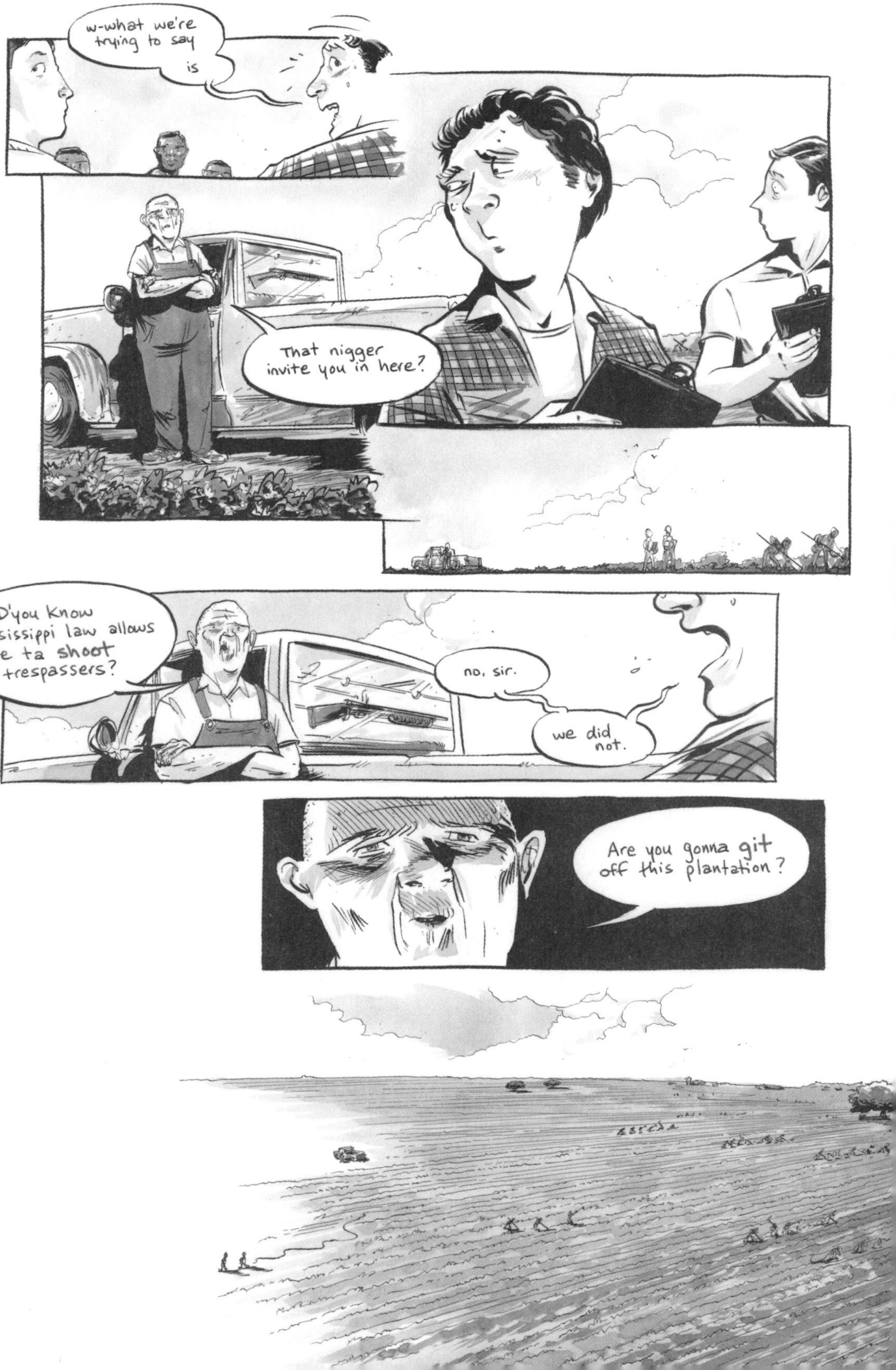
w-what we're trying to say is
That nigger invite you in here?
D'you know Mississippi law allows me ta shoot trespassers?
no, sir.
we did not.
Are you gonna git off this plantation?

BY THE MIDDLE OF JULY, NEARLY ALL OF THE FREEDOM SCHOOLS WERE UP AND RUNNING.

FREEDOM SCHOOL CHURCH

THE TEACHERS HAD TO MAKE DO WITH ONLY A HANDFUL OF BOOKS AND A FEW SUPPLIES, BUT IN MANY PLACES THEY HAD FAR MORE STUDENTS THAN EXPECTED.

IN THE WEEKS AFTER THE SIGNING OF THE CIVIL RIGHTS ACT, THE NAACP AND OTHERS BECAME INCREASINGLY CONCERNED ABOUT OUR CONTINUED PROTESTS--

--AND WHAT THAT COULD MEAN FOR PRESIDENT JOHNSON'S CHANCES AMONG SOUTHERN VOTERS IN THE FALL ELECTION.

Roosevelt Hotel

I WAS SUMMONED TO A MEETING OF THE "BIG SIX" BY A TELEGRAM FROM ROY WILKINS, WHO SAID HE WANTED TO DISCUSS THESE CONCERNS-- AND THE POTENTIAL RISKS "IF WE DO NOT PLAY OUR HAND COOLLY AND INTELLIGENTLY."

THE PROTESTS HAVE TO STOP!

WHAT WILKINS REALLY WANTED WAS FOR US TO AGREE TO A TOTAL BAN ON FURTHER DEMONSTRATIONS, WHICH WE COULD NOT ACCEPT.

THAT'S AN EASY POSITION FOR YOU TO TAKE--

IT'S NOT OFTEN THAT YOU'RE THE ONE IN THE STREETS PROTESTING.

I WAS SURPRISED THAT JAMES FARMER STOOD WITH ME, BUT THE RIGHT TO DEMONSTRATE WAS SOMETHING I BELIEVED WE COULD NEVER COMPROMISE.

Perhaps a broad curtailment, if not a total moratorium...

...would be a better way forward.

IN MISSISSIPPI THAT SUMMER WE SUFFERED MORE THAN 1000 ARRESTS,

80 BEATINGS,

35 SHOOTINGS,

35 CHURCH BURNINGS,

AND 30 BOMBINGS.

DOCTORS WHO EVALUATED VOLUNTEERS RETURNING HOME FROM FREEDOM SUMMER DESCRIBED THE SYMPTOMS OF THE EMOTIONAL AND PHYSICAL TOLL AS "BATTLE FATIGUE," MARKING "A CRISIS IN THE LIVES OF THOSE YOUTHS WHO EXPERIENCE THEM."

DEMONSTRATIONS MUST CONTINUE.

THE PRESSURE MUST BE KEPT ON.

A MOVEMENT IS FUELED BY **PASSION**,

AND WE HAD **PLENTY**.

CHK

IN THE MOVIES, BEING THROWN TOGETHER IN A DANGEROUS SITUATION IS ROMANTIC-- BUT TO BE HONEST, ROMANCE WAS USUALLY THE **LAST** THING ON OUR MINDS.

WE WERE IN A **WAR**.

KA-
TSHHT!

POP TOP!

PEOPLE LIKED TO SPECULATE ABOUT **SEX** IN THE MOVEMENT. IT HAPPENED, SURE, BUT IT WASN'T AS RAMPANT AS A LOT OF PEOPLE THOUGHT.

STILL, WE WERE SO **YOUNG**--

--SPARKS WERE BOUND TO **FLY**.

I REMEMBER ONE NIGHT THAT SUMMER, IN THE MIDDLE OF EVERYTHING GOING ON,

THE MOVIE STAR **SHIRLEY MACLAINE** CAME TO VISIT SNCC IN ATLANTA, AND EVEN CAME TO ONE OF OUR PARTIES.

SHE WOULD LATER WRITE THAT I WAS TOO SWEET TO MAKE A MOVE.

SHE WAS **RIGHT**.

BUT THAT NIGHT, I DANCED WITH SHIRLEY MACLAINE FOR ALMOST AN HOUR.

Of course, by the end of it,

I had two beers and passed out.

AUGUST 4, 1964
NESHOBA COUNTY

ANYTHING?

NO--

BUT THAT SMELL IS GETTING WORSE.

OKAY BERT, AGAIN!

STOP!

STOP!

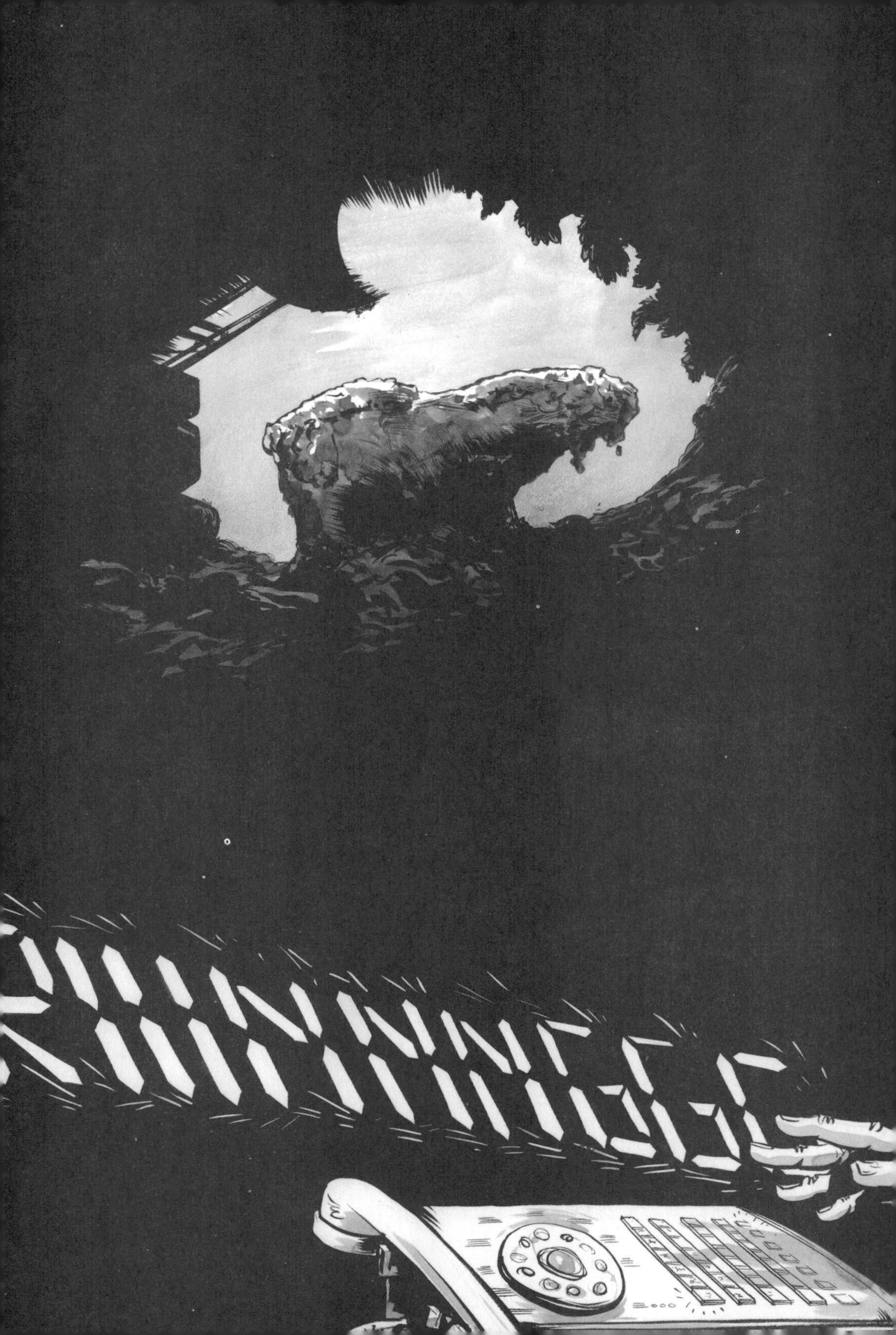

THE WHITE HOUSE.

MR. PRESIDENT?

YEAH?

A DISCUSSION OF THE BREWING MILITARY CONFLICT IN THE GULF OF TONKIN WAS INTERRUPTED BY A PHONE CALL FROM FBI DEPUTY DIRECTOR DELOACH.

MR. HOOVER WANTED ME TO CALL YOU, SIR, IMMEDIATELY AND TELL YOU THAT THE FBI HAS FOUND **THREE BODIES**--

AT THE TIME, WE HAD NO WAY OF KNOWING HOW MUCH THE SIMMERING CRISIS IN SOUTHEAST ASIA WOULD DEFINE THE REST OF THE DECADE.

SIX MILES SOUTHEAST OF PHILADELPHIA, MISSISSIPPI. SIX MILES WEST OF WHERE THE CIVIL RIGHTS WORKERS WERE LAST SEEN ON THE NIGHT OF JUNE 21ST.

A SEARCH PARTY OF AGENTS TURNED UP THE BODIES JUST ABOUT FIFTEEN MINUTES AGO, WHILE THEY WERE DIGGING IN THE WOODS AND UNDERBRUSH SEVERAL HUNDRED YARDS OFF ROUTE 21, IN THAT AREA.

WE'RE GOING TO GET A CORONER THERE RIGHT AWAY, SIR-- AND WE'RE GOING TO MOVE THESE BODIES TO JACKSON, WHERE THEY CAN BE **IDENTIFIED**.

WE HAVE **NOT** IDENTIFIED THEM AS YET AS THE THREE MISSING MEN-- BUT WE HAVE EVERY REASON TO BELIEVE THAT THEY **ARE** THE THREE MISSING MEN.

THEY WERE UNDER A-- THEY WERE AT THE SITE OF A DAM THAT HAD BEEN CONSTRUCTED NEAR PHILADELPHIA, MISSISSIPPI.

Wanted to let you know right away, sir.

When are you gonna make the announcement?

WITHIN TEN MINUTES, SIR, IF IT'S ALL RIGHT WITH YOU.

All right.

96

AUGUST 6, 1964 --
JACKSON, MS.

FREEDOM DEMOCRATIC PARTY

TWO DAYS AFTER THE BODIES OF SCHWERNER, CHANEY, AND GOODMAN WERE FOUND, THE MFDP HELD ITS STATE CONVENTION TO ELECT DELEGATES TO SEND TO ATLANTIC CITY.

JOE RAUH WAS AN ATTORNEY FOR THE MFDP, AND HE OUTLINED ITS STRATEGY FOR THE COMING CHALLENGES AT THE ATLANTIC CITY CONVENTION.

I HAD GOTTEN TO KNOW JOE THAT SUMMER-- HE CAME TO MISSISSIPPI AS GENERAL COUNSEL FOR THE LEADERSHIP CONFERENCE ON CIVIL RIGHTS, AND WORKED EXTENSIVELY WITH BOTH THE UAW AND NAACP.

I RESPECTED JOE RAUH--

HE BELIEVED DEEPLY IN WHAT WE WERE TRYING TO DO, AND IN FUNDAMENTAL HUMAN RIGHTS.

WE NEEDED HIM TO HELP THE MFDP NAVIGATE THE COMPLICATED MAZE OF PRECINCT, COUNTY, AND STATE ELECTIONS. AFTER ALL WE'D BEEN THROUGH, THE CHALLENGE AT THE DEMOCRATIC CONVENTION WOULD REST ALMOST ENTIRELY ON THE LEGAL STRATEGY RAUH AND HIS TEAM CREATED.

OUR MAGIC NUMBERS ARE ELEVEN AND EIGHT!

SEAT THE FREEDOM DEMOCRATIC PARTY!

"ELEVEN AND EIGHT"-- THAT BECAME OUR RALLYING CRY.

THE KEY TO OUR STRATEGY WAS A **HEARING** BEFORE THE 108-MEMBER CREDENTIALS COMMITTEE ON THE FIRST DAY OF THE CONVENTION.

NO ONE EXPECTED THEM TO JUST **GIVE** US MISSISSIPPI'S DELEGATES, BUT PARTY RULES ALLOWED SEATING DISPUTES TO BE TAKEN TO THE CONVENTION FLOOR IF AS FEW AS **ELEVEN** COMMITTEE MEMBERS VOTED FOR IT.

NESHOBA

MARSHALL

SUNFLOWER

WE BELIEVED IF WE GOT **THAT** FAR, WE WOULD WIN IN A **LANDSLIDE.**

AT THAT POINT, ONLY **EIGHT** STATES WOULD BE NEEDED TO REQUEST A **FLOOR VOTE** FOR A **FULL ROLL CALL** VOTE OF THE CONVENTION.

MANY PRO-SEGREGATION DEMOCRATS, SOMETIMES CALLED **DIXIECRATS,** WERE PLANNING TO **SKIP** THE CONVENTION AND PLEDGE THEIR SUPPORT FOR THE **REPUBLICAN** NOMINEE.

WHEN YOU HAVE **TWO** THAT CLAIM TO REPRESENT THE REGULAR PARTY--

YOU TAKE THE **LOYAL** ONE.

I SPOKE THAT DAY.

WE'VE COME TO THIS STATE WITH A SPIRIT OF **LOVE** AND **BROTHERHOOD.**

WE HAVE SUFFERED THE **BEATINGS** AND **ARRESTS.** WE HAVE WITNESSED THE **BURNING** OF OUR CHURCHES AND HOMES.

WE HAVE DEMANDED **ANSWERS** AS OUR FRIENDS AND COLLEAGUES HAVE BEEN **MURDERED.**

HOW LONG WILL IT TAKE THE FEDERAL GOVERNMENT TO SEE WHAT IS HAPPENING?!

IF THEY DO NOT **WANT** TO SEE, WE'LL GO TO ATLANTIC CITY AND WE WILL <u>MAKE</u> THEM SEE!

THE CAPSTONE OF THE JACKSON CONVENTION THAT DAY WAS **ELLA BAKER**'S KEYNOTE ADDRESS.

SHE WAS INSTRUMENTAL IN THE CREATION OF SNCC, AND SO MUCH OF THE MOVEMENT ITSELF, AND YET AGAIN SHE WAS THERE TO LIGHT THE FIRES OF FREEDOM.

A POLITICAL PARTY SHOULD BE OPEN TO **ALL** THE PEOPLE WHO WISH TO SUBSCRIBE TO ITS PRINCIPLES...

AT **NO** POINT WERE THE SOUTHERN STATES **DENIED** THEIR REPRESENTATION ON THE BASIS OF THE FACT THAT THEY HAD DENIED **OTHER** PEOPLE THE RIGHT TO **PARTICIPATE** IN THE ELECTION OF THOSE WHO GOVERN THEM.

NOW THIS IS **NOT** THE KIND OF KEYNOTE SPEECH, PERHAPS, YOU LIKE. BUT I'M NOT TRYING TO MAKE YOU FEEL GOOD.

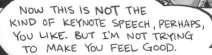

YOUNG MEN AND WOMEN WANT SOME **MEANING** IN THEIR LIVES.

UNTIL THE KILLING OF BLACK MOTHERS' SONS IS AS IMPORTANT AS THE KILLING OF WHITE MOTHERS' SONS--

--WE MUST <u>KEEP ON.</u>

FOLLOWING THE RULES OF THE DEMOCRATIC PARTY, A FULL SLATE OF **68** DELEGATES WAS ELECTED, INCLUDING THE MFDP'S VICE-CHAIR, **FANNIE LOU HAMER.**

AUGUST 7, 1964.

FIRST UNION MISSIONARY BAPTIST CHURCH-- MERIDIAN, MS.

THE NEXT DAY, I WENT TO JAMES CHANEY'S FUNERAL.

DAVE DENNIS, CO-DIRECTOR OF **COFO**, DELIVERED THE EULOGY.

AS I STAND HERE, I NOT ONLY BLAME THE PEOPLE WHO PULLED THE TRIGGER, OR DID THE BEATING, OR DUG THE HOLE WITH A SHOVEL.

I BLAME THE PEOPLE IN WASHINGTON, D.C. --

--AND ON DOWN IN THE STATE OF MISSISSIPPI FOR WHAT HAPPENED JUST AS MUCH AS I BLAME THOSE WHO PULLED THE TRIGGER.

YOU SEE, I KNOW WHAT'S GOING TO HAPPEN.

I FEEL THAT, EVEN IF THEY **FIND** THE PEOPLE WHO KILLED THOSE GUYS IN THE SUMMERTIME, YOU GOT TO COME BACK TO THE STATE OF MISSISSIPPI AND HAVE A JURY, ALL THEIR COUSINS, THEIR AUNTS, THEIR UNCLES.

AND I **KNOW** WHAT THEY'RE GOING TO SAY-- 'NOT GUILTY', BECAUSE NO ONE SAW THEM PULL THE TRIGGER.

I'M TIRED OF THAT.

SEE, **ANOTHER** THING THAT MAKES ME EVEN **TIREDER**, THOUGH,

IS THAT WE, AS PEOPLE HERE IN THIS **STATE** AND THE COUNTRY--

ARE ALLOWING THIS TO **CONTINUE** TO HAPPEN.

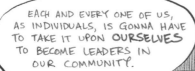

EACH AND EVERY ONE OF US, AS INDIVIDUALS, IS GONNA HAVE TO TAKE IT UPON **OURSELVES** TO BECOME LEADERS IN OUR COMMUNITY.

TAKING OUR BLACK BROTHERS BY THE **HAND**--

BLOCK BY BLOCK, HOUSE BY HOUSE, CITY BY CITY, COUNTY BY COUNTY, STATE BY STATE THROUGH THIS ENTIRE **COUNTRY**.

HOLDING OUR HANDS UP **HIGH**, TELLIN' THEM THAT IF THEY'RE NOT READY FOR US, **TOO BAD**, BABY,

'CAUSE WE'RE COMING **ANYWAY**, YOU SEE.

THE BEST THING THAT WE CAN **DO** FOR MR. CHANEY, FOR MICKEY SCHWERNER, FOR ANDREW GOODMAN, IS TO **STAND UP** AND DEMAND OUR **RIGHTS**.

ALL THESE PEOPLE WHO **AREN'T** REGISTERED VOTERS SHOULD BE IN **LINE** IN THE MORNING, DEMANDING TO BECOME A REGISTERED VOTER-- **DEMAND!**

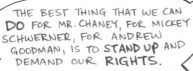

SAY, "BABY, I'M **HERE**."

...DON'T BOW DOWN **ANYMORE**. HOLD YOUR HEADS UP!

WE WANT OUR FREEDOM-- **NOW!!**

I DON'T WANT TO GO TO ANOTHER MEMORIAL-- I'M **TIRED** OF FUNERALS! **TIRED** OF IT!

WE GOT TO **STAND UP!**

JULY 14, 1964--
DALY CITY, CA.

AT THE 1964 REPUBLICAN NATIONAL CONVENTION, NEW YORK GOVERNOR **NELSON ROCKEFELLER** TRIED TO SWAY THE PARTY OF LINCOLN TO **STAND UP** TO THE GROWING INFLUENCE OF CONSERVATIVE EXTREMISTS.

IT IS **ESSENTIAL** THAT THIS CONVENTION REPUDIATE, HERE AND NOW, ANY DOCTRINAIRE, MILITANT MINORITY-- WHETHER COMMUNIST, KU KLUX KLAN, OR BIRCHER-- WHICH WOULD **SUBVERT** THIS PARTY TO PURPOSES ALIEN TO THE VERY **BASIC TENETS** WHICH GAVE THIS PARTY BIRTH.

PRECISELY ONE YEAR AGO TODAY ON JULY 14, 1963, I ISSUED A STATEMENT WHEREIN I WARNED THAT:

"THE REPUBLICAN PARTY IS IN **REAL DANGER** OF SUBVERSION BY A RADICAL, WELL-FINANCED, AND HIGHLY DISCIPLINED MINORITY.

AT THE TIME, I POINTED OUT THAT THE PURPOSES OF THIS MINORITY WERE:

"WHOLLY ALIEN TO THE SOUND AND HONEST CONSERVATISM THAT HAS FIRMLY BASED THE REPUBLICAN PARTY IN THE **BEST** OF A CENTURY'S TRADITIONS,

"WHOLLY ALIEN TO THE SOUND AND HONEST REPUBLICAN LIBERALISM THAT HAS KEPT THE PARTY ABREAST OF **HUMAN NEEDS** IN A CHANGING WORLD,

"WHOLLY ALIEN TO THE **BROAD MIDDLE COURSE** THAT ACCOMODATES THE MAINSTREAM OF REPUBLICAN PRINCIPLES."

BOOOO

BOOOO!

BOOoo

BOOOO

HISSSSS HA!

BOOO

OUR SOLE CONCERN MUST BE THE FUTURE **WELL-BEING** OF AMERICA, AND OF FREEDOM AND RESPECT FOR **HUMAN DIGNITY**--

THE PRESERVATION AND ENHANCEMENT OF THESE PRINCIPLES UPON WHICH THIS NATION HAS ACHIEVED ITS GREATNESS.

BOOOO

BOOOO

BOOOoo

BOOoo

BOOoooo!

BOOoo

THE REPUBLICAN PARTY NOMINATED **BARRY GOLDWATER**-- A SENATOR FROM ARIZONA WHO HAD VOTED **AGAINST** THE CIVIL RIGHTS ACT-- FOR PRESIDENT.

THOSE WHO SEEK ABSOLUTE POWER-- EVEN THOUGH THEY SEEK IT TO DO WHAT THEY REGARD AS **GOOD**--ARE SIMPLY DEMANDING THE RIGHT TO ENFORCE THEIR **OWN** VERSION OF HEAVEN ON EARTH.

AND LET ME REMIND YOU THEY ARE THE **VERY ONES** WHO CREATE THE MOST HELLISH **TYRANNIES**.

ABSOLUTE POWER **DOES** CORRUPT, AND THOSE WHO SEEK IT MUST BE SUSPECT AND MUST BE **OPPOSED**.

THEIR MISTAKEN COURSE STEMS FROM **FALSE NOTIONS** OF **EQUALITY**, LADIES AND GENTLEMEN.

EQUALITY, **RIGHTLY** UNDERSTOOD AS OUR FOUNDING FATHERS UNDERSTOOD IT, LEADS TO LIBERTY AND TO THE EMANCIPATION OF CREATIVE DIFFERENCES.

WRONGLY UNDERSTOOD-- AS IT HAS BEEN SO **TRAGICALLY** IN OUR TIME-- IT LEADS FIRST TO CONFORMITY, AND THEN TO DESPOTISM.

GOLDWATER'S ACCEPTANCE SPEECH SIGNALED A DANGEROUS **SHIFT** IN THE REPUBLICAN PARTY.

I WOULD REMIND YOU THAT **EXTREMISM** IN THE DEFENSE OF LIBERTY IS NO VICE--

AND LET ME REMIND YOU, ALSO, THAT **MODERATION** IN THE PURSUIT OF JUSTICE IS NO **VIRTUE**.

IT WAS IN THIS SHADOW THAT PRESIDENT JOHNSON MAPPED HIS PATH TO **RE-ELECTION**.

AUGUST 14, 1964.

...WE BETTER JUST REALLY TRY TO SEE IF THE NEGROES DON'T REALIZE THAT THEY'VE GOT THE PRESIDENT, THEY'VE GOT THE VICE PRESIDENT,

THEY'LL HAVE THE GOVERNMENT FOR FOUR YEARS, THAT WE'LL BE FAIR AND JUST WITH THEM--

--AND WHY IN THE LIVING HELL DO THEY WANT TO HAND-SHOVEL FIFTEEN STATES TO GOLDWATER?!

DO YOU SEE ANY GOOD THAT CAN COME FROM IT?

A WEEK BEFORE WE WERE SET TO ARRIVE IN ATLANTIC CITY, PRESIDENT JOHNSON CALLED SENATOR HUBERT HUMPHREY OF MINNESOTA TO DISCUSS OUR ACTIONS--

--AND ENLIST HUMPHREY'S SUPPORT IN STOPPING US.

CAN IT GET US ANY VOTES, ANYWHERE?

NOT ONE DAMN BIT OF GOOD. NOT ONE BIT.

WE'RE JUST NOT DEALING WITH WHAT I CALL EMOTIONALLY STABLE PEOPLE ON THIS, MR. PRESIDENT.

PASSED OVER BY PRESIDENT KENNEDY AS A RUNNING-MATE, SENATOR HUMPHREY HAD LONG HELD AMBITIONS FOR THE PRESIDENCY.

STILL UNDECIDED, PRESIDENT JOHNSON WAS TO ANNOUNCE HIS RUNNING-MATE IN A MATTER OF DAYS AT THE DEMOCRATIC NATIONAL CONVENTION.

NOW IF WE, ON THE OTHER HAND, HAVE A FIGHT ON THIS--

AND WIN--

-- AND WE SUPPORT MISSISSIPPI, IT SEEMS TO ME THAT ALL THE POOR NEGROES IN ATLANTA AND HARLEM WILL SAY, "WELL, JOHNSON AND HUMPHREY-- LOOK AT THEM.

"THEY STOOD UP FOR MISSISSIPPI AT THE CONVENTION, SO WE HAVEN'T GOT MUCH CHOICE BETWEEN GOLDWATER AND HIM--

"AND SO WE JUST WON'T VOTE."

well...

...WE'VE GOT TO SETTLE IT BEFORE THE CONVENTION. I KNOW THAT.

AUGUST 21, 1964.

THE DELEGATES ARRIVED BY BUS AT THE OLD GEM HOTEL IN ATLANTIC CITY.

THEY WERE A SIGHT TO BEHOLD--

THE EPITOME OF AMERICAN DEMOCRACY.

DR. KING, MYSELF, AND MANY OTHERS WOULD COME ALONG TO SUPPORT THE DELEGATES--

-- TO STAGE RALLIES, TALK TO THE PRESS, AND SHOW THE WORLD WHAT WE STOOD FOR.

WE EVEN BROUGHT A BURNED-OUT CAR TO REPRESENT THE ONE DRIVEN BY GOODMAN, SCHWERNER, AND CHANEY.

MEANWHILE, JOE RAUH WAS MAKING FINAL PREPARATIONS FOR THE NEXT DAY'S TESTIMONY BEFORE THE CREDENTIALS COMMITTEE.

JOE-- THEY'VE **SCREWED** YOU!

MY GOD, ALREADY?

CONVENTION ORGANIZERS HAD SCHEDULED THE MEETING IN A ROOM **TOO SMALL** TO ACCOMMODATE THE TELEVISION CAMERAS THAT WERE SO **ESSENTIAL** TO OUR PLANNING.

WE WERE MAKING OUR CASE TO THE **NATION** JUST AS MUCH AS TO THE COMMITTEE.

RAUH **PREVAILED**, AND THE MEETING TOOK PLACE IN A BALLROOM LARGE ENOUGH TO ACCOMMODATE CAMERAS FROM **ALL** THE MAJOR NETWORKS.

WE ONLY HAVE AN HOUR...

HE WAS A WASHINGTON INSIDER-- AND A **MEMBER** OF THE CREDENTIALS COMMITTEE IN HIS OWN RIGHT. HIS OPENING STATEMENT ESTABLISHED OUR **ATTACK** ON THE "REGULAR" MISSISSIPPI DELEGATION.

...TO TELL YOU A STORY OF **TRAGEDY** AND **TERROR** IN MISSISSIPPI.

I WATCHED FROM A ROOM DOWN THE HALL AS RAUH CALLED A SERIES OF WITNESSES, INCLUDING AARON HENRY AND REV. ED KING, WHOSE TESTIMONY APPEALED TO THE **MORAL CONSCIOUSNESS** OF THE COMMITTEE MEMBERS.

BUT ONE TESTIMONY SHOOK THE **NATION.**

MR. CHAIRMAN,

AND TO THE CREDENTIALS COMMITTEE--

MY NAME IS MRS. FANNIE LOU HAMER--

I LIVE AT 626 EAST LAFAYETTE STREET; RULEVILLE, MISSISSIPPI; SUNFLOWER COUNTY-- THE HOME OF SENATOR JAMES O. EASTLAND AND SENATOR STENNIS.

IT WAS THE 31ST OF AUGUST, 1962-- EIGHTEEN OF US TRAVELED **26** MILES TO THE COUNTY COURTHOUSE IN INDIANOLA, TO TRY TO REGISTER TO BECOME **FIRST-CLASS CITIZENS.**

WE WAS MET IN INDIANOLA BY POLICEMEN-- **HIGHWAY PATROLMEN--** AND THEY ONLY ALLOWED **TWO** OF US TO TAKE THE LITERACY TEST AT THE TIME.

CREDENTIALS COMMITTEE

AFTER WE HAD TAKEN THIS TEST AND STARTED BACK TO RULEVILLE, WE WAS HELD UP BY THE CITY POLICE AND THE STATE HIGHWAY PATROLMEN, AND CARRIED BACK TO INDIANOLA--

WHERE THE BUS DRIVER WAS CHARGED WITH DRIVING A BUS THE WRONG COLOR.

AFTER WE PAID THE FINE AMONG US, WE CONTINUED ON TO RULEVILLE. REVEREND JEFF SUNNY CARRIED ME FOUR MILES IN THE RURAL AREA WHERE I HAD WORKED AS A TIMEKEEPER AND SHARECROPPER FOR 18 YEARS.

I WAS MET THERE BY MY CHILDREN, WHO TOLD ME THAT THE PLANTATION OWNER WAS ANGRY--

BECAUSE I'D GONE DOWN TO TRY TO REGISTER.

AFTER THEY TOLD ME, MY HUSBAND CAME, AND SAID THE PLANTATION OWNER WAS RAISING CAIN BECAUSE I'D TRIED TO REGISTER.

BUT BEFORE HE QUIT TALKING, THE PLANTATION OWNER CAME AND SAID, "FANNIE LOU, DID PAP TELL YOU WHAT I SAID?"

AND I SAID, "YES, SIR."

HE SAID, "WELL, I MEAN THAT."

HE SAID, "IF YOU DON'T GO DOWN AND WITHDRAW YOUR REGISTRATION, YOU WILL HAVE TO LEAVE--

I ADDRESSED HIM AND SAID, "I DIDN'T TRY TO REGISTER FOR YOU. I TRIED TO REGISTER FOR MYSELF."

I HAD TO LEAVE THAT SAME NIGHT.

"--THEN IF YOU GO DOWN AND WITHDRAW, YOU STILL MIGHT HAVE TO GO,

BECAUSE WE'RE NOT READY FOR THAT IN MISSISSIPPI."

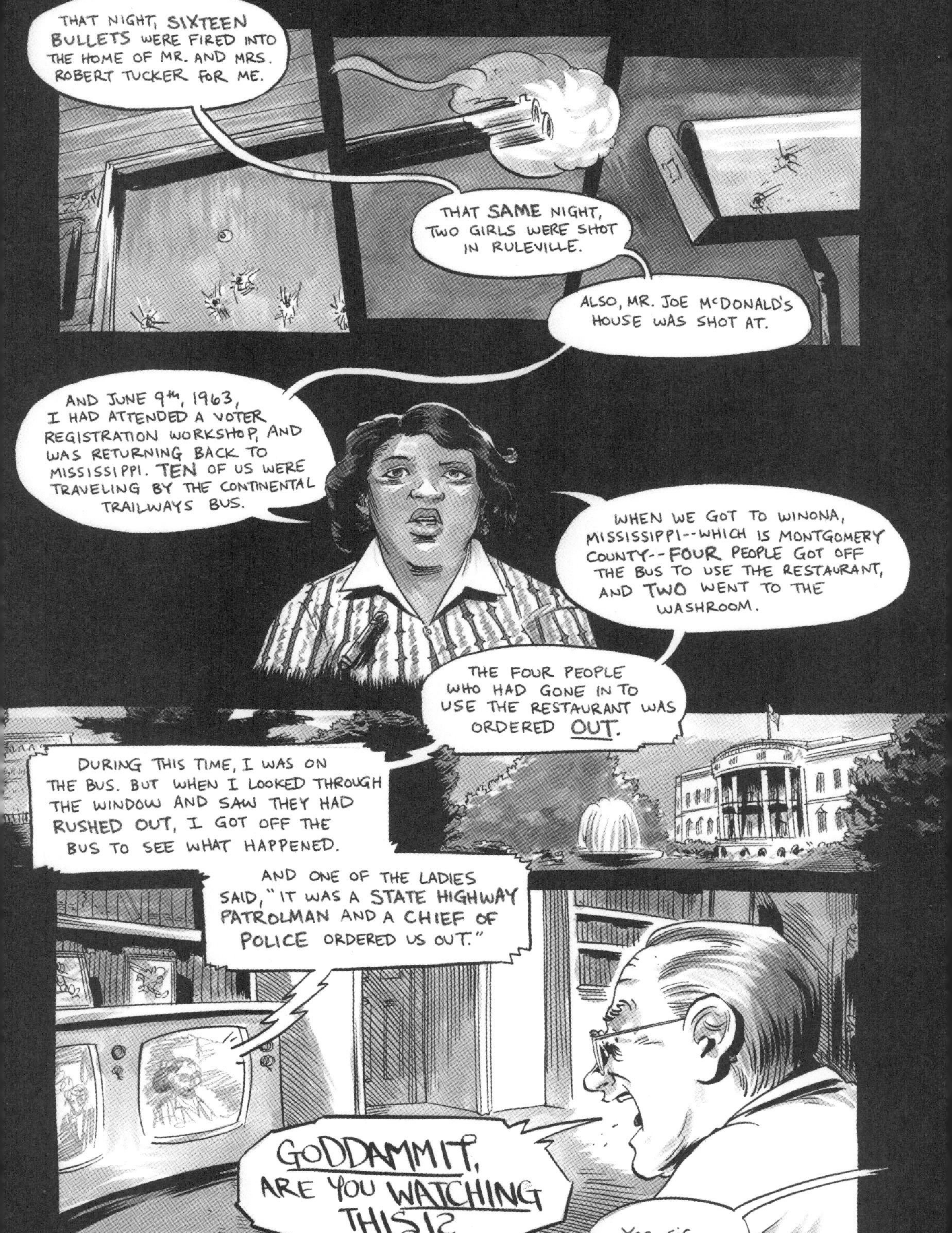
THAT NIGHT, SIXTEEN BULLETS WERE FIRED INTO THE HOME OF MR. AND MRS. ROBERT TUCKER FOR ME.
THAT SAME NIGHT, TWO GIRLS WERE SHOT IN RULEVILLE.
ALSO, MR. JOE McDONALD'S HOUSE WAS SHOT AT.
AND JUNE 9th, 1963, I HAD ATTENDED A VOTER REGISTRATION WORKSHOP, AND WAS RETURNING BACK TO MISSISSIPPI. TEN OF US WERE TRAVELING BY THE CONTINENTAL TRAILWAYS BUS.
WHEN WE GOT TO WINONA, MISSISSIPPI--WHICH IS MONTGOMERY COUNTY--FOUR PEOPLE GOT OFF THE BUS TO USE THE RESTAURANT, AND TWO WENT TO THE WASHROOM.
THE FOUR PEOPLE WHO HAD GONE IN TO USE THE RESTAURANT WAS ORDERED OUT.
DURING THIS TIME, I WAS ON THE BUS. BUT WHEN I LOOKED THROUGH THE WINDOW AND SAW THEY HAD RUSHED OUT, I GOT OFF THE BUS TO SEE WHAT HAPPENED.
AND ONE OF THE LADIES SAID, "IT WAS A STATE HIGHWAY PATROLMAN AND A CHIEF OF POLICE ORDERED US OUT."
GODDAMMIT, ARE YOU WATCHING THIS!?
Yes, sir.

I GOT BACK ON THE BUS, AND ONE OF THE PERSONS WHO'D USED THE WASHROOM GOT BACK ON, TOO. AS SOON AS I WAS SEATED, I SAW WHEN THEY BEGAN TO PUT THE FIVE PEOPLE IN A HIGHWAY PATROLMAN'S CAR.

WE'VE GOT TO DO SOMETHING!

I STEPPED OFF THE BUS TO SEE WHAT WAS HAPPENING, AND SOMEBODY SCREAMED FROM THE CAR THAT THE FIVE WORKERS WAS IN AND SAID, "GET THAT ONE THERE."

what should we do, sir?

WHEN THE MAN TOLD ME I WAS UNDER ARREST AND I WENT TO GET IN THE CAR, HE KICKED ME.

We've got to get that woman OFF the television.

I WAS CARRIED TO THE COUNTY JAIL AND PUT IN THE BOOKING ROOM... AFTER I WAS PLACED IN THE CELL, I BEGAN TO HEAR SOUNDS OF LICKS AND SCREAMS.

I COULD HEAR THE SOUNDS OF LICKS AND HORRIBLE SCREAMS.

AND I COULD HEAR SOMEBODY SAY, "CAN YOU SAY 'YES, SIR', NIGGER? CAN YOU SAY 'YES, SIR'?"

AND THEY WOULD SAY OTHER HORRIBLE NAMES.

SHE WOULD SAY, "YES, I CAN SAY 'YES, SIR.'"

"SO, WELL-- SAY IT."

SHE SAID, "I DON'T KNOW YOU WELL ENOUGH."

CALL A PRESS CONFERENCE.

What should I say the press conference is about, sir?

THEY BEAT HER I DON'T KNOW **HOW** LONG.

AND AFTER A WHILE SHE BEGAN TO PRAY, AND ASKED GOD TO HAVE MERCY ON THOSE PEOPLE.

AND IT WASN'T TOO LONG BEFORE THREE WHITE MEN CAME TO <u>MY</u> CELL.

WE'LL FIGURE IT OUT.

ONE OF THESE MEN WAS A STATE HIGHWAY PATROLMAN, AND HE ASKED WHERE I WAS FROM.

I TOLD HIM RULEVILLE AND HE SAID, "WE ARE GOING TO CHECK ON THIS."

THEY LEFT MY CELL, AND IT WASN'T TOO LONG BEFORE THEY CAME BACK.

HE SAID, "YOU'RE FROM RULEVILLE ALL RIGHT," AND HE USED A CURSE WORD.

And he said, "We are going to make you wish you was dead."

I WAS CARRIED INTO ANOTHER CELL WHERE THEY HAD TWO NEGRO PRISONERS. THE STATE HIGHWAY PATROLMAN ORDERED THE FIRST NEGRO TO TAKE THE BLACKJACK.

THE FIRST NEGRO PRISONER ORDERED ME-- BY ORDERS FROM THE STATE HIGHWAY PATROLMAN-- FOR ME TO LAY DOWN ON A BUNK BED ON MY FACE.

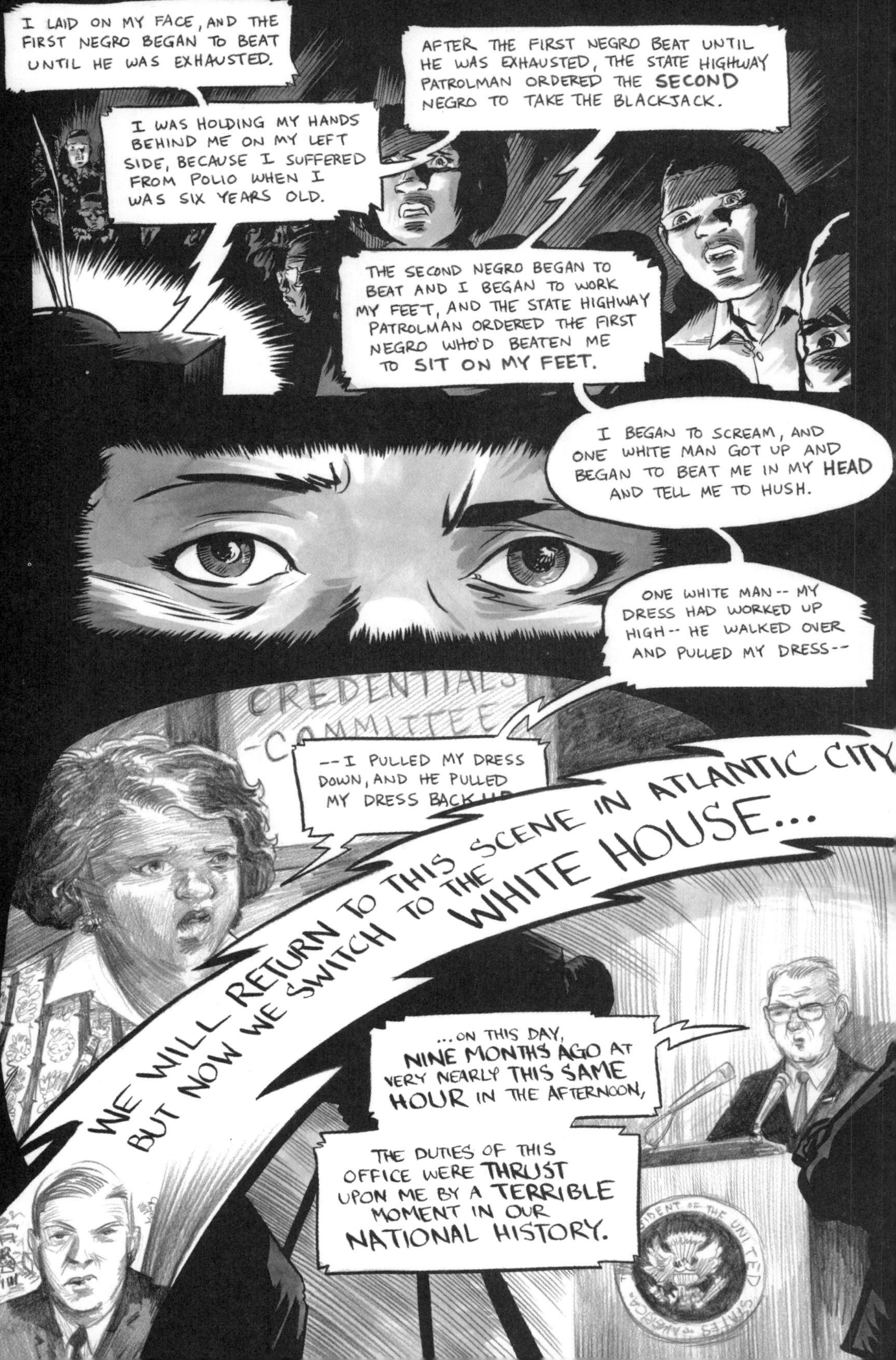
I LAID ON MY FACE, AND THE FIRST NEGRO BEGAN TO BEAT UNTIL HE WAS EXHAUSTED.
I WAS HOLDING MY HANDS BEHIND ME ON MY LEFT SIDE, BECAUSE I SUFFERED FROM POLIO WHEN I WAS SIX YEARS OLD.
AFTER THE FIRST NEGRO BEAT UNTIL HE WAS EXHAUSTED, THE STATE HIGHWAY PATROLMAN ORDERED THE SECOND NEGRO TO TAKE THE BLACKJACK.
THE SECOND NEGRO BEGAN TO BEAT AND I BEGAN TO WORK MY FEET, AND THE STATE HIGHWAY PATROLMAN ORDERED THE FIRST NEGRO WHO'D BEATEN ME TO SIT ON MY FEET.
I BEGAN TO SCREAM, AND ONE WHITE MAN GOT UP AND BEGAN TO BEAT ME IN MY HEAD AND TELL ME TO HUSH.
ONE WHITE MAN -- MY DRESS HAD WORKED UP HIGH -- HE WALKED OVER AND PULLED MY DRESS --
CREDENTIALS
-- I PULLED MY DRESS DOWN, AND HE PULLED MY DRESS BACK
WE WILL RETURN TO THIS SCENE IN ATLANTIC CITY BUT NOW WE SWITCH TO THE WHITE HOUSE...
...ON THIS DAY, NINE MONTHS AGO AT VERY NEARLY THIS SAME HOUR IN THE AFTERNOON,
THE DUTIES OF THIS OFFICE WERE THRUST UPON ME BY A TERRIBLE MOMENT IN OUR NATIONAL HISTORY.

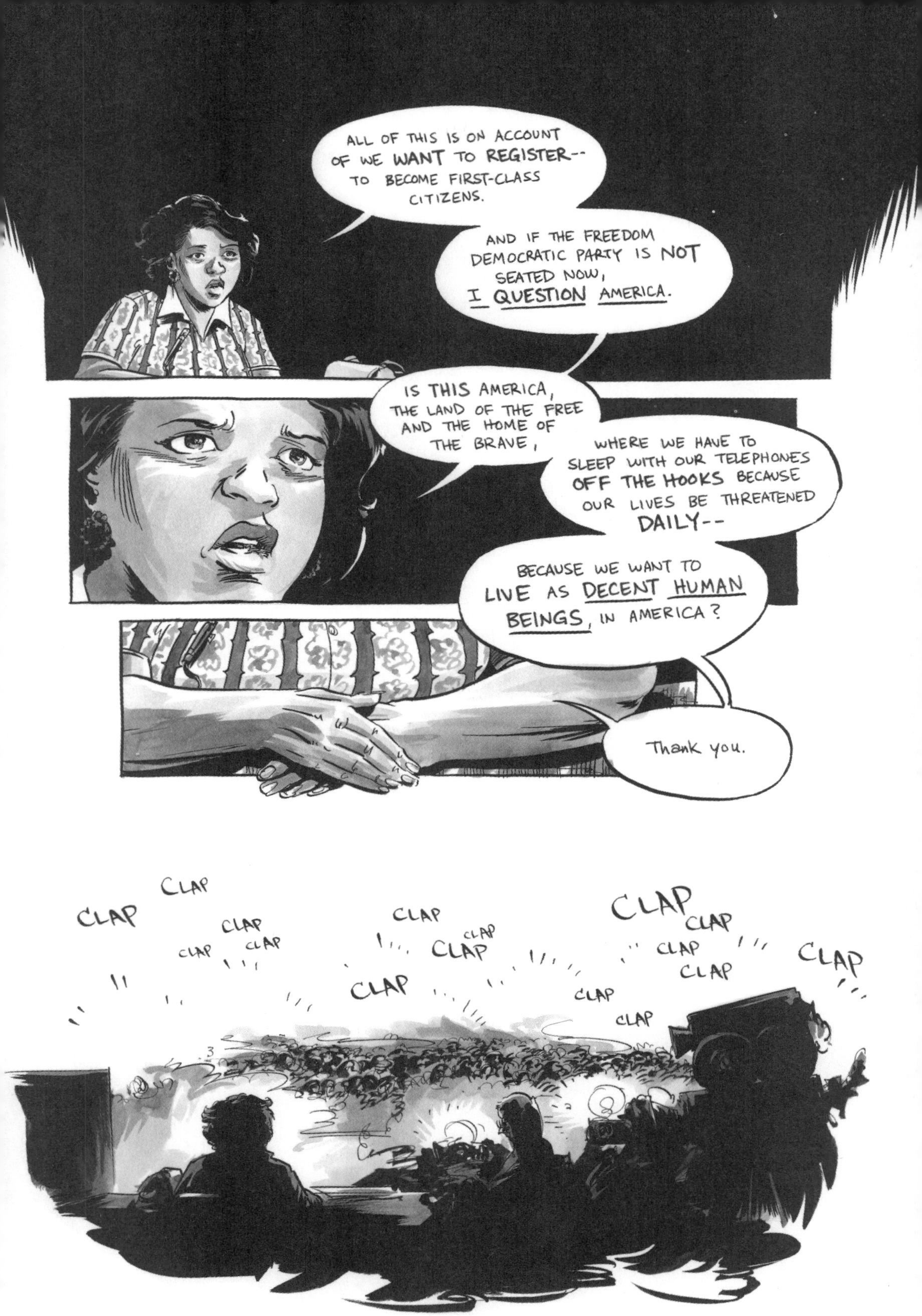
ALL OF THIS IS ON ACCOUNT OF WE WANT TO REGISTER-- TO BECOME FIRST-CLASS CITIZENS.
AND IF THE FREEDOM DEMOCRATIC PARTY IS NOT SEATED NOW, I QUESTION AMERICA.
IS THIS AMERICA, THE LAND OF THE FREE AND THE HOME OF THE BRAVE,
WHERE WE HAVE TO SLEEP WITH OUR TELEPHONES OFF THE HOOKS BECAUSE OUR LIVES BE THREATENED DAILY--
BECAUSE WE WANT TO LIVE AS DECENT HUMAN BEINGS, IN AMERICA?
Thank you.
CLAP CLAP CLAP CLAP CLAP CLAP CLAP CLAP CLAP CLAP CLAP CLAP CLAP CLAP CLAP CLAP CLAP

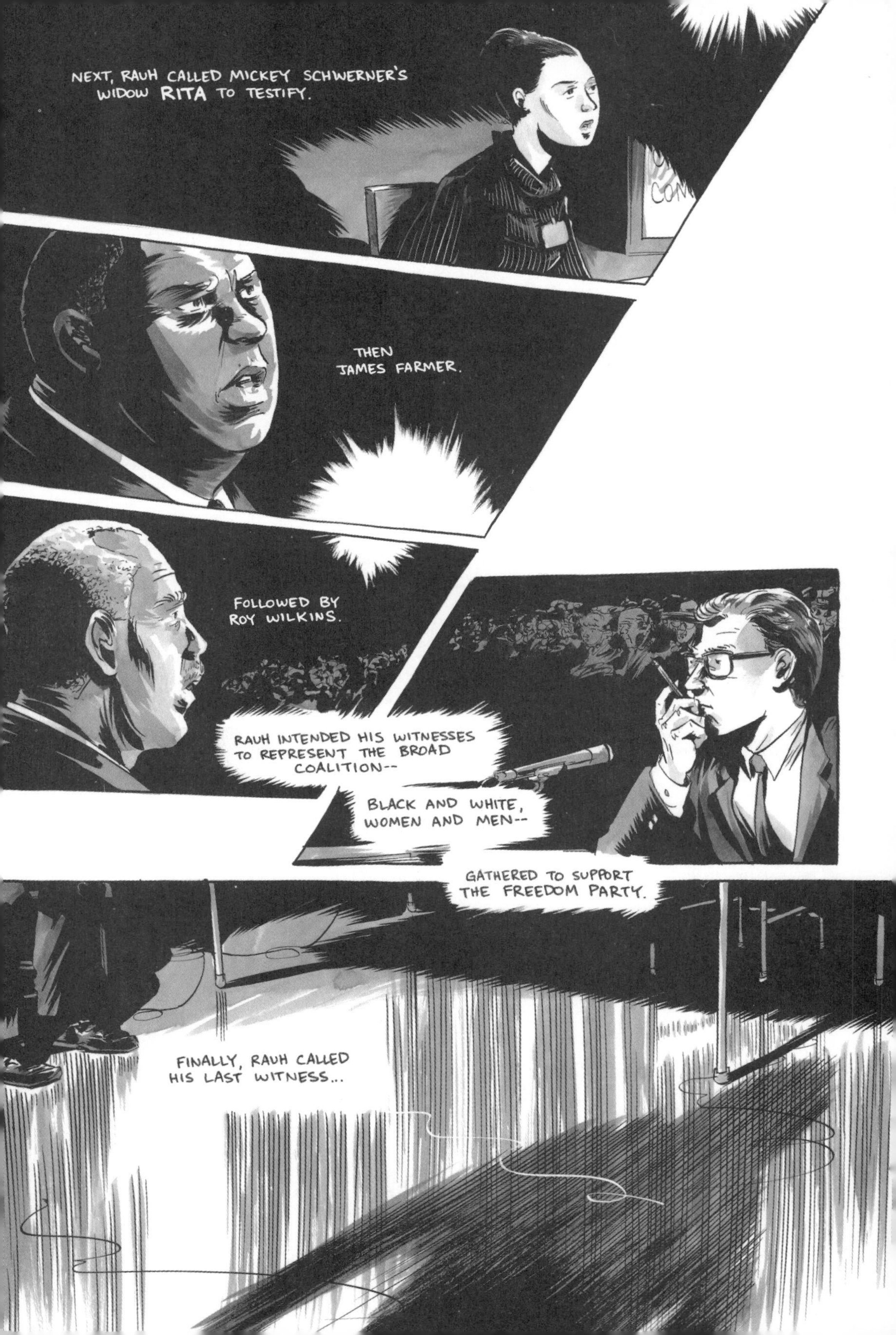
NEXT, RAUH CALLED MICKEY SCHWERNER'S WIDOW RITA TO TESTIFY.
THEN JAMES FARMER.
FOLLOWED BY ROY WILKINS.
RAUH INTENDED HIS WITNESSES TO REPRESENT THE BROAD COALITION--
BLACK AND WHITE, WOMEN AND MEN--
GATHERED TO SUPPORT THE FREEDOM PARTY.
FINALLY, RAUH CALLED HIS LAST WITNESS...

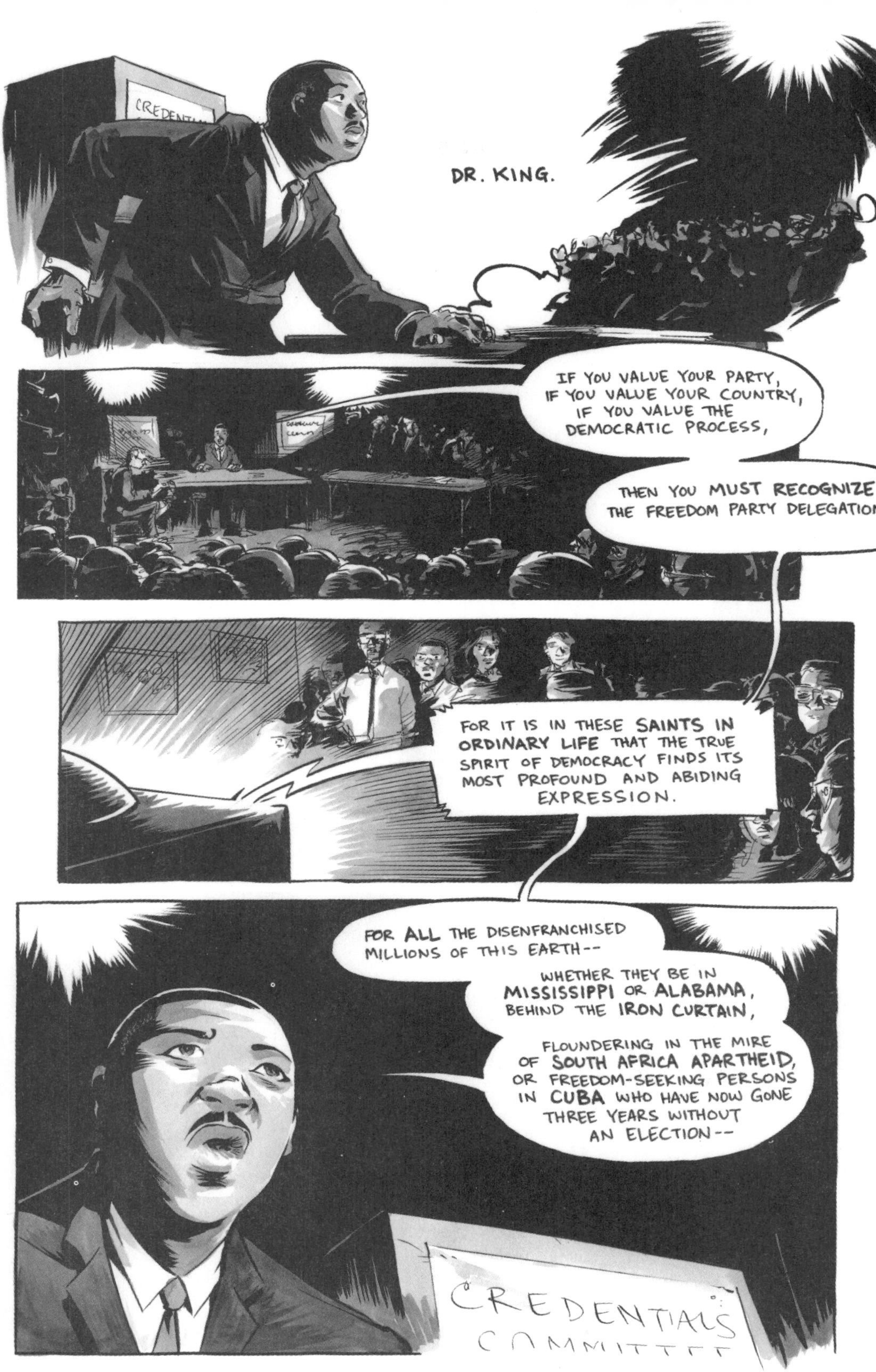
CREDENTIALS
DR. KING.
IF YOU VALUE YOUR PARTY, IF YOU VALUE YOUR COUNTRY, IF YOU VALUE THE DEMOCRATIC PROCESS,
THEN YOU MUST RECOGNIZE THE FREEDOM PARTY DELEGATION,
FOR IT IS IN THESE SAINTS IN ORDINARY LIFE THAT THE TRUE SPIRIT OF DEMOCRACY FINDS ITS MOST PROFOUND AND ABIDING EXPRESSION.
FOR ALL THE DISENFRANCHISED MILLIONS OF THIS EARTH--
WHETHER THEY BE IN MISSISSIPPI OR ALABAMA, BEHIND THE IRON CURTAIN,
FLOUNDERING IN THE MIRE OF SOUTH AFRICA APARTHEID, OR FREEDOM-SEEKING PERSONS IN CUBA WHO HAVE NOW GONE THREE YEARS WITHOUT AN ELECTION--
CREDENTIALS

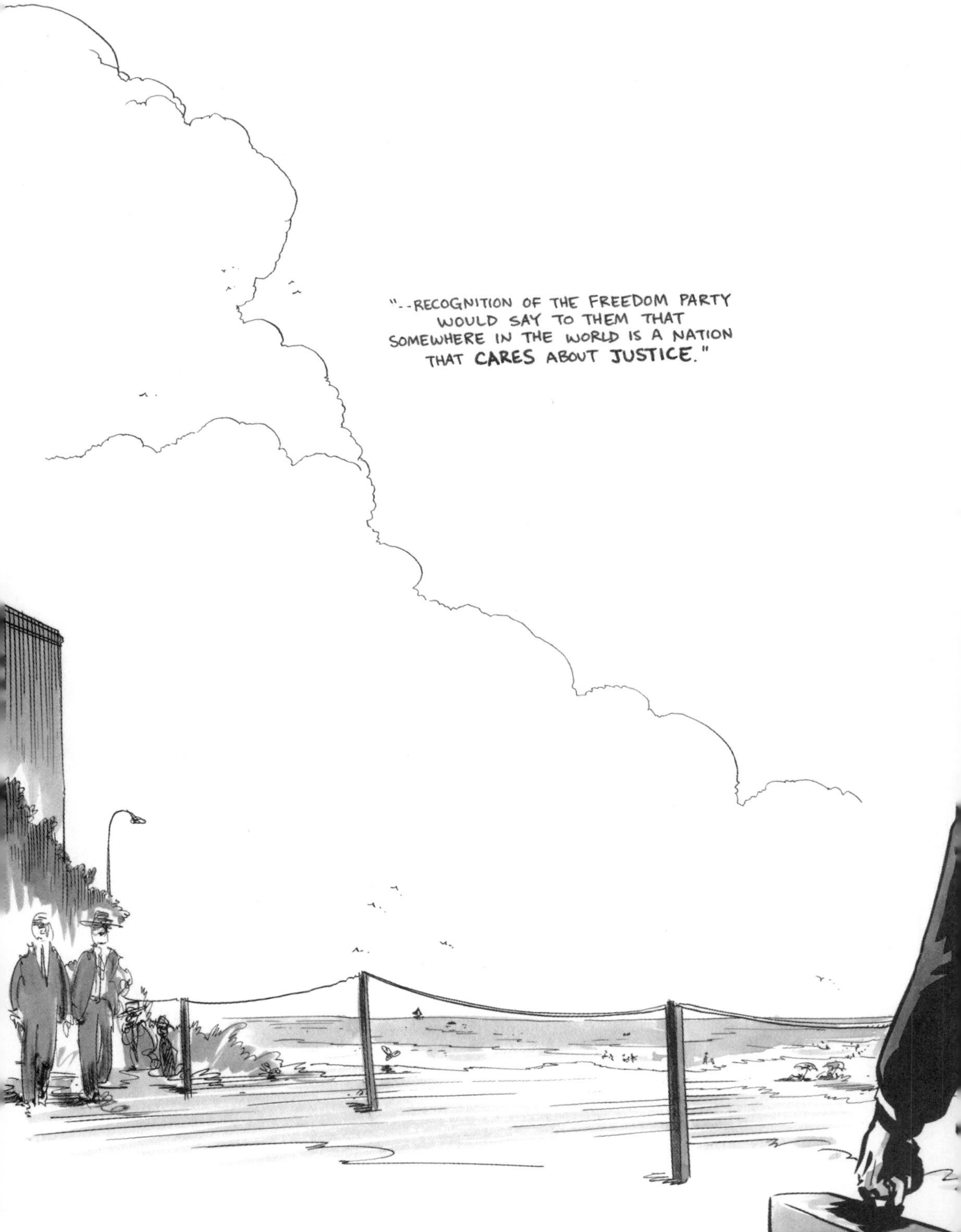
"--RECOGNITION OF THE FREEDOM PARTY WOULD SAY TO THEM THAT SOMEWHERE IN THE WORLD IS A NATION THAT CARES ABOUT JUSTICE."

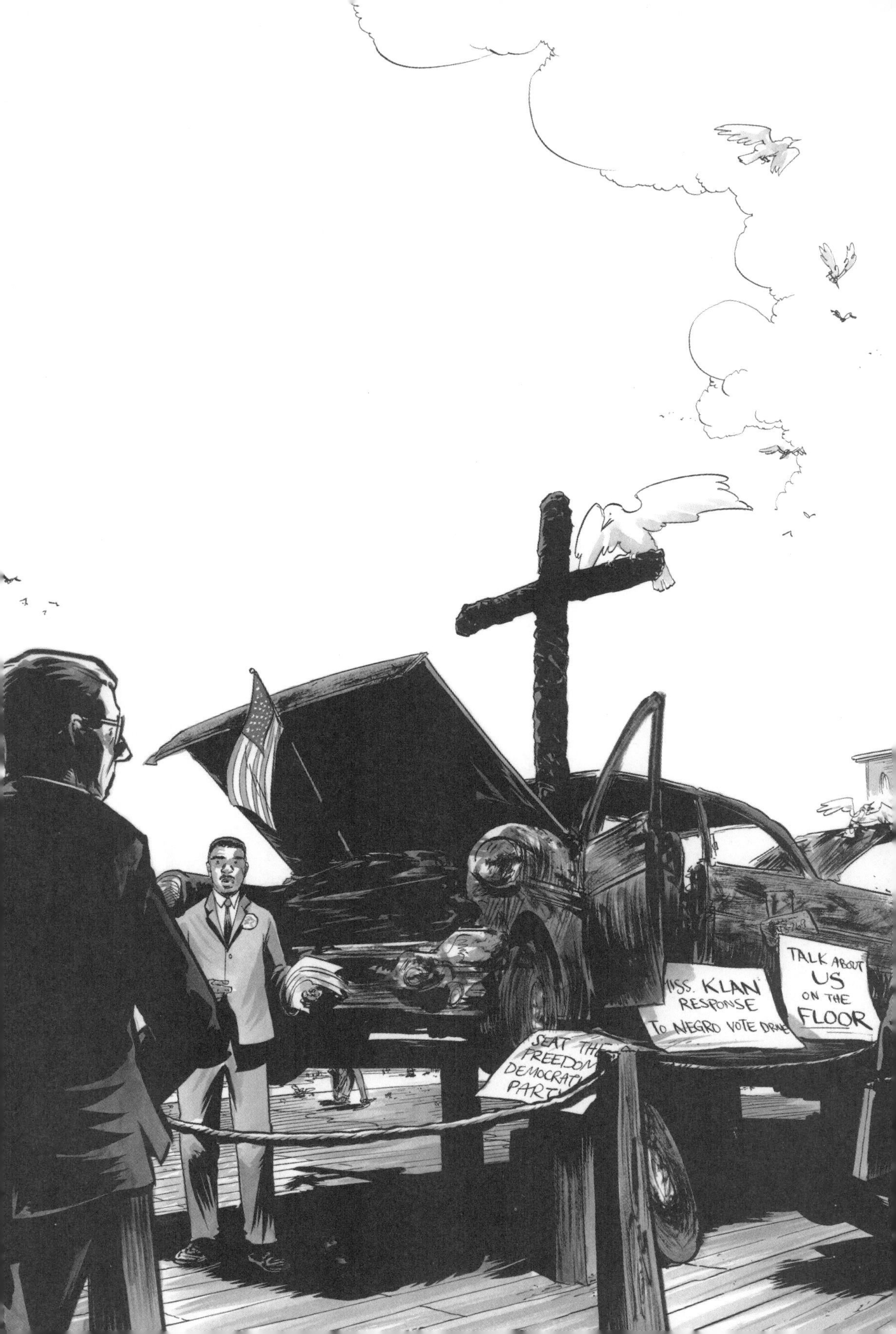
SEAT THE
FREEDOM
DEMOCRAT
PART
ISS. KLAN RESPONSE TO NEGRO VOTE DRI
TALK ABOUT US ON THE FLOOR

AFTER THEIR TESTIMONY, THE DELEGATES
WENT BACK TO THEIR HOTEL--

WHERE THEY LEARNED THAT PRESIDENT
JOHNSON HAD PRE-EMPTED MRS. HAMER'S
TESTIMONY WITH A TRUMPED-UP
PRESS CONFERENCE.

THEY WERE INCENSED.

hey,
LOOK!

BUT PRESIDENT JOHNSON'S
GAMBIT BACKFIRED.

NETWORKS THAT CUT AWAY TO COVER
THE PRESS CONFERENCE AT THE WHITE
HOUSE MADE UP FOR IT BY LEADING
THEIR EVENING NEWS BROADCAST
WITH MRS. HAMER'S TESTIMONY.

THAT'S WHY I LIKE
THAT SONG, "GO TELL IT
ON THE MOUNTAIN"--

I FEEL LIKE I'M
TALKING TO THE WORLD.

THE PRESIDENT COULD FEEL THE SOUTH *SLIPPING AWAY.*

THE THING'S OUTTA HAND NOW!!

TO BE PERFECTLY FRANK, THE PARTY IN MISSISSIPPI NEARLY ENDORSED GOLDWATER ALREADY.

MOST OF OUR DELEGATES DON'T EVEN WANNA GO TO ATLANTIC CITY!

SENATOR JAMES O. EASTLAND

JOHNSON WAS BACKED INTO A CORNER, BUT HE WASN'T AFRAID OF USING HARDBALL POLITICS TO FIGHT HIS WAY OUT.

THE NEXT DAY, THE CREDENTIALS COMMITTEE VOTE WAS POSTPONED, AND JOHNSON APPOINTED AN "EMERGENCY SUBCOMMITTEE" TO CREATE A PROPOSAL TO ADDRESS THE MISSISSIPPI SITUATION.

WE LATER LEARNED THAT PRESIDENT JOHNSON'S MEN WERE USING FBI WIRETAPS ON THE MFDP OFFICE-- AS WELL AS DR. KING'S AND BAYARD RUSTIN'S HOTEL ROOMS--

--TO DO ANYTHING IN THEIR POWER TO INFLUENCE THE OUTCOME.

AS RUMORS SPREAD ABOUT A POSSIBLE **OFFER**, WE TOOK UP A **PICKET** OUTSIDE THE CONVENTION.

♪ WE SHALL OVERCOME... WE SHALL OVERCOME SOMEDAY ♪

IT BECAME CLEAR THAT JOHNSON HAD DIRECTED SENATOR HUBERT HUMPHREY TO FORCE A **COMPROMISE**. HUMPHREY HAD VOTED FOR THE CIVIL RIGHTS ACT, AND WAS SEEN AS **SYMPATHETIC** TO THE CAUSE.

YOU'RE A GOOD MAN, SENATOR HUMPHREY--

HUMPHREY PLED HIS CASE WITH FREEDOM PARTY DELEGATES, EVEN INDICATING THAT HIS CHANCES OF BEING ADDED TO THE JOHNSON TICKET **HINGED** ON A SOLUTION.

I BEEN PRAYING ABOUT YOU AND I BEEN THINKING ABOUT YOU, AND YOU'RE A **GOOD MAN**.

THE TROUBLE IS,

YOU'RE AFRAID TO DO WHAT YOU **KNOW** IS <u>RIGHT</u>.

BUT...

but I've been a long-time supporter of civil rights... I believe--

I'm gonna pray for you.

MEANWHILE, JOHNSON'S PEOPLE WERE WORKING IN BACK CHANNELS, TWISTING ARMS AND CALLING IN FAVORS TO **ERODE** OUR SUPPORT ON THE CREDENTIALS COMMITTEE.

GONNA BE REAL H... GET THAT APPROVED... DOESN'T QUIET DOWN...

...AND YOU KN... PRESIDENT...ED... SUPPORT ON THIS...

YOU DO WANT HUMPHREY ON THE TICKET... DON'T YOU?

IF WE COULDN'T GET OUR **ELEVEN** COMMITTEE MEMBERS, WE'D NEVER GET THE CHANCE TO TRY FOR **EIGHT** STATES -- OR **FULL RECOGNITION.**

FINALLY, A MEETING WAS CALLED TO DISCUSS A **PROPOSAL.**

AS WE GATHERED, RUMORS SWIRLED THAT A "FIX" HAD BEEN ACCEPTED, UNDERCUTTING THE **MFDP'S** POSITION FROM THE OUTSET-- IT WAS "**TAKE IT OR LEAVE IT.**"

THE COMMITTEE PROPOSED TO BAN SEGREGATED DELEGATIONS IN THE FUTURE--

BUT FOR **THIS** YEAR, THEY WOULD HONOR THE "REGULAR" MISSISSIPPI DELEGATES -- AS LONG AS THEY PROMISED TO SUPPORT **JOHNSON.**

ONLY **TWO** MFDP DELEGATES WOULD BE RECOGNIZED (WITH SPECIAL "AT-LARGE" SEATS), WHILE THE OTHER **66** WOULD BE NON-VOTING "GUESTS."

THE ROOM WAS **SPLIT.**

WE SHOULD BE SATISFIED WITH THIS--

TWO SEATS IS A VICTORY.

WE DIDN'T COME ALL THE WAY HERE FOR NO **TWO** SEATS.

BUT THIS **IS** A VICTORY. THE PARTY **WILL** HAVE SEATS AT THE CONVENTION.

HAVING HUMPHREY AS **V.P.** IS A **WIN** FOR CIVIL RIGHTS--

--WHEN THEY WON'T EVEN **LET** US REPRESENT MISSISSIPPI?!

WE CAME TO BRING OUR MORALITY TO POLITICS, NOT POLITICS TO OUR MORALITY.

WE'VE SHED TOO MUCH BLOOD.

WE'VE COME **TOO FAR** TO BACK DOWN NOW.

THE SNCC CONTINGENT DID **NOT** PUSH OUR POINT OF VIEW ON THE MFDP DELEGATES. WE STATED OUR THOUGHTS ABOUT THE PROS AND CONS, THEN STEPPED BACK AND LET PEOPLE LIKE FANNIE LOU HAMER, VICTORIA GRAY, UNITA BLACKWELL, E.W. STEPTOE, JAMES TRAVIS, ANNIE DEVINE-- AND SO MANY OTHERS--

SPEAK FOR THEMSELVES AND ULTIMATELY DECIDE FOR THEMSELVES.

WHEN THE VOTE WAS TAKEN, ALL **68** MFDP DELEGATES UNANIMOUSLY **REJECTED** THE PROPOSAL.

YOU PEOPLE HAVE **PUT YOUR POINT ACROSS!**

ROY!

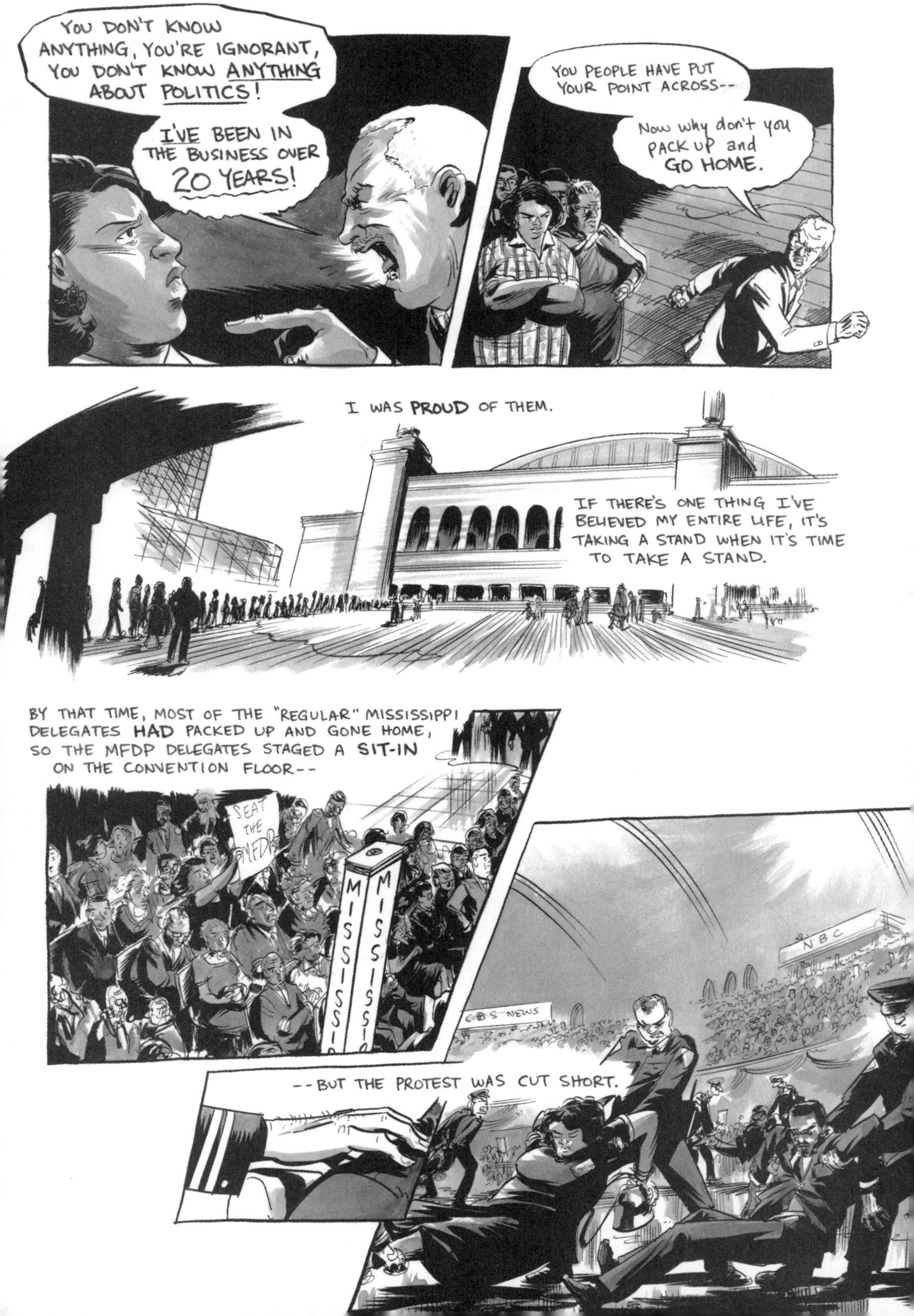
YOU DON'T KNOW ANYTHING, YOU'RE IGNORANT, YOU DON'T KNOW ANYTHING ABOUT POLITICS!
I'VE BEEN IN THE BUSINESS OVER 20 YEARS!
YOU PEOPLE HAVE PUT YOUR POINT ACROSS--
Now why don't you PACK UP and GO HOME.
I WAS PROUD OF THEM.
IF THERE'S ONE THING I'VE BELIEVED MY ENTIRE LIFE, IT'S TAKING A STAND WHEN IT'S TIME TO TAKE A STAND.
BY THAT TIME, MOST OF THE "REGULAR" MISSISSIPPI DELEGATES HAD PACKED UP AND GONE HOME, SO THE MFDP DELEGATES STAGED A SIT-IN ON THE CONVENTION FLOOR--
SEAT THE MFDP
MISSISSI
MISSISSI
NBC
CBS NEWS
--BUT THE PROTEST WAS CUT SHORT.

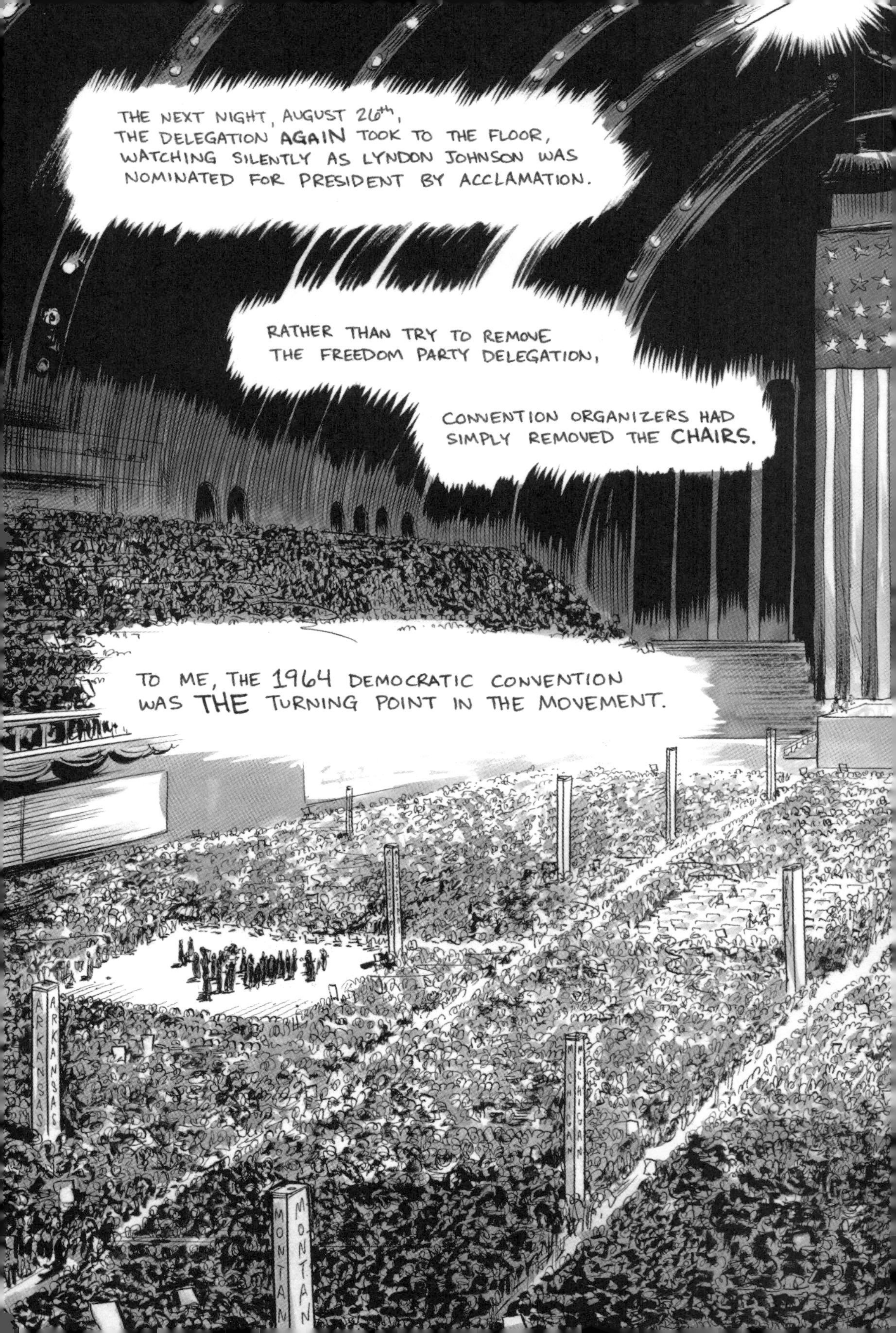
THE NEXT NIGHT, AUGUST 26th, THE DELEGATION AGAIN TOOK TO THE FLOOR, WATCHING SILENTLY AS LYNDON JOHNSON WAS NOMINATED FOR PRESIDENT BY ACCLAMATION.
RATHER THAN TRY TO REMOVE THE FREEDOM PARTY DELEGATION,
CONVENTION ORGANIZERS HAD SIMPLY REMOVED THE CHAIRS.
TO ME, THE 1964 DEMOCRATIC CONVENTION WAS THE TURNING POINT IN THE MOVEMENT.
ARKANSAS
MICHIGAN
MONTANA

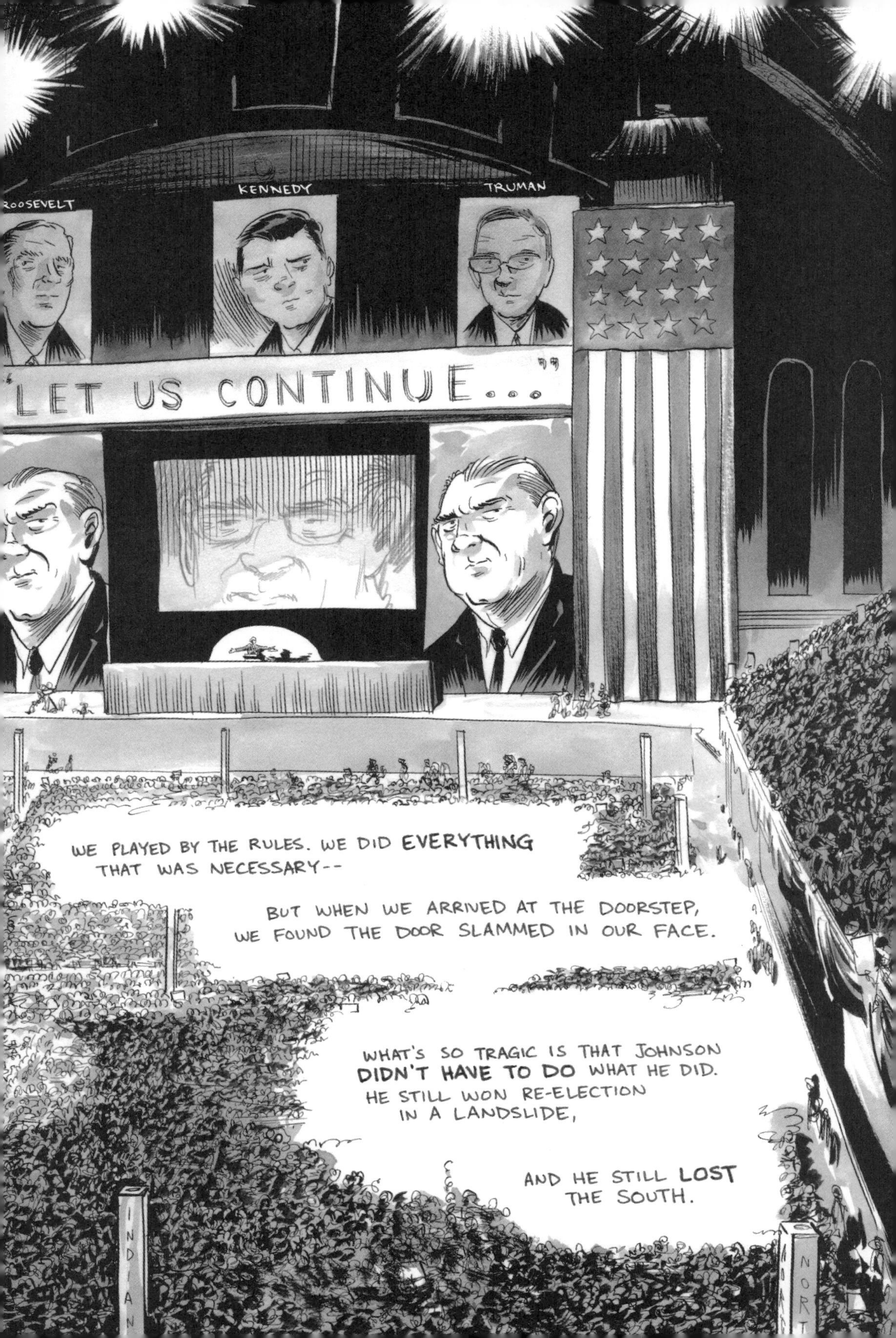
ROOSEVELT
KENNEDY
TRUMAN
"LET US CONTINUE..."
WE PLAYED BY THE RULES. WE DID EVERYTHING THAT WAS NECESSARY--
BUT WHEN WE ARRIVED AT THE DOORSTEP, WE FOUND THE DOOR SLAMMED IN OUR FACE.
WHAT'S SO TRAGIC IS THAT JOHNSON DIDN'T HAVE TO DO WHAT HE DID. HE STILL WON RE-ELECTION IN A LANDSLIDE,
AND HE STILL LOST THE SOUTH.
INDIAN
NORT

WHEN THE DUST SETTLED, MANY "WHITE LIBERALS" WERE SEEN AS VILLAINS--

AND YOU HEARD THOSE WHO URGED **COMPROMISE** CALLED "DOUBLE-CROSSER" OR "UNCLE TOM."

LINGERING FEELINGS OF CYNICISM, MISTRUST OF GOVERNMENT, AND DEEP RESENTMENT OF "WHITE LIBERALS" WOULD CAST SHADOWS OVER SOUTHERN POLITICS FOR **DECADES** TO COME.

I WAS DEVASTATED.

I FELT SO NAÏVE.

I WAS NEVER SHAKEN IN MY
BELIEF IN A MULTI-RACIAL SOCIETY,

BUT FOR THE FIRST TIME, I WAS
SURROUNDED BY FRIENDS AND COLLEAGUES
WHO FELT DIFFERENT.

THOSE WHO ONCE FOUGHT PASSIONATELY
TO INCORPORATE WHITES, TO CREATE A
TRULY INTERRACIAL MOVEMENT,

WERE NOW SET ADRIFT.

SNCC WAS FALLING APART.

WE WERE BURNED OUT.

HARRY BELAFONTE, A LONGTIME SNCC SUPPORTER,
COULD SEE THE STRAIN TAKING ITS TOLL
AND WANTED TO **HELP.**

BELAFONTE INVITED A DELEGATION FROM SNCC TO ACCOMPANY HIM ON A THREE-WEEK TRIP TO **AFRICA** TO SPEAK TO YOUNG PEOPLE AND SHARE IDEAS ABOUT WHAT WE WERE DOING IN THE AMERICAN SOUTH.

WE JUMPED AT THE CHANCE.

DAKAR, SENEGAL.

IT WAS MY FIRST VISIT TO AFRICA-- REALLY, IT WAS THE FIRST TIME I EVER LEFT THE UNITED STATES.

FANNIE LOU HAMER WENT. SO DID BOB AND DONNA MOSES, BILL HANSEN, PRATHIA HALL, MATTHEW JONES, RUBY ROBINSON, AND JIM FORMAN, OF COURSE. MY CLOSE FRIENDS JULIAN BOND AND DON HARRIS WENT, TOO.

SOMETIMES WHEN YOU LEARN A WORD IN ANOTHER LANGUAGE,

IT CHANGES THE MEANING OF THAT WORD FOR YOU IN YOUR OWN LANGUAGE.

A TOAST-- UHURU!

UHURU!

UHURU MEANS FREEDOM.

HEARING THAT WORD OVER AND OVER, I BEGAN TO UNDERSTAND MORE DEEPLY THAN EVER HOW WE ARE ALL CONNECTED IN THE UNENDING QUEST TO BE **FREE**.

WELCOME ABOARD.

I HAD BEEN ON AIRPLANE AFTER AIRPLANE IN THE UNITED STATES, BUT NEVER BEFORE IN MY LIFE HAD I SEEN A BLACK PILOT,

LET ALONE TWO.

FROM DAKAR, WE FLEW SOUTH TO GUNEA.

AND THAT WAS JUST THE BEGINNING.

GUINEA WAS BASICALLY A **VACATION** FOR OUR GROUP.

BUT DON HARRIS AND I MADE ARRANGEMENTS WITH AN ORGANIZATION CALLED THE **AMERICAN COMMITTEE ON AFRICA** TO EXTEND OUR STAY. WHILE THE OTHERS WENT HOME, WE WOULD VISIT OTHER AFRICAN NATIONS TO MEET WITH OTHER YOUNG ACTIVISTS LIKE OURSELVES.

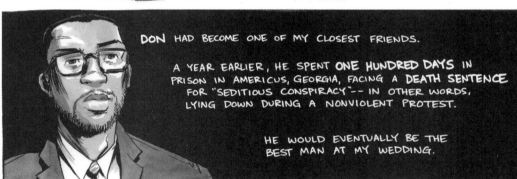

DON HAD BECOME ONE OF MY CLOSEST FRIENDS.

A YEAR EARLIER, HE SPENT **ONE HUNDRED DAYS** IN PRISON IN AMERICUS, GEORGIA, FACING A **DEATH SENTENCE** FOR "SEDITIOUS CONSPIRACY"-- IN OTHER WORDS, LYING DOWN DURING A NONVIOLENT PROTEST.

HE WOULD EVENTUALLY BE THE BEST MAN AT MY WEDDING.

WE TRAVELED FIRST TO LIBERIA, THEN GHANA AND ETHIOPIA.

IT WAS LIBERATING TO BE TWO YOUNG BLACK MEN, AMERICANS,

MEETING SO MANY OTHER YOUNG PEOPLE AWASH IN THE RISING GLOBAL TIDE OF **REVOLUTION.**

THIS IS JOHN LEWIS AND DON HARRIS -- THEY ARE LEADERS OF THE STUDENT NONVIOLENT COORDINATING COMMITTEE... IN AMERICA.

THE YOUNG PEOPLE WE MET WERE VERY ASTUTE, AND FAR MORE RADICAL THAN THOSE OF US IN **SNCC**.

WHAT IS YOUR ORGANIZATION'S RELATIONSHIP WITH MALCOLM'S?

UHHH, WELLLL...

MALCOLM X. THEY ALWAYS ASKED. HE STRUCK A CHORD WITH THE YOUNG REVOLUTIONARIES.

LOOK, YOU GUYS MIGHT BE REALLY **DOING** SOMETHING.

BUT IF YOU'RE TO THE RIGHT OF MALCOLM, YOU MIGHT AS WELL START PACKING **NOW**, BECAUSE NO ONE WILL LISTEN TO YOU.

IT WAS EYE-OPENING.

BACK HOME, **WE** WERE CONSIDERED THE RADICALS, BY THE PRESS, BY MOST OF SOCIETY...

...EVEN BY THE MOVEMENT.

ON OUR WAY FROM ETHIOPIA TO ZAMBIA, OUR PLANE HAD MECHANICAL TROUBLE AND WE WERE FORCED TO LAND IN **KENYA**.

THE AIRLINE PUT US UP IN THE NEW STANLEY HOTEL IN NAIROBI.

I'LL NEVER FORGET...

Hello, John...

What are you doing here?

IT WAS MALCOLM X.

MALCOLM! IT'S GOOD TO SEE YOU... THIS IS MY FRIEND, DON HARRIS.

Please, sit down.

Thank you.

EARLIER THAT YEAR, MALCOLM HAD **SPLIT** FROM ELIJAH MUHAMMAD'S NATION OF ISLAM.

HE SEEMED A LITTLE **ANXIOUS**. MALCOLM HAD COME FROM A CONFERENCE IN CAIRO, WHERE HE SPOKE ABOUT BRINGING THE PROBLEMS OF BLACK PEOPLE IN AMERICA BEFORE THE **UNITED NATIONS**.

HE SAID WE HAVE TO **IDENTIFY** WITH THE PEOPLE OF AFRICA,

"... AND THAT THEY MUST IDENTIFY WITH **US**.

THE STRUGGLE IN AFRICA IS **INSEPARABLE** FROM OUR STRUGGLE IN AMERICA.

WHAT MOVED ME AND IMPRESSED ME WAS HIS SENSITIVITY TO THE FACT THAT OUR BEING IN AFRICA WAS VERY **DANGEROUS** FOR US.

HE KNEW THERE WERE PEOPLE BACK IN AMERICA WHO DID **NOT** LIKE US TRYING TO LINK THE MOVEMENT IN AFRICA TO WHAT WAS HAPPENING IN AMERICA.

ON SEVERAL OCCASIONS, HE SUGGESTED THAT WE SIT WITH OUR BACKS TO THE WALL SO WE COULD SEE ANYONE APPROACHING US.

WOULD YOU...

...like to continue this conversation in my room, where we can speak in private?

HE TALKED ABOUT HIS IMPRESSIONS OF CAIRO AND ABOUT CERTAIN AFRICAN LEADERS,

BUT MOSTLY HE TALKED TO US ABOUT WHAT **WE** WERE DOING.

MALCOLM TALKED ABOUT THE NEED TO SHIFT OUR FOCUS FROM RACE TO **CLASS**, BOTH AMONG ONE ANOTHER AND BETWEEN OURSELVES AND THE WHITE COMMUNITY.

HE SAID HE BELIEVED **THAT** WAS THE ROOT OF OUR PROBLEMS, NOT JUST IN AMERICA,

BUT ALL OVER THE WORLD.

MALCOLM WAS SAYING, IN EFFECT, THAT IT IS A STRUGGLE FOR THE **POOR**-- FOR THOSE WHO HAVE BEEN LEFT OUT AND LEFT BEHIND--

AND THAT IT **TRANSCENDS** RACE.

I SUPPORT WHAT YOU'RE DOING IN THE SOUTH.

DON'T GIVE UP. THIS IS AN **ONGOING** STRUGGLE. BE PREPARED FOR THE WORST, BUT KEEP IT UP-- KEEP FIGHTING.

PEOPLE ARE **CHANGING**.

THERE ARE PEOPLE ALL OVER THE WORLD SUPPORTING YOU.

I HAD NO WAY OF KNOWING THEN, BUT THAT WAS THE LAST TIME I WOULD SEE MALCOLM ALIVE.

AFTER THREE DAYS, OUR PLANE WAS READY AND WE WENT TO ZAMBIA, THEN BACK THROUGH KENYA AND ETHIOPIA.

WE ARRIVED IN ADDIS ABABA JUST IN TIME FOR THE PRESIDENTIAL ELECTION BACK IN THE STATES. WE LISTENED TO THE RESULTS ON A "VOICE OF AMERICA" BROADCAST.

IT APPEARS JOHNSON IS ON HIS WAY TO A LANDSLIDE VICTORY-- WINNING 44 OF 50 STATES, AND DOMINATING THE ELECTORAL COLLEGE!

DESPITE EVERYTHING, I WAS HAPPY THAT JOHNSON WON, AND PARTICULARLY EXCITED WHEN IT WAS ANNOUNCED THAT **ROBERT KENNEDY** HAD WON THE SENATE SEAT IN NEW YORK.

OUR LAST STOP IN AFRICA WAS CAIRO, WHERE WE DECIDED IT WAS TIME TO PLAY TOURIST.

AS THE SUN SET BEHIND THE PYRAMIDS, WE RODE IN SILENCE.

I COULDN'T HELP BUT FEEL LONELY, EVEN A LITTLE SAD, AT THE THOUGHT OF WHAT AWAITED US BACK IN AMERICA.

AFTER **72** DAYS OF TRAVELS, WE
RETURNED HOME ON NOVEMBER 22nd.

A LOT HAD CHANGED WHILE WE WERE GONE--
MANY PEOPLE THOUGHT I'D BEEN AWAY TOO LONG.

SNCC WAS THREATENING TO
COLLAPSE UNDER ITS OWN WEIGHT.

ALL THE THINGS THAT MADE
SNCC WHAT IT WAS--

DECENTRALIZED LEADERSHIP,
CONSENSUS-DRIVEN DECISION
MAKING, RESPECT FOR
INDIVIDUALITY--

--WERE NOW TEARING
IT APART.

WE HAD ALWAYS BEEN A CLOSE-KNIT GROUP. I THOUGHT OF US AS
A BAND OF BROTHERS AND SISTERS, A CIRCLE OF TRUST... BUT THE
MISSISSIPPI SUMMER PROJECT HAD SWELLED OUR NUMBERS SIGNIFICANTLY.

THE INTIMACY THAT HAD ALLOWED FOR DECISION-MAKING
BY CONSENSUS HAD ALL BUT **DISAPPEARED.**

SALT-OF-THE-EARTH FIELD STAFF **CHAFED** AGAINST
COLLEGE-EDUCATED INTELLECTUALS PUSHING A
MORE POLITICAL AGENDA.

JUST BEFORE I GOT BACK, **SNCC** HELD A STAFF RETREAT IN WAVELAND, MISSISSIPPI, TO ADDRESS SOME OF THESE CHALLENGES.

MARY KING AND CASEY HAYDEN SUBMITTED A PAPER CALLED "THE POSITION OF WOMEN IN THE MOVEMENT".

"ASSUMPTIONS OF **MALE SUPERIORITY** ARE AS WIDESPREAD AND DEEP-ROOTED, AND EVERY MUCH AS CRIPPLING TO THE **WOMAN** AS ASSUMPTIONS OF **WHITE SUPREMACY** ARE TO THE **NEGRO**."

AS MORE AND MORE WOMEN JOINED THE MOVEMENT, THE QUESTION OF **GENDER EQUALITY** TOOK HOLD AS POWERFULLY AS ANY CHALLENGE WITHIN SNCC.

AFTER ALL THE PAPERS WERE PRESENTED AND THE RETREAT HAD ADJOURNED FOR THE DAY, **STOKELY CARMICHAEL** AND SOME SNCC STAFFERS WERE BLOWING OFF STEAM.

WHAT IS THE POSITION OF WOMEN IN SNCC?

THE POSITION OF WOMEN IN SNCC IS **PRONE..!**

IT WAS A **JOKE**, REALLY--

BUT IT SO PERFECTLY CAPTURED WHAT **SO MANY** WERE FEELING THAT THE COMMENT TOOK ON A LIFE OF ITS OWN.

BACK IN ATLANTA, DON AND I WROTE LENGTHY REPORTS ON OUR EXPERIENCES IN AFRICA THAT WERE DISSEMINATED AMONG THE SNCC LEADERSHIP.

TIK TIK
TAKKA
TAK TIK

THEN I GAVE A SERIES OF INTERVIEWS TO THE PRESS TO SPREAD OUR MESSAGE AND COMBAT DANGEROUS RUMORS SWIRLING ABOUT OUR TACTICS AND MEMBERSHIP.

CAN YOU TELL ME WHY A DELEGATION OF HIGH-RANKING SNCC MEMBERS TRAVELED TO AFRICA?

IT MATTERS **NOT** WHETHER IT IS IN ANGOLA, MOZAMBIQUE, SOUTHWEST AFRICA, OR MISSISSIPPI, ALABAMA, GEORGIA, AND HARLEM, U.S.A.--

THE STRUGGLE IS THE SAME.

IT IS THE STRUGGLE AGAINST A **VICIOUS** AND **EVIL** SYSTEM THAT IS CONTROLLED AND KEPT IN ORDER **FOR**, AND **BY**, A FEW WHITE MEN THROUGHOUT THE WORLD.

NESHOBA COUNTY

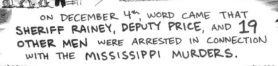

ON DECEMBER 4th, WORD CAME THAT SHERIFF RAINEY, DEPUTY PRICE, AND **19** OTHER MEN WERE ARRESTED IN CONNECTION WITH THE MISSISSIPPI MURDERS.

AT A HEARING SIX DAYS LATER, JUDGE HAROLD COX--

-- THE **SAME** JUDGE WHO EARLIER CALLED US "A BUNCH OF CHIMPANZEES"--

141

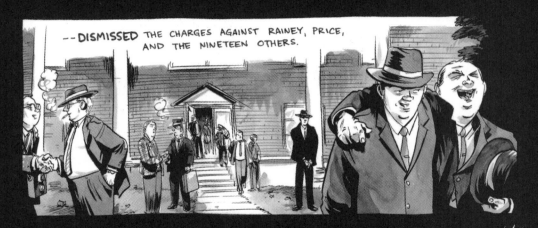

--DISMISSED THE CHARGES AGAINST RAINEY, PRICE, AND THE NINETEEN OTHERS.

THAT SAME DAY, DR. KING BECAME THE YOUNGEST PERSON TO EVER RECEIVE A **NOBEL PEACE PRIZE.**

AND ONLY THE SECOND AFRICAN-AMERICAN AFTER DIPLOMAT RALPH BUNCHE IN 1950.

I WAS OVERJOYED FOR DR. KING'S HONOR, BUT MOST OF MY COLLEAGUES IN SNCC **RESENTED** IT.

FRANKLY, A LOT OF MY COLLEAGUES RESENTED **ME.**

I COULD FEEL **SNCC** BECOMING MORE AND MORE **ISOLATED** FROM THE MOVEMENT.

I DIDN'T GET TO STAY HOME LONG--

CLINK

SNCC WAS RUNNING OUT OF **MONEY**. DONORS WHO'D SUPPORTED US THROUGH THE SUMMER PROJECT WERE INCREASINGLY **HESITANT** TO CONTINUE OFFERING FUNDING.

RUMORS SWIRLED THAT SNCC HAD BEEN TAKEN OVER BY **COMMUNISTS**, AND THAT OUR RECENT TRIP WAS A RUSE TO COVER A SECRET VISIT TO **CHINA**.

IT'S CALLED "**RED-BAITING**," AND IT'S ALWAYS DEEPLY BOTHERED ME.

IF YOU'RE GOING TO CALL SOMEONE A NAME, OR SLAP A LABEL ON THEM, HAVE A REASON-- EVEN IF IT'S RACIST, I CAN **RESPECT** THAT.

BUT CALLING SOMEONE A "COMMUNIST" OR A "SOCIALIST" IS THE INTELLECTUAL EQUIVALENT OF THROWING FROM YOUR BACK FOOT. YOU'RE NOT PUTTING MUCH ON THE BALL.

I WENT ON A FUND-RAISING TRIP TO PHILADELPHIA AND NEW YORK TO TRY AND TURN THINGS **AROUND**.

JOHN, YOU **HAVE** TO TELL ME--

I HEARD SNCC IS GOING TO **BREAK UP**. IS IT TRUE?

NO, NO, IT'S **NOT** TRUE.

WHAT'S THIS I'VE BEEN HEARING ABOUT AN ATTEMPTED "COUP" AGAINST SNCC LEADERSHIP?

NO, JUST SOME VERY...

SPIRITED MEETINGS AT A RECENT CONFERENCE.

WHEN I GOT BACK FROM THE TRIP,

I DECIDED TO WRITE A LETTER TO THE ENTIRE MEMBERSHIP, ADDRESSING MANY OF THE RUMORS I'D HEARD. I WASN'T PANICKING,

TIKKA
TIK TAKKA
TAK

BUT I WAS AS CLOSE TO IT AS I THINK I'VE EVER BEEN.

TIK
TIK
TAKKA
DING!

I TRIED TO ADDRESS THE RUMORS AS DIRECTLY AS POSSIBLE, DISPEL ANY NOTION THAT I MIGHT BE **LEAVING** AS CHAIRMAN, AND LAY OUT MY PLAN FOR VISITING ALL THE SNCC-LED PROJECTS OVER THE NEXT FEW WEEKS.

I'VE ALWAYS SEEN MYSELF AS A **DOER**,

CARL--

ZZ-ZZZIIP!

AND IN MOMENTS LIKE THAT

YOU MIND HELPING ME MAKE COPIES OF THIS LETTER TO SEND OUT?

THE ONLY THING THAT MADE SENSE TO ME WAS TO **KEEP MOVING.**

RIGHT ON. WHO WE SENDING IT TO?

EVERYBODY.

SO I WENT ON THE ROAD FOR THE NEXT SEVERAL WEEKS, UNTIL I FOUND MYSELF BACK IN THE HEART OF DALLAS COUNTY, ALABAMA...

SELMA.

AS SIGNIFICANT AS IT WAS, THE CIVIL RIGHTS ACT OF 1964
MADE **NO** PROVISION TO ENSURE THE RIGHTS OF AFRICAN-AMERICANS
TO REGISTER TO VOTE. IN MORE THAN TWO YEARS OF SNCC-LED
WORK ORGANIZING AND PROTESTING IN SELMA, WE REGISTERED
FEWER THAN **100** NEW VOTERS.

AND THANKS TO JUDGE HARE'S INJUNCTION AGAINST PUBLIC GATHERINGS,
SNCC'S OPERATION IN SELMA HAD GROUND TO A HALT.

DR. KING MET WITH PRESIDENT JOHNSON IN DECEMBER,
SHORTLY AFTER RECEIVING THE NOBEL PEACE PRIZE.
THEY DISCUSSED THE NEED FOR A **VOTING RIGHTS ACT,**
BUT PRESIDENT JOHNSON SAID IT WAS **IMPOSSIBLE.**
THE VOTES IN CONGRESS WERE SIMPLY NOT THERE.

JOHNSON SAID, IN EFFECT:

IF YOU **WANT** A VOTING RIGHTS ACT,
MAKE ME DO IT.

WHEN DR. KING RETURNED TO ATLANTA, HE ACCEPTED AN INVITATION
FROM AN ORGANIZATION CALLED THE **DALLAS COUNTY IMPROVEMENT
ASSOCIATION,** REQUESTING **SCLC** TO HELP THE PEOPLE OF SELMA.

ON DECEMBER 28, 1964, DR. KING CONVENED A MEETING OF THE GROUPS ORGANIZING IN SELMA TO PRESENT A PLAN:

THE PROJECT FOR AN ALABAMA POLITICAL FREEDOM MOVEMENT.

WE WILL HOLD A MASS MEETING ON JANUARY 2nd TO **BREAK** JUDGE HARE'S **INJUNCTION**, AND CONCENTRATE OUR EFFORTS ON VOTER REGISTRATION AND MASS DEMONSTRATIONS IN DALLAS COUNTY.

SELMA HAD JUST ELECTED A NEW MAYOR-- **JOE SMITHERMAN**, A REFRIGERATOR SALESMAN. HE WAS CONSIDERED A **MODERATE**-- A MODERATE SEGREGATIONIST, THAT IS-- AND HE WAS HOPING TO ATTRACT NORTHERN BUSINESS INVESTMENT TO THE AREA, SOMETHING HE **COULDN'T** DO IF PUBLIC CONFRONTATIONS WITH PROTESTORS BROUGHT NEGATIVE MEDIA ATTENTION.

MAYOR SMITHERMAN QUICKLY APPOINTED **WILSON BAKER** AS SELMA'S **CHIEF OF POLICE.** BAKER HAD NARROWLY LOST TO JIM CLARK IN THE RACE FOR SHERIFF, PARTIALLY DUE TO BAKER'S **LESS VIOLENT** ATTITUDES TOWARDS DEALING WITH PROTESTORS.

THIS PITTED CLARK AND BAKER IN A BATTLE OVER **JURISDICTION**-- BAKER'S OFFICERS PATROLLED THE CITY, WHILE CLARK AND HIS DEPUTIES CONTROLLED THE COURTHOUSE.

WE CHOSE TO LAUNCH OUR CAMPAIGN ON **JANUARY 2nd** BECAUSE SHERIFF CLARK WAS GOING TO BE OUT OF TOWN ATTENDING THE ORANGE BOWL, AND CHIEF BAKER HAD SAID HE WOULD **NOT** ENFORCE JUDGE HARE'S INJUNCTION FORBIDDING GATHERINGS OF MORE THAN THREE PEOPLE.

JANUARY 2, 1965.

ONLY ONE CHURCH IN SELMA WAS WILLING TO RISK THE POTENTIAL **RETRIBUTION** FOR HOSTING THE KICK-OFF MASS MEETING:

BROWN CHAPEL AME.

AT FIRST, WE WERE WORRIED NO ONE WOULD SHOW UP--

--BUT BY THE TIME THE MEETING STARTED, WE HAD MORE PEOPLE THAN THE CHURCH COULD HOLD.

TODAY MARKS THE BEGINNING OF A DETERMINED, ORGANIZED, MOBILIZED CAMPAIGN TO GET THE RIGHT TO VOTE **EVERYWHERE** IN ALABAMA.

IF WE ARE REFUSED, WE WILL APPEAL TO **GOVERNOR GEORGE WALLACE.**

IF **HE** REFUSES TO LISTEN, WE WILL APPEAL TO THE LEGISLATURE.

IF **THEY** DON'T LISTEN, WE WILL APPEAL TO THE **CONSCIENCE** OF THE **CONGRESS.**

WE MUST BE READY TO **MARCH.** WE MUST BE READY TO GO TO JAIL BY THE **THOUSANDS.**

OUR <u>CRY</u> TO THE STATE OF ALABAMA IS A <u>SIMPLE</u> ONE--

--GIVE US THE BALLOT!

THE INJUNCTION HAD BEEN BROKEN.

NO ONE WAS ARRESTED.

THAT EVENING A MEETING WAS HELD AT AMELIA BOYNTON'S HOME, AND THE DATE OF OUR FIRST MASS PROTEST WAS SET:

JANUARY 18th.

SHERIFF CLARK WOULD BE BACK IN TOWN.

WITHIN **SNCC** THERE WERE STRONG FEELINGS THAT WE HAD DONE THE HARD, NECESSARY WORK LAYING THE FOUNDATION--

--BUT NOW DR. KING AND **SCLC** WOULD SWOOP IN AND GRAB HEADLINES WITHOUT BUILDING STRONG TIES TO THE COMMUNITY.

I UNDERSTOOD WHY THEY FELT THAT WAY--

THE SNCC STAFF WORKING IN ALABAMA HAD ALREADY BEEN NEGLECTED BY THE EMPHASIS WE PUT ON **MISSISSIPPI**, AND NOW THEY WERE BEING **PUSHED ASIDE** BY SCLC.

AS THE CHAIRMAN OF SNCC **AND** A MEMBER OF SCLC'S BOARD, I WAS CAUGHT IN THE MIDDLE.

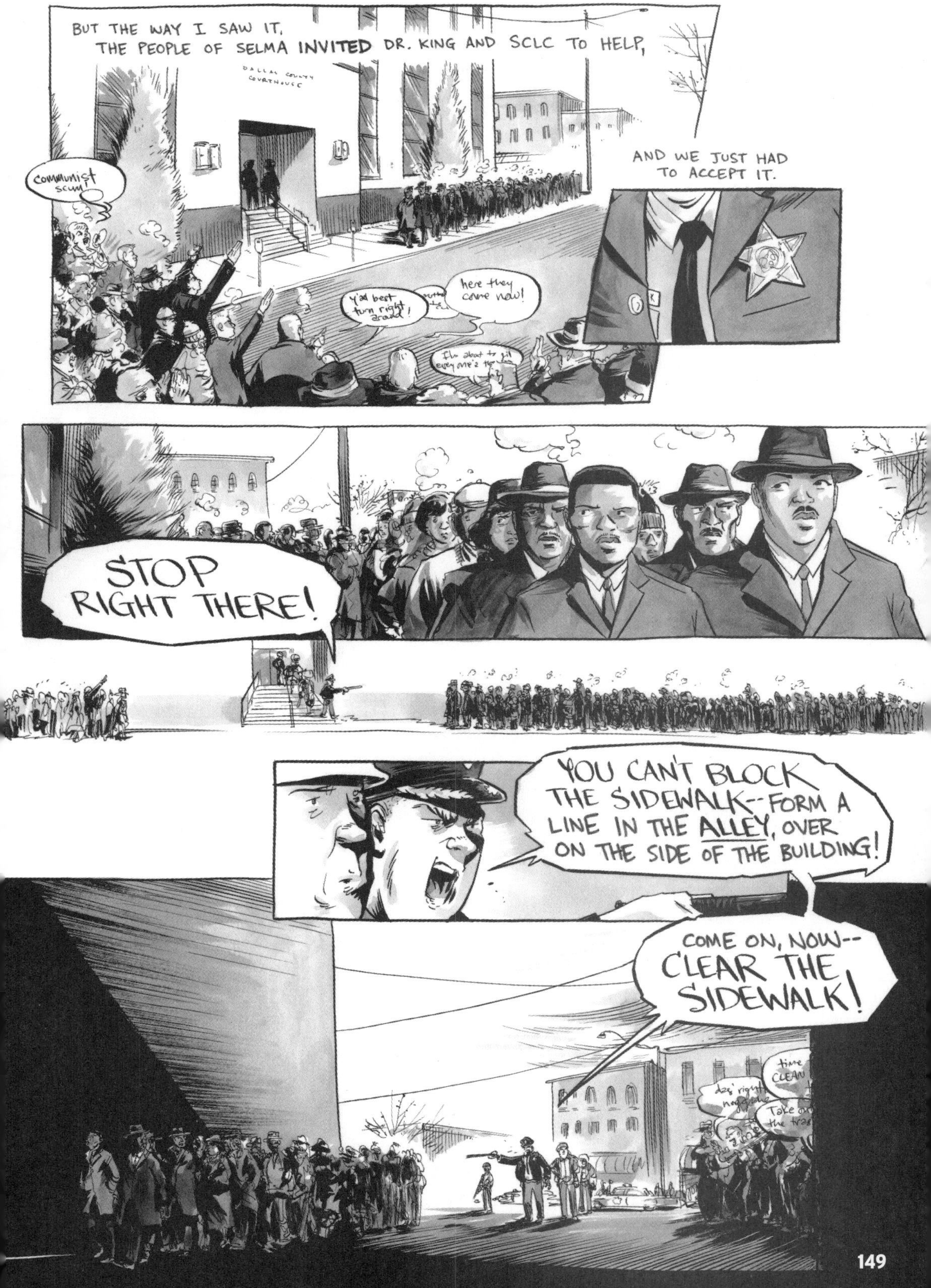
BUT THE WAY I SAW IT, THE PEOPLE OF SELMA **INVITED** DR. KING AND SCLC TO HELP,
DALLAS COUNTY COURTHOUSE
Communist scum!
y'all best turn right around!
here they come now!
AND WE JUST HAD TO ACCEPT IT.
STOP RIGHT THERE!
YOU CAN'T BLOCK THE SIDEWALK-- FORM A LINE IN THE ALLEY, OVER ON THE SIDE OF THE BUILDING!
COME ON, NOW-- CLEAR THE SIDEWALK!

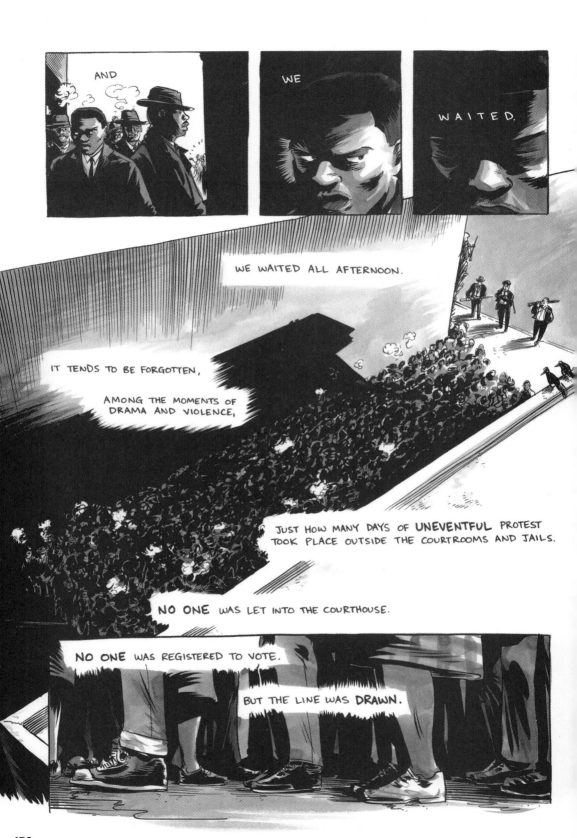

AND

WE

WAITED.

WE WAITED ALL AFTERNOON.

IT TENDS TO BE FORGOTTEN,

AMONG THE MOMENTS OF DRAMA AND VIOLENCE,

JUST HOW MANY DAYS OF **UNEVENTFUL** PROTEST TOOK PLACE OUTSIDE THE COURTROOMS AND JAILS.

NO ONE WAS LET INTO THE COURTHOUSE.

NO ONE WAS REGISTERED TO VOTE.

BUT THE LINE WAS **DRAWN.**

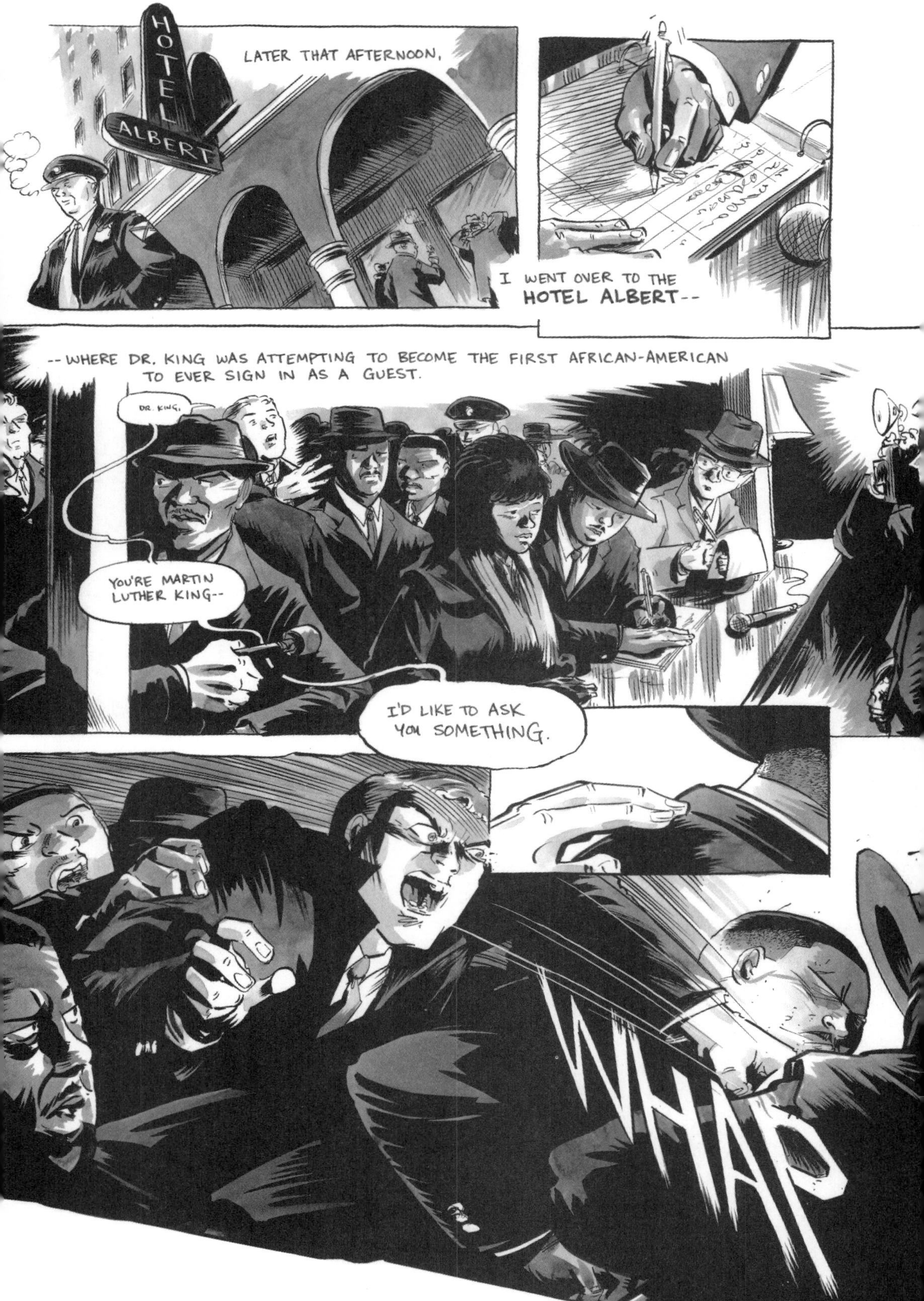
HOTEL ALBERT
LATER THAT AFTERNOON,
I WENT OVER TO THE HOTEL ALBERT--
--WHERE DR. KING WAS ATTEMPTING TO BECOME THE FIRST AFRICAN-AMERICAN TO EVER SIGN IN AS A GUEST.
DR. KING,
YOU'RE MARTIN LUTHER KING--
I'D LIKE TO ASK YOU SOMETHING.
WHAP

I DON'T KNOW WHAT CAME OVER ME.

I DIDN'T HIT HIM,

THOUGH I MAY HAVE **THOUGHT** ABOUT IT FOR A SPLIT-SECOND.

IT WAS THE CLOSEST I'VE **EVER** COME TO LAYING DOWN MY NONVIOLENCE.

I FOUND OUT THAT DAY, EVEN I HAVE **LIMITS.**

WE MARCHED AGAIN THE VERY NEXT DAY, BUT THIS TIME WE WERE **NOT** GOING TO COMPLY WITH SHERIFF CLARK IF HE ORDERED US DOWN THE ALLEY.

DR. KING HAD TO ATTEND A SPEAKING ENGAGEMENT ELSEWHERE, SO A YOUNG MAN FROM SCLC NAMED **HOSEA WILLIAMS** LED THE MARCH WITH ME.

Y'ALL STOP RIGHT THERE--

YOU HAVE TO LINE UP IN THE ALLEY AND GO THROUGH THE **SIDE DOOR.**

SHERIFF CLARK, WE WANT TO ENTER THROUGH THE **FRONT DOOR.**

IZZAT SO?!

Y'ALL **ALL** UNDER ARREST!

KLIK

AMELIA BOYNTON, WHO WAS THERE TO **VOUCH** FOR ANYONE WHO MIGHT MAKE IT INTO THE COURTHOUSE TO REGISTER, CAUGHT SHERIFF CLARK'S **ATTENTION**.

MRS. BOYNTON WAS A RESPECTED BUSINESSWOMAN AND ORGANIZER--

BUT THAT DIDN'T STOP HIM.

YOU'RE ALL UNDER ARREST!

me, too?

Are they arrestin' me?

shhhhh--

Don't be scared.

Just stay close.

Don't let go of my hand.

LETS GO, LETS GO!

DALLAS COUNTY COURTHOUSE

MORE THAN **60** OF US WERE ARRESTED, INCLUDING LOCAL THIRD-GRADE TEACHER MARGARET MOORE AND HER STUDENT SHEYANN WEBB.

BUT THANKS TO THE UNBELIEVABLE LAWYERS FROM THE NAACP LEGAL DEFENSE FUND, WE WERE RELEASED LATER THAT DAY.

JANUARY 20, 1965.

THE NEXT DAY, I LED YET **ANOTHER** MARCH TO THE COUNTY COURTHOUSE.

IN WASHINGTON, IT WAS INAUGURATION DAY. THE NATION'S POLITICAL ESTABLISHMENT GATHERED AT THE CAPITOL TO SWEAR IN JOHNSON TO HIS FIRST FULL PRESIDENTIAL TERM, BUT IT COULDN'T HAVE SEEMED FARTHER AWAY.

JOHN LEWIS! YOU STOP THESE PEOPLE RIGHT NOW!

AGAIN-- GO LINE UP IN THE ALLEY, AND WHEN **WE SAYS SO,** THESE PEOPLE CAN GO THROUGH THE **SIDE** DOOR.

SHERIFF CLARK, WE WANT TO ENTER THROUGH THE **FRONT** DOOR.

AGITATOR!

YOU'RE THE LOWEST FORM OF HUMANITY.

YOU HAVE **ONE MINUTE** TO MOVE.

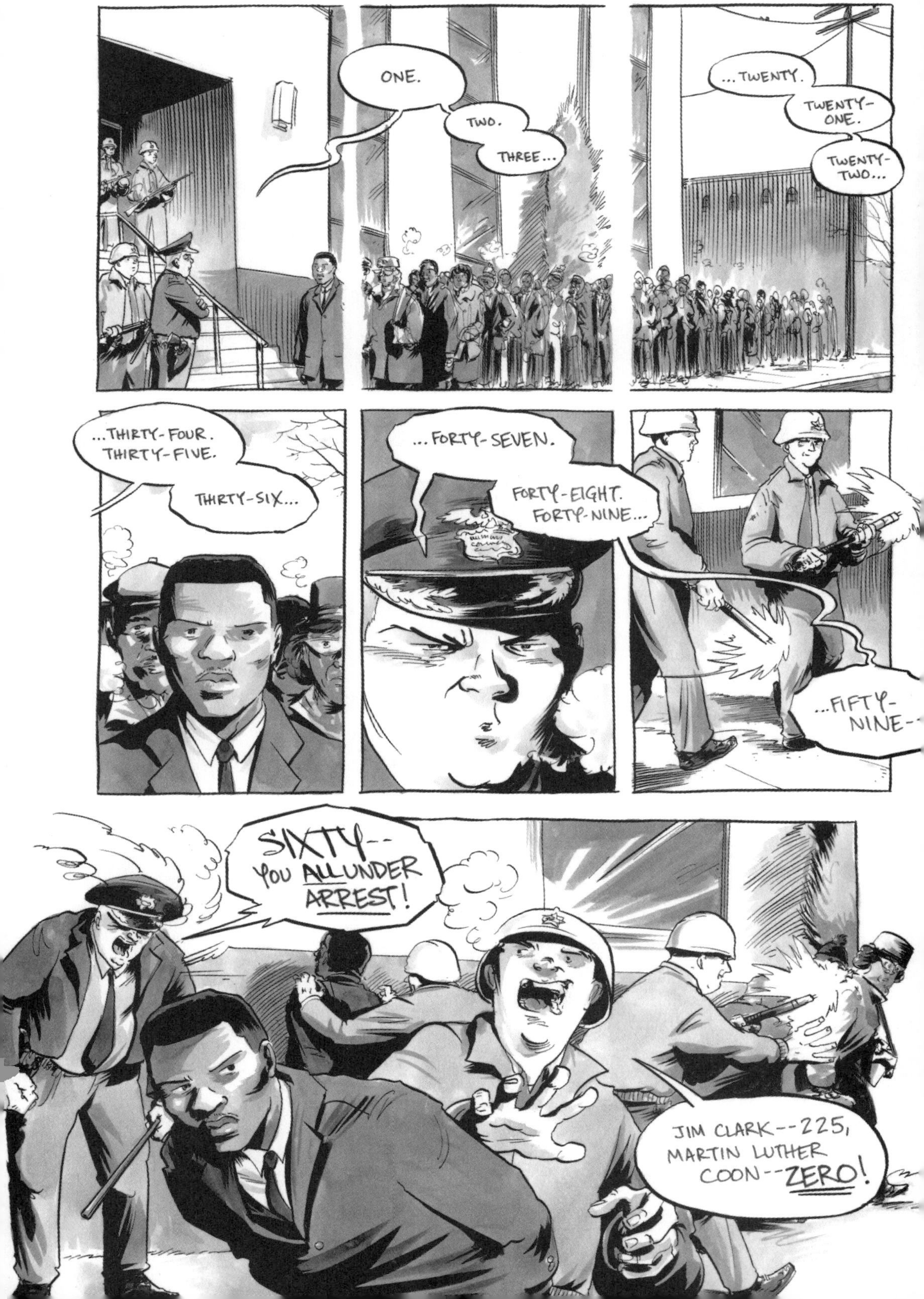
ONE.
TWO.
THREE...
...TWENTY.
TWENTY-ONE.
TWENTY-TWO...
...THIRTY-FOUR. THIRTY-FIVE.
THIRTY-SIX...
...FORTY-SEVEN.
FORTY-EIGHT. FORTY-NINE...
...FIFTY-NINE--
SIXTY-- YOU ALL UNDER ARREST!
JIM CLARK--225, MARTIN LUTHER COON--ZERO!

JANUARY 22, 1965.

I WAS RELEASED FROM JAIL IN TIME TO SEE SOMETHING TRULY **REMARKABLE**.

COME ON, **YOU** HAVE TO COME, TOO--!

THEY'RE GONNA **FIRE** US, RHODA.

I'VE GOT TWO KIDS, AND MY HUSBAND HASN'T HAD WORK IN SIX MONTHS. I CAN'T LOSE MY JOB, AND I **CAN'T** GO TO **JAIL**.

KLAP

THEY... PROBABLY... WON'T FIRE US. WHO'S GONNA **TEACH**?!

IF WE'RE **NOT** IN THE CLASSROOM, THEN THE KIDS'LL BE OUT IN THE STREETS-- PROBABLY **PROTESTING** TOO.

BESIDES, HOW CAN WE **TEACH** AMERICAN CIVICS WHEN **WE** **CAN'T** **VOTE**?!

OKAY. I'LL COME.

REVEREND F.D. REESE WAS PRESIDENT OF THE DALLAS COUNTY VOTER LEAGUE, BUT HE WAS ALSO A **SCHOOL TEACHER**, AND HE ACTIVELY ORGANIZED HIS COLLEAGUES' PARTICIPATION.

NEVER BEFORE HAD SCHOOL TEACHERS GATHERED TO **MARCH**. SOME HAD JOINED US HERE AND THERE, BUT **THIS** WAS SOMETHING TO BEHOLD.

MARGARET MOORE'S PARTICIPATION EARLIER IN THE WEEK SERVED AS INSPIRATION -- NEARLY EVERY BLACK SCHOOL TEACHER IN SELMA TURNED OUT.

MANY OF THEM CARRIED **TOOTHBRUSHES** TO SHOW THEY WEREN'T AFRAID OF GOING TO **JAIL**.

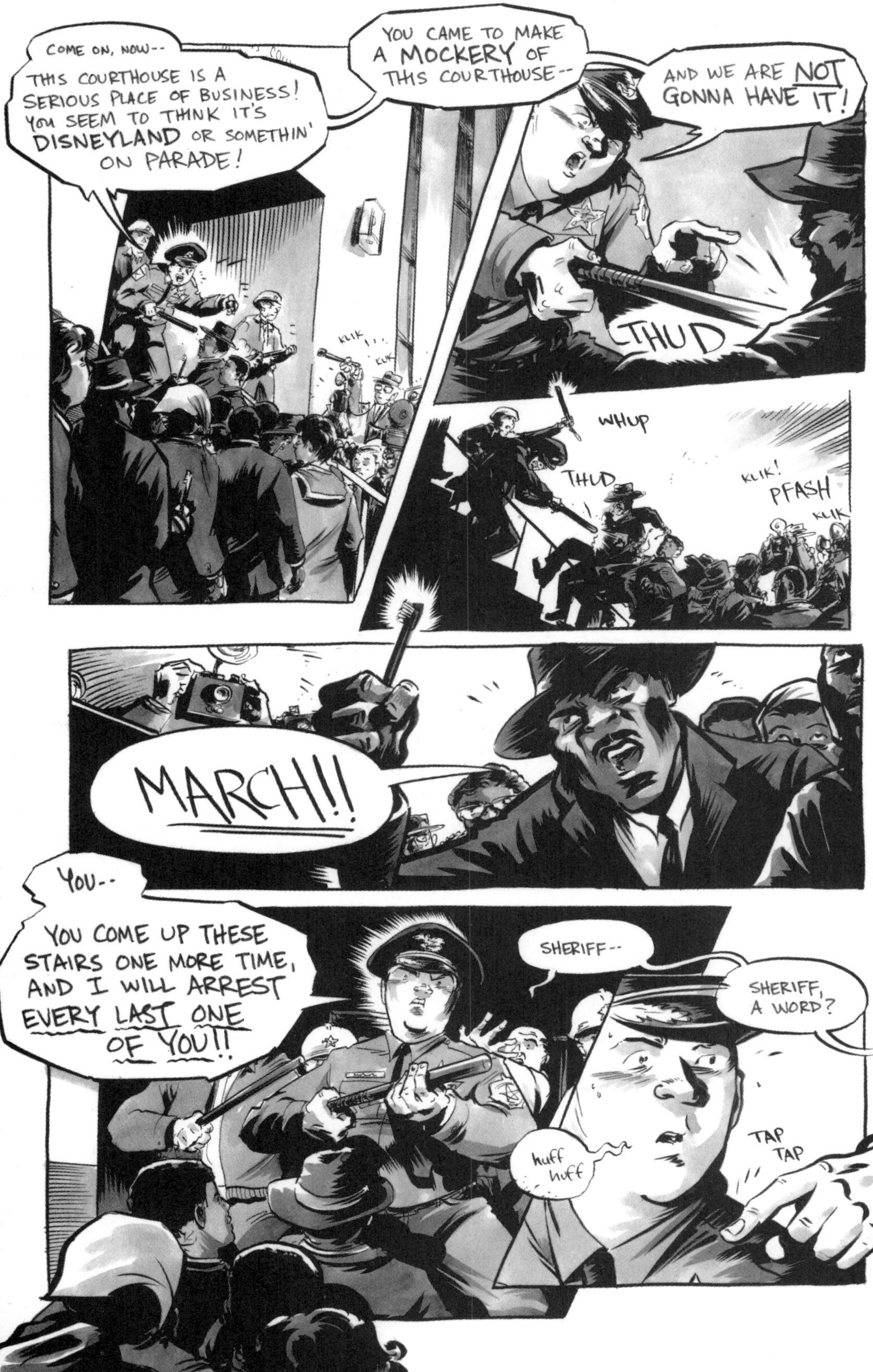
COME ON, NOW--
THIS COURTHOUSE IS A SERIOUS PLACE OF BUSINESS! YOU SEEM TO THINK IT'S DISNEYLAND OR SOMETHIN' ON PARADE!
YOU CAME TO MAKE A MOCKERY OF THIS COURTHOUSE--
AND WE ARE NOT GONNA HAVE IT!
THUD
WHUP
THUD
KLIK!
PFASH
KLIK
MARCH!!
YOU--
YOU COME UP THESE STAIRS ONE MORE TIME, AND I WILL ARREST EVERY LAST ONE OF YOU!!
SHERIFF--
SHERIFF, A WORD?
huff huff
TAP TAP

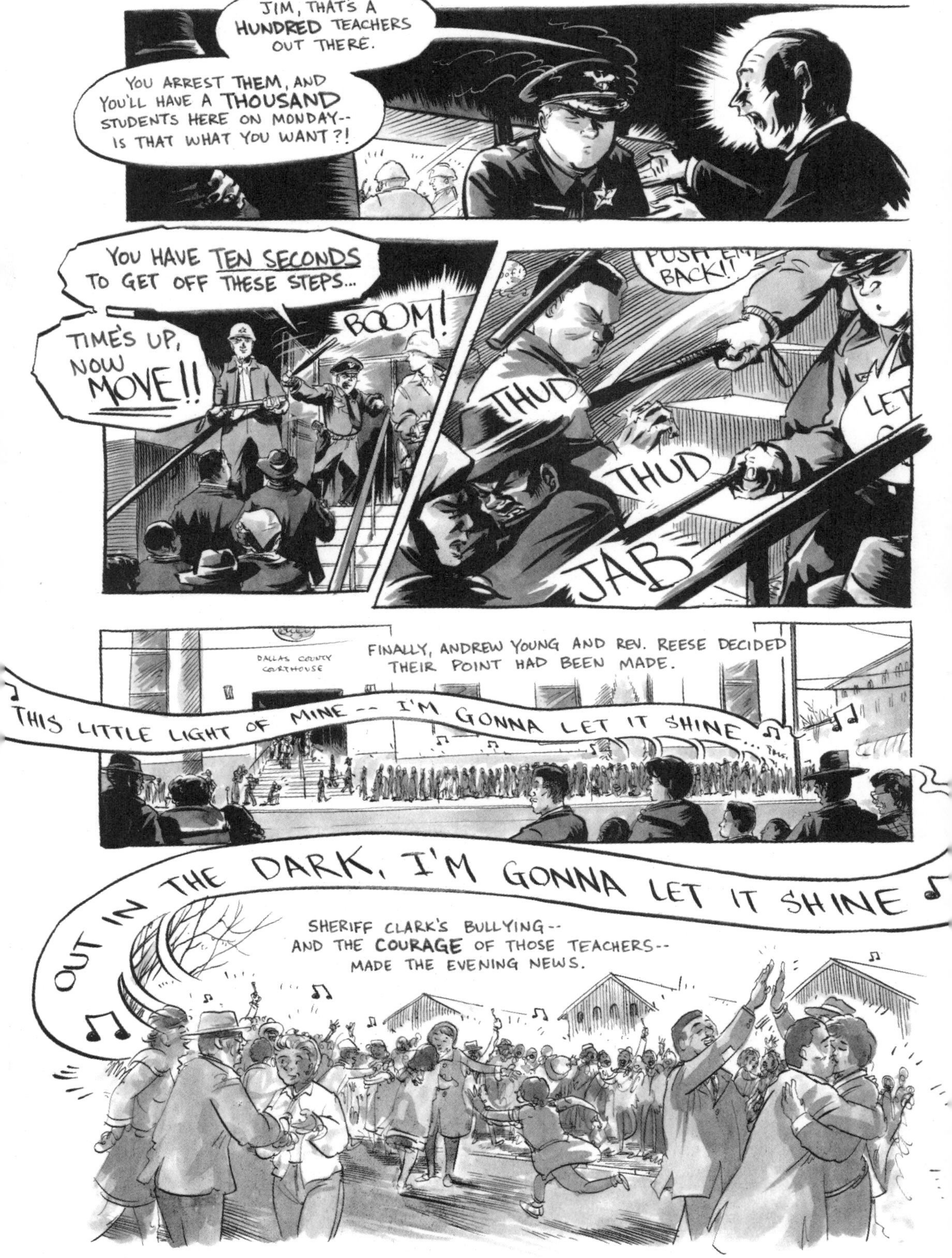

JIM, THAT'S A HUNDRED TEACHERS OUT THERE.
YOU ARREST THEM, AND YOU'LL HAVE A THOUSAND STUDENTS HERE ON MONDAY-- IS THAT WHAT YOU WANT?!
YOU HAVE TEN SECONDS TO GET OFF THESE STEPS...
TIME'S UP, NOW MOVE!!
BOOM!
PUSH 'EM BACK!!
THUD
THUD
JAB
FINALLY, ANDREW YOUNG AND REV. REESE DECIDED THEIR POINT HAD BEEN MADE.
DALLAS COUNTY COURTHOUSE
THIS LITTLE LIGHT OF MINE-- I'M GONNA LET IT SHINE...
OUT IN THE DARK, I'M GONNA LET IT SHINE
SHERIFF CLARK'S BULLYING-- AND THE COURAGE OF THOSE TEACHERS-- MADE THE EVENING NEWS.

OVER THE WEEKEND,

WORD OF THE TEACHERS' MARCH SPREAD,

AND OUR NUMBERS EXPANDED AS OTHER PROFESSIONAL GROUPS DECIDED THEY, TOO, WOULD MARCH.

LOOKING AROUND, I COULDN'T HELP BUT NOTICE THAT SO MANY PEOPLE FROM THOSE EARLY DAYS IN **NASHVILLE** WERE NOW PITCHING IN WITH THE EFFORT IN **SELMA**.

DIANE AND BEVEL WERE WORKING WITH SCLC NOW.

NO--NO, I NEED **THEM** BY **MONDAY!**

BERNARD LAFAYETTE WAS THERE, WORKING FOR SCLC TOO-- EVEN C.T. VIVIAN CAME DOWN TO HELP.

ONLY A HANDFUL OF SNCC STAFF WERE THERE, AND MANY OF MY COLLEAGUES SAW THE OPERATION AS SCLC'S SHOW--

BUT IF THE **PEOPLE** OF SELMA WANTED TO MARCH,

I WAS GOING TO MARCH **WITH** THEM.

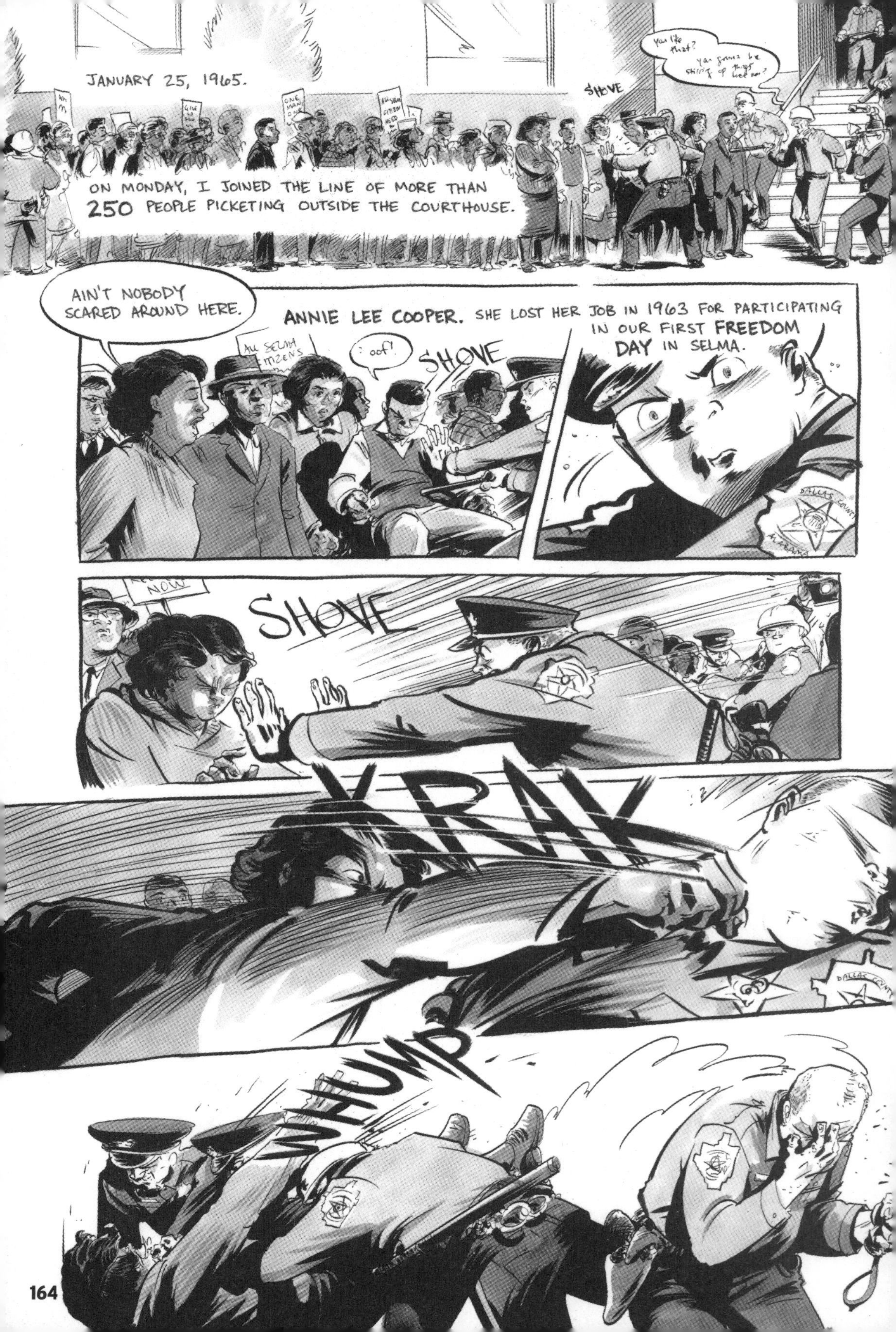
JANUARY 25, 1965.
You like that?
SHOVE
ON MONDAY, I JOINED THE LINE OF MORE THAN 250 PEOPLE PICKETING OUTSIDE THE COURTHOUSE.
AIN'T NOBODY SCARED AROUND HERE.
ANNIE LEE COOPER. SHE LOST HER JOB IN 1963 FOR PARTICIPATING IN OUR FIRST FREEDOM DAY IN SELMA.
ALL SELMA CITIZENS
oof!
SHOVE
DALLAS COUNTY ALABAMA
NOW
SHOVE
KRAK
DALLAS COUNTY
WHUMP

THE NEXT DAY, PHOTOS OF ANNIE LEE COOPER'S BATTERED FACE APPEARED IN NEWSPAPERS ACROSS THE COUNTRY.

SOME YEARS LATER, SHE WOULD BE ELECTED TO THE SELMA CITY COUNCIL.

THE VERY NEXT DAY, WE WERE BACK AGAIN.

AND I GOT ARRESTED.

I WAS RELEASED FROM JAIL IN TIME TO JOIN THE **NEXT** DAY'S PROTEST,

AND I GOT ARRESTED... AGAIN.

AS I WENT TO JAIL, ATLANTA'S ELITE WERE PREPARING A BLACK-TIE DINNER TO HONOR DR. KING FOR RECEIVING THE NOBEL PEACE PRIZE. DESPITE ATLANTA'S **PROGRESSIVE** REPUTATION, THE DINNER WAS ALMOST AN EMBARRASSMENT WHEN MANY BUSINESS LEADERS **REFUSED** TO ATTEND--

-- THAT IS, UNTIL COCA-COLA CHAIRMAN **ROBERT WOODRUFF**, ARGUABLY THE MOST POWERFUL PERSON IN THE CITY, MADE IT CLEAR THAT ATLANTA **WOULD** PROPERLY HONOR ITS NEWEST NOBEL LAUREATE.

BACK IN SELMA, DESPITE HEADLINES GENERATED BY SHERIFF CLARK'S **BRUTALITY**, THE MOVEMENT CONTINUED TO **LOSE STEAM.**

BY THE END OF THE MONTH, FEWER THAN **60** PEOPLE HAD EVEN BEEN ALLOWED INTO THE COURTHOUSE TO ATTEMPT TO REGISTER--

AND **EVERY** SINGLE ONE OF THEM WAS **REJECTED.**

TO MAKE MATTERS WORSE, **SNCC** WAS NEARLY BROKE. I HAD LEFT SELMA FOR AN URGENT FUND-RAISING TRIP TO CALIFORNIA WHEN, ON FEBRUARY 1ST--

FIVE YEARS SINCE THOSE FIRST SIT-INS IN GREENSBORO--

THIS IS A DELIBERATE ATTEMPT TO **DRAMATIZE** CONDITIONS IN THIS CITY, STATE, AND COMMUNITY.

--DR. KING DECIDED TO **STEP UP** THE PRESSURE BY GOING TO JAIL HIMSELF.

LATER THAT WEEK, WHILE DR. KING WAS STILL IN JAIL AND THE COURTHOUSE MARCHES CONTINUED,

MALCOLM X VISITED SELMA.

I'M A FIELD NEGRO--

IF THE MASTER WON'T TREAT ME RIGHT, AND HE'S **SICK**, I'LL TELL THE DOCTOR TO GO THE **OTHER WAY**.

NOW I'M NOT INTENDING TO TRY AND **STIR YOU UP**, AND MAKE YOU DO SOMETHING YOU WOULDN'T HAVE DONE **ANYWAY**--

I PRAY THAT GOD WILL **BLESS** YOU IN EVERYTHING THAT YOU DO.

I PRAY THAT YOU WILL GROW INTELLECTUALLY, SO THAT YOU CAN UNDERSTAND THE PROBLEMS OF THE **WORLD**--

-- AND WHERE **YOU** FIT INTO THAT WORLD PICTURE.

167

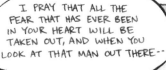

I PRAY THAT ALL THE FEAR THAT HAS EVER BEEN IN YOUR HEART WILL BE TAKEN OUT, AND WHEN YOU LOOK AT THAT MAN OUT THERE--

--IF YOU KNOW HE'S NOTHING BUT A **COWARD**, YOU WON'T FEAR HIM.

THEY FUNCTION IN MOBS--**THAT'S** A COWARD. THEY PUT ON A **SHEET** SO YOU WON'T KNOW WHO THEY ARE-- **THAT'S A COWARD.**

THE TIME **WILL** COME WHEN THAT SHEET WILL BE RIPPED OFF--

AND IF THE FEDE GOVERNMENT DOES TAKE IT OFF, **WE** TAKE IT OFF.

CAN YOU TELL US WHY YOU'RE HERE TODAY?

I AM **100 PERCENT** FOR ANY EFFORT PUT FORTH BY BLACK PEOPLE IN THIS COUNTRY TO HAVE ACCESS TO THE **BALLOT.**

AND I FRANKLY BELIEVE THAT, SINCE THE BALLOT IS OUR **RIGHT,** WE ARE **WITHIN** THAT RIGHT TO USE **WHATEVER MEANS NECESSARY** TO SECURE THOSE RIGHTS.

PEOPLE WOULD DO WELL TO **LISTEN** TO DR. KING AND GIVE HIM WHAT HE'S ASKING FOR-- AND GIVE IT TO HIM **FAST**-- BEFORE SOME **OTHER** FACTIONS COME ALONG AND TRY TO DO IT ANOTHER WAY.

WHAT HE'S ASKING FOR IS <u>RIGHT</u>.

--THEN I THINK THE INTELLIGENCE OF THE **BLACK** PEOPLE IN THIS AREA WILL COMPEL THEM TO DEVISE **ANOTHER** METHOD THAT **WILL** GET RESULTS.

ARE YOU SAYING THAT NONVIOLENCE OUGHT TO BE ABANDONED HERE IN SELMA--

DR. KING AND HIS FOLLOWERS ARE VERY **INTELLIGENTLY** TRYING TO IMPRESS THE PEOPLE OF THIS AREA THAT THEY SHOULD GIVE THE BLACK MAN THE RIGHT TO VOTE.

NOW, IF THOSE PEOPLE ARE **NOT** INTELLIGENT ENOUGH **THEMSELVES** TO RECOGNIZE WHAT THEY CONSIDER AN INTELLIGENT APPROACH--

NOK NOK

MRS. KING--?

MRS. KING, WILL YOU TELL DR. KING THAT I HAD PLANNED TO VISIT WITH HIM IN JAIL? I WON'T GET A CHANCE NOW, I'M AFRAID...

I WANT DR. KING TO KNOW THAT I **DIDN'T** COME TO SELMA TO MAKE HIS JOB DIFFICULT.

HELLO, MALCOLM.

I REALLY DO THINK MY PRESENCE COULD MAKE IT **EASIER**--

IF THE WHITE PEOPLE REALIZE WHAT THE **ALTERNATIVE** IS, PERHAPS THEY'LL BE MORE WILLING TO HEAR HIM OUT.

SCLC PUBLISHED DR. KING'S "A **LETTER FROM A SELMA JAIL**" IN THE <u>NEW YORK TIMES</u>. WHILE IT DIDN'T PROVOKE THE SAME PUBLIC OUTCRY AS EARLIER LETTERS, PRESIDENT JOHNSON **DID** ADDRESS THE EVENTS IN SELMA DURING A NATIONAL PRESS CONFERENCE.

ALL AMERICANS SHOULD BE INDIGNANT WHEN ONE AMERICAN IS DENIED THE RIGHT TO **VOTE**.

THE LOSS OF THAT RIGHT TO A SINGLE CITIZEN UNDERMINES THE FREEDOM OF **EVERY** CITIZEN. THIS IS WHY **ALL** OF US SHOULD BE CONCERNED WITH THE EFFORTS OF OUR FELLOW AMERICANS TO REGISTER TO VOTE IN ALABAMA.

THE NEXT DAY, DR. KING WAS RELEASED FROM JAIL, AND I FLEW BACK FROM CALIFORNIA TO JOIN HIM.

WE GREETED A DELEGATION OF **CONGRESSMEN** WHO HAD COME TO SELMA TO SEE FOR THEMSELVES WHAT WAS HAPPENING.

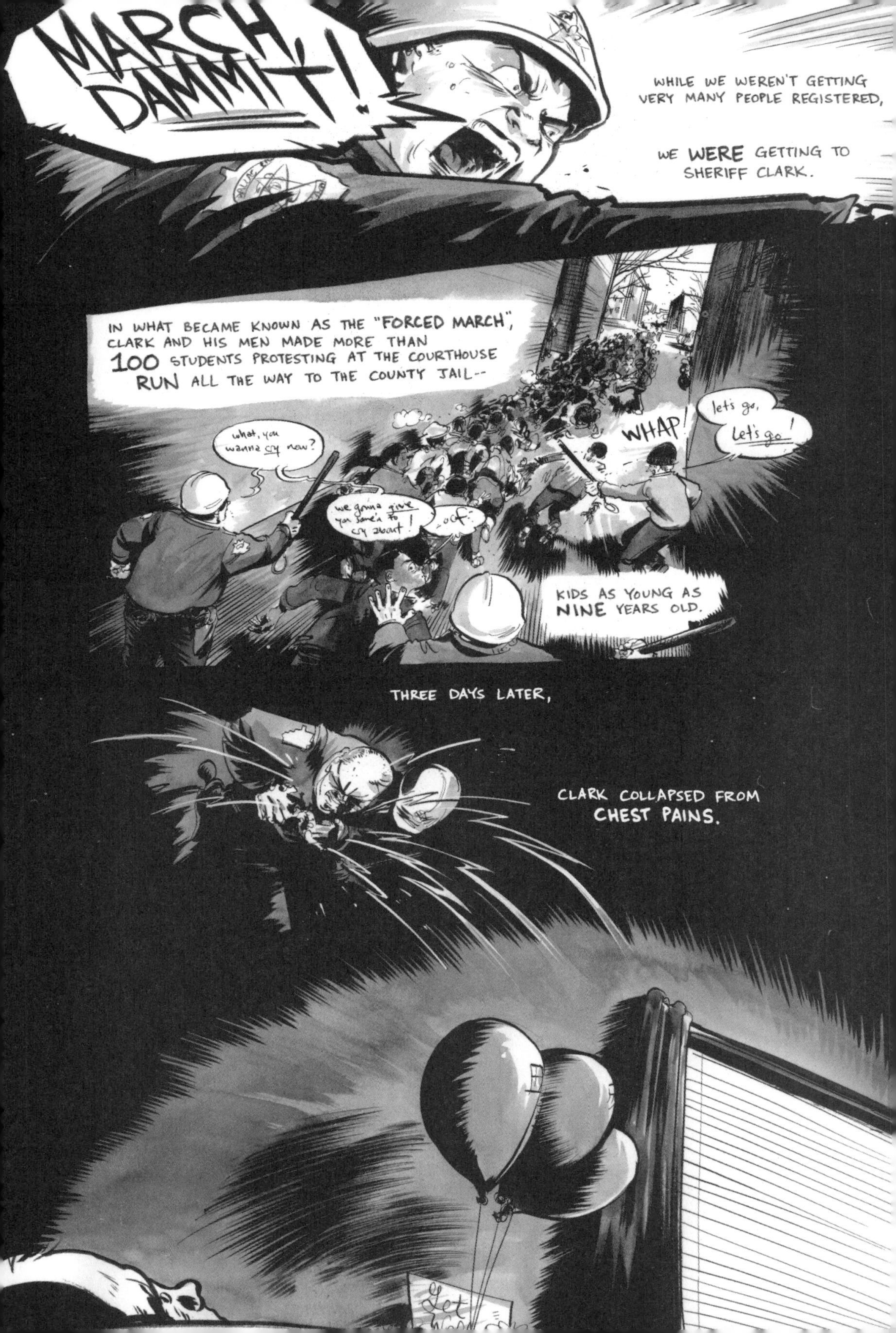
MARCH, DAMMIT!
WHILE WE WEREN'T GETTING VERY MANY PEOPLE REGISTERED,
WE WERE GETTING TO SHERIFF CLARK.
IN WHAT BECAME KNOWN AS THE "FORCED MARCH", CLARK AND HIS MEN MADE MORE THAN 100 STUDENTS PROTESTING AT THE COURTHOUSE RUN ALL THE WAY TO THE COUNTY JAIL--
what, you wanna cry now?
we gonna give you some'n to cry about!
oof
WHAP!
let's go, Let's go!
KIDS AS YOUNG AS NINE YEARS OLD.
THREE DAYS LATER,
CLARK COLLAPSED FROM CHEST PAINS.

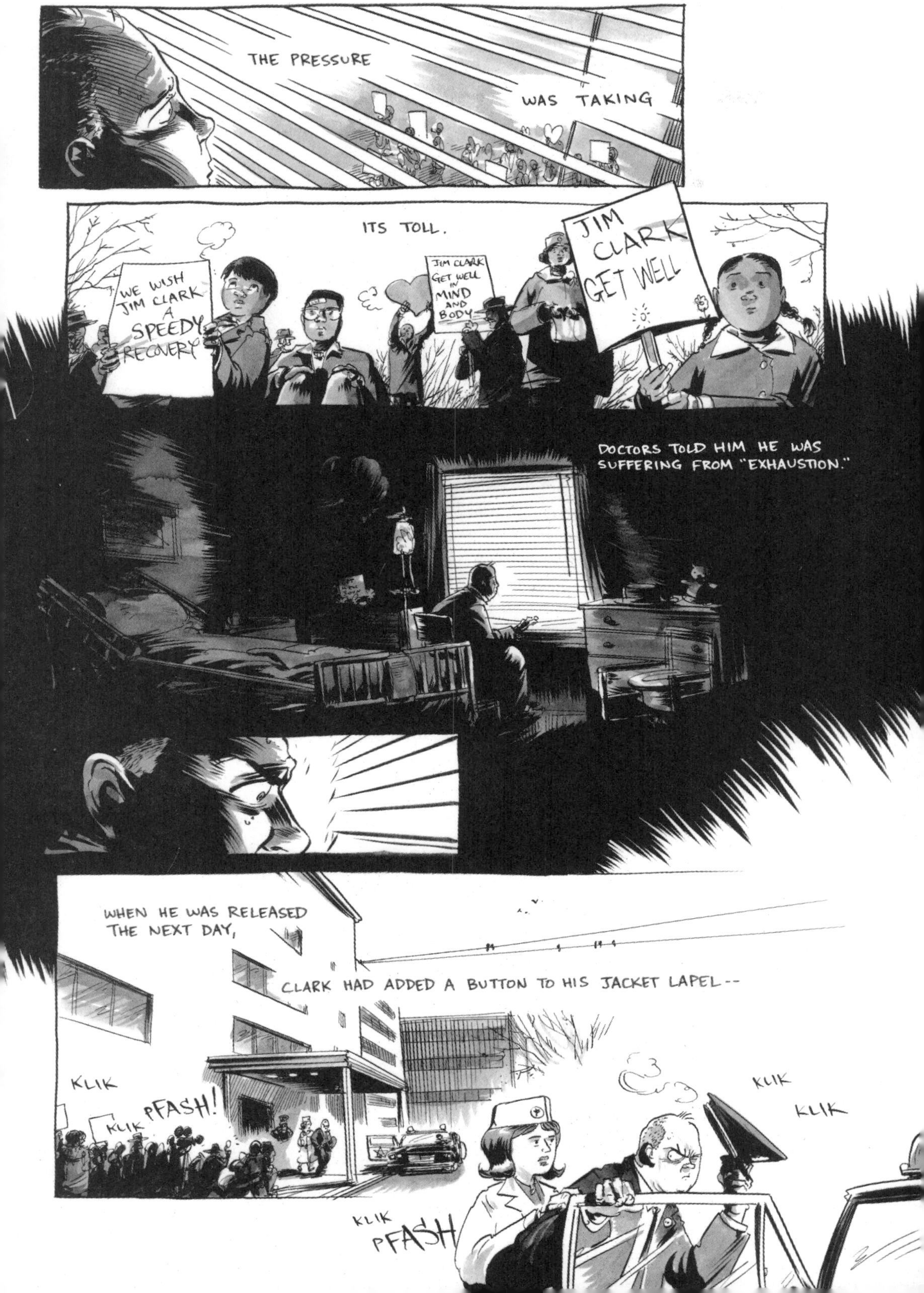
THE PRESSURE
WAS TAKING
ITS TOLL.
WE WISH JIM CLARK A SPEEDY RECOVERY
JIM CLARK GET WELL IN MIND AND BODY
JIM CLARK GET WELL
DOCTORS TOLD HIM HE WAS SUFFERING FROM "EXHAUSTION."
WHEN HE WAS RELEASED THE NEXT DAY,
CLARK HAD ADDED A BUTTON TO HIS JACKET LAPEL--
KLIK
KLIK
pFASH!
KLIK
KLIK
KLIK
pFASH

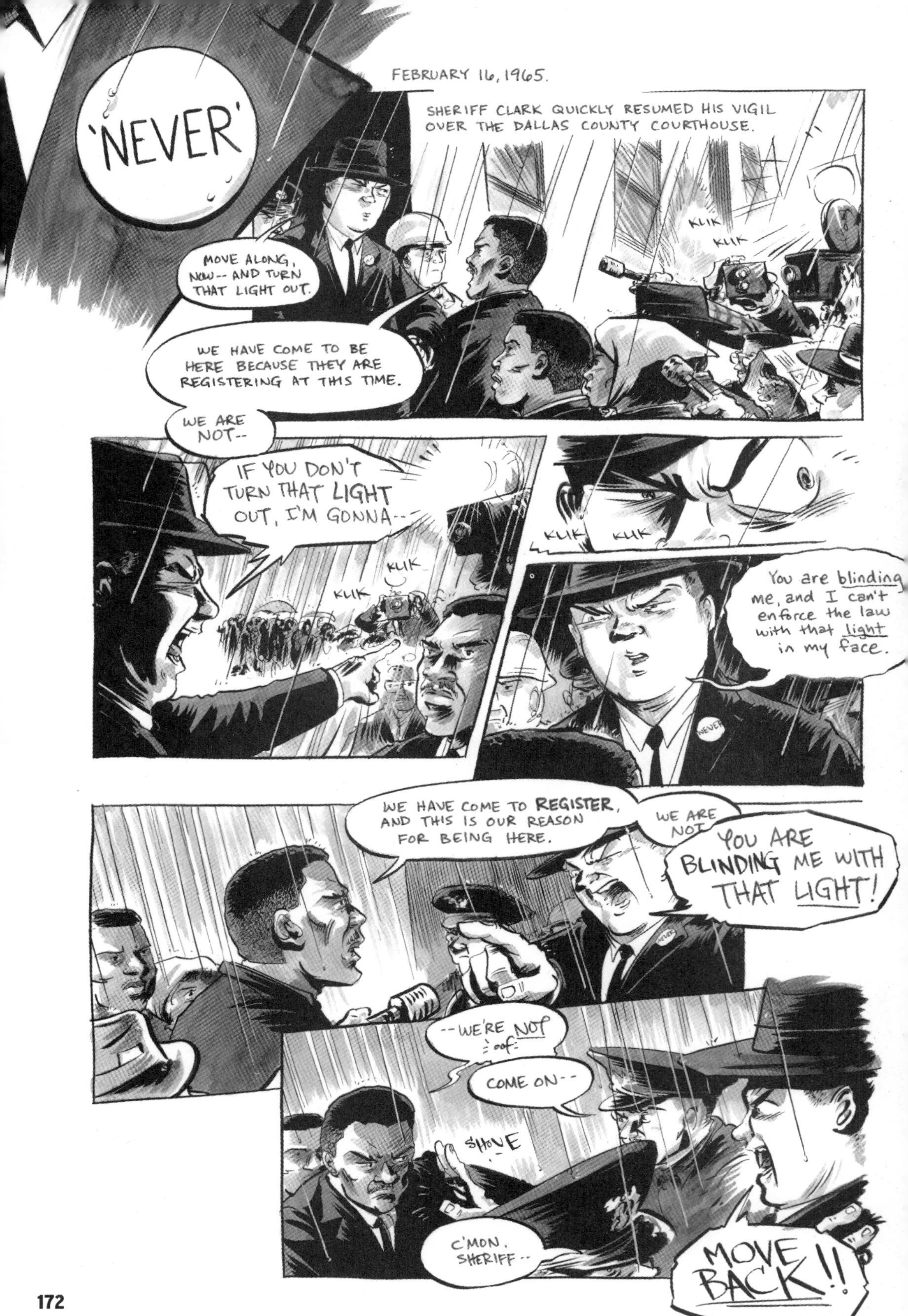
'NEVER'
FEBRUARY 16, 1965.
SHERIFF CLARK QUICKLY RESUMED HIS VIGIL OVER THE DALLAS COUNTY COURTHOUSE.
KLIK
KLIK
MOVE ALONG, NOW-- AND TURN THAT LIGHT OUT.
WE HAVE COME TO BE HERE BECAUSE THEY ARE REGISTERING AT THIS TIME.
WE ARE NOT--
IF YOU DON'T TURN THAT LIGHT OUT, I'M GONNA--
KLIK
KLIK
KLIK
KLIK
You are blinding me, and I can't enforce the law with that light in my face.
NEVER
WE HAVE COME TO REGISTER, AND THIS IS OUR REASON FOR BEING HERE.
WE ARE NOT
YOU ARE BLINDING ME WITH THAT LIGHT!
--WE'RE NOT
oof-
COME ON--
SHOVE
C'MON. SHERIFF--
MOVE BACK!!

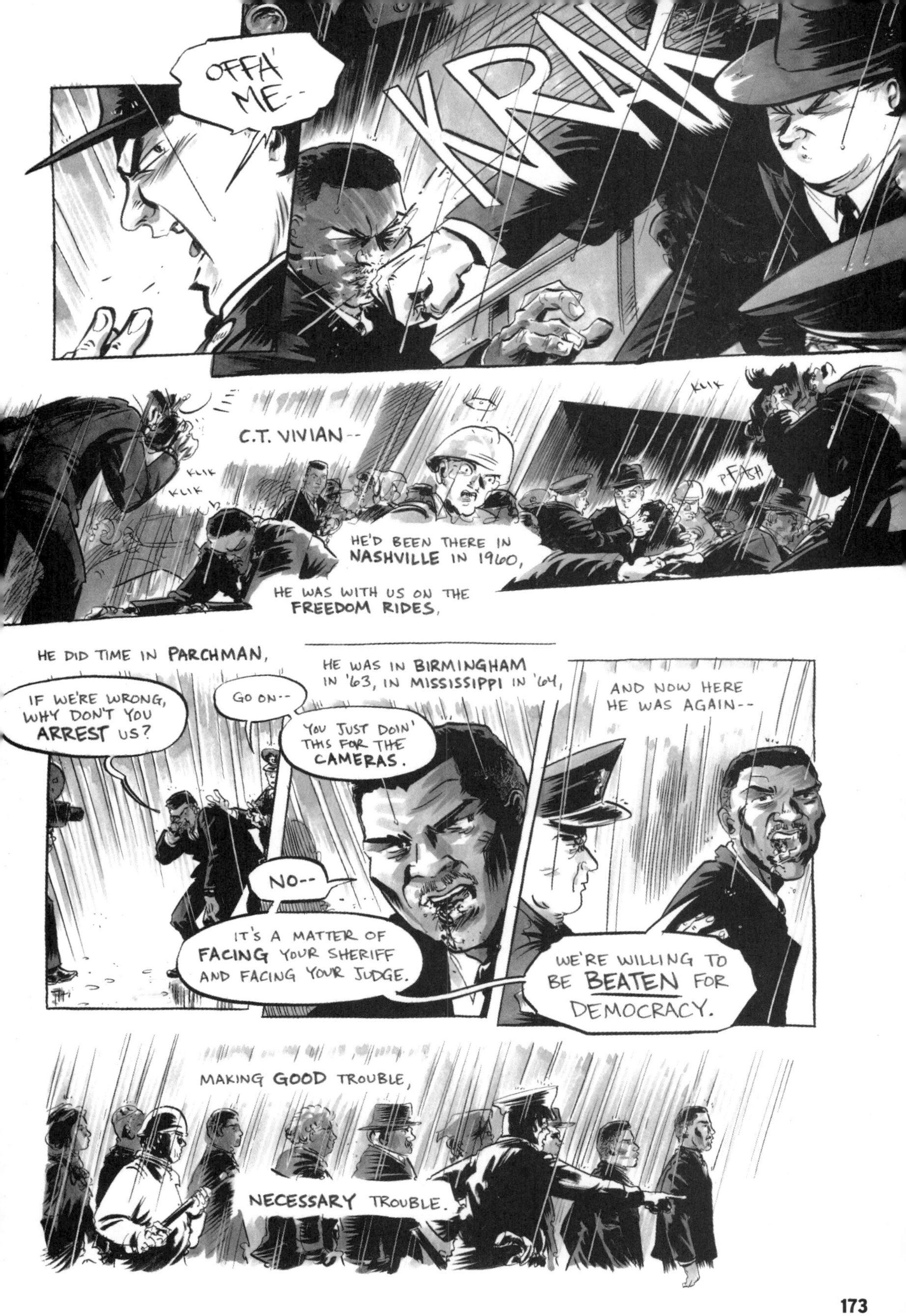
OFFA' ME--
KRAK
C.T. VIVIAN--
KLIK
KLIK
KLIK
PFASH
HE'D BEEN THERE IN NASHVILLE IN 1960,
HE WAS WITH US ON THE FREEDOM RIDES,
HE DID TIME IN PARCHMAN,
IF WE'RE WRONG, WHY DON'T YOU ARREST US?
GO ON--
HE WAS IN BIRMINGHAM IN '63, IN MISSISSIPPI IN '64,
YOU JUST DOIN' THIS FOR THE CAMERAS.
NO--
IT'S A MATTER OF FACING YOUR SHERIFF AND FACING YOUR JUDGE.
AND NOW HERE HE WAS AGAIN--
WE'RE WILLING TO BE BEATEN FOR DEMOCRACY.
MAKING GOOD TROUBLE,
NECESSARY TROUBLE.

FEBRUARY 18--
MARION, AL, 30 MILES FROM SELMA.

AFTER BEING RELEASED FROM JAIL, C.T. VIVIAN SPOKE AT A RALLY PROTESTING THE ARREST OF A SCLC WORKER NAMED JAMES ORANGE.

AFTER C.T. SPOKE, HUNDREDS OF PEOPLE WERE READY TO MARCH TO THE CITY JAIL AND **SING** OUTSIDE ORANGE'S CELL.

HOLD IT--

DOZENS OF ALABAMA STATE TROOPERS HAD BEEN SENT TO MARION AS REINFORCEMENTS TO RESTORE "PEACE" TO THE "SOUTHERN WAY OF LIFE."

YOU <u>MUST</u> TURN AROUND-- GO BACK TO YOUR <u>CHURCH</u> OR TO <u>YOUR HOME!</u>

THIS WAS A DANGEROUS MARCH. UNDER COVER OF DARKNESS,

TZZZZ'-

TOO MANY THINGS COULD HAPPEN.

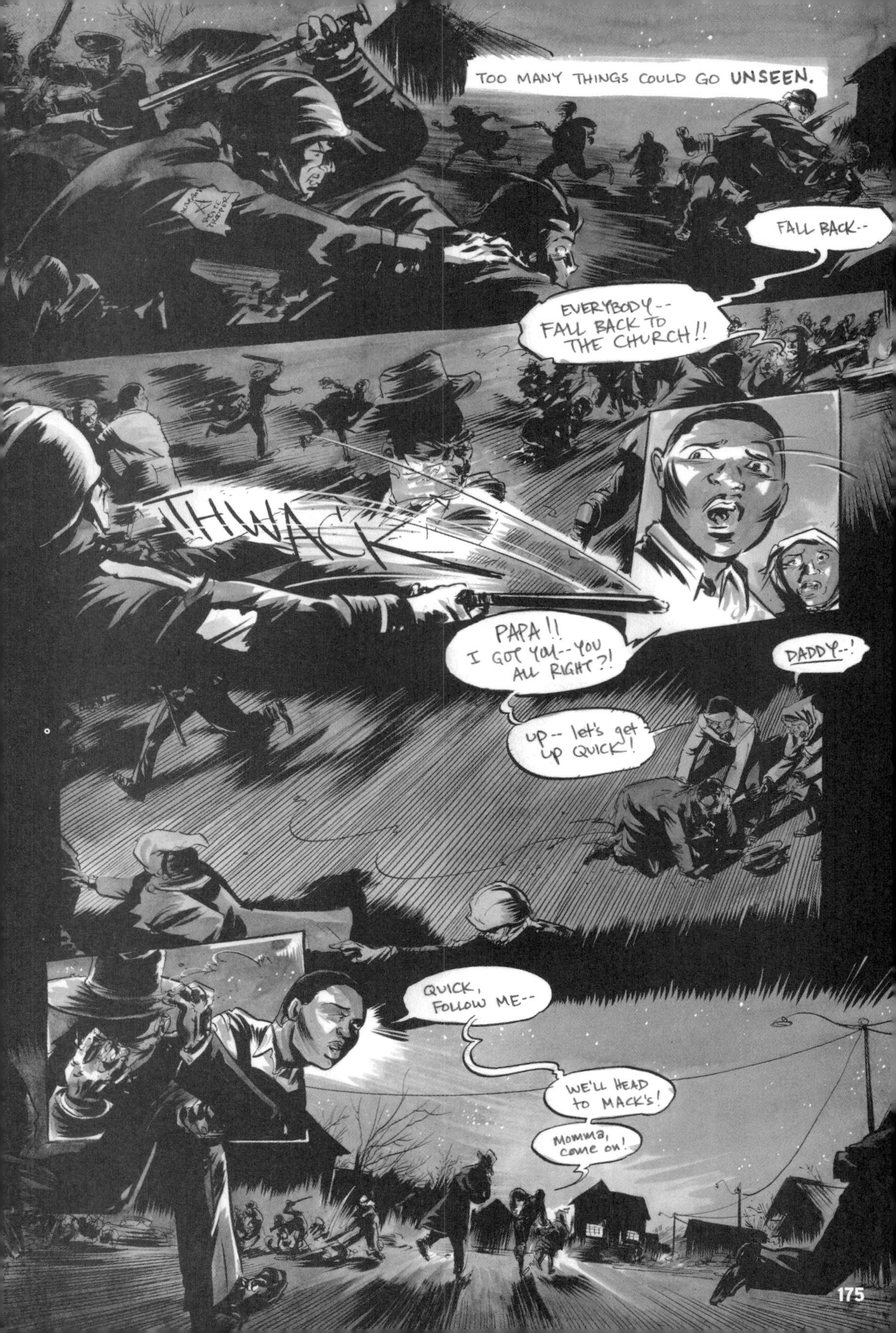
TOO MANY THINGS COULD GO UNSEEN.
FALL BACK--
EVERYBODY-- FALL BACK TO THE CHURCH!!
THWACK
PAPA!! I GOT YOU--YOU ALL RIGHT?!
DADDY--!
up-- let's get up QUICK!
QUICK, FOLLOW ME--
WE'LL HEAD to MACK's!
Momma, come on!

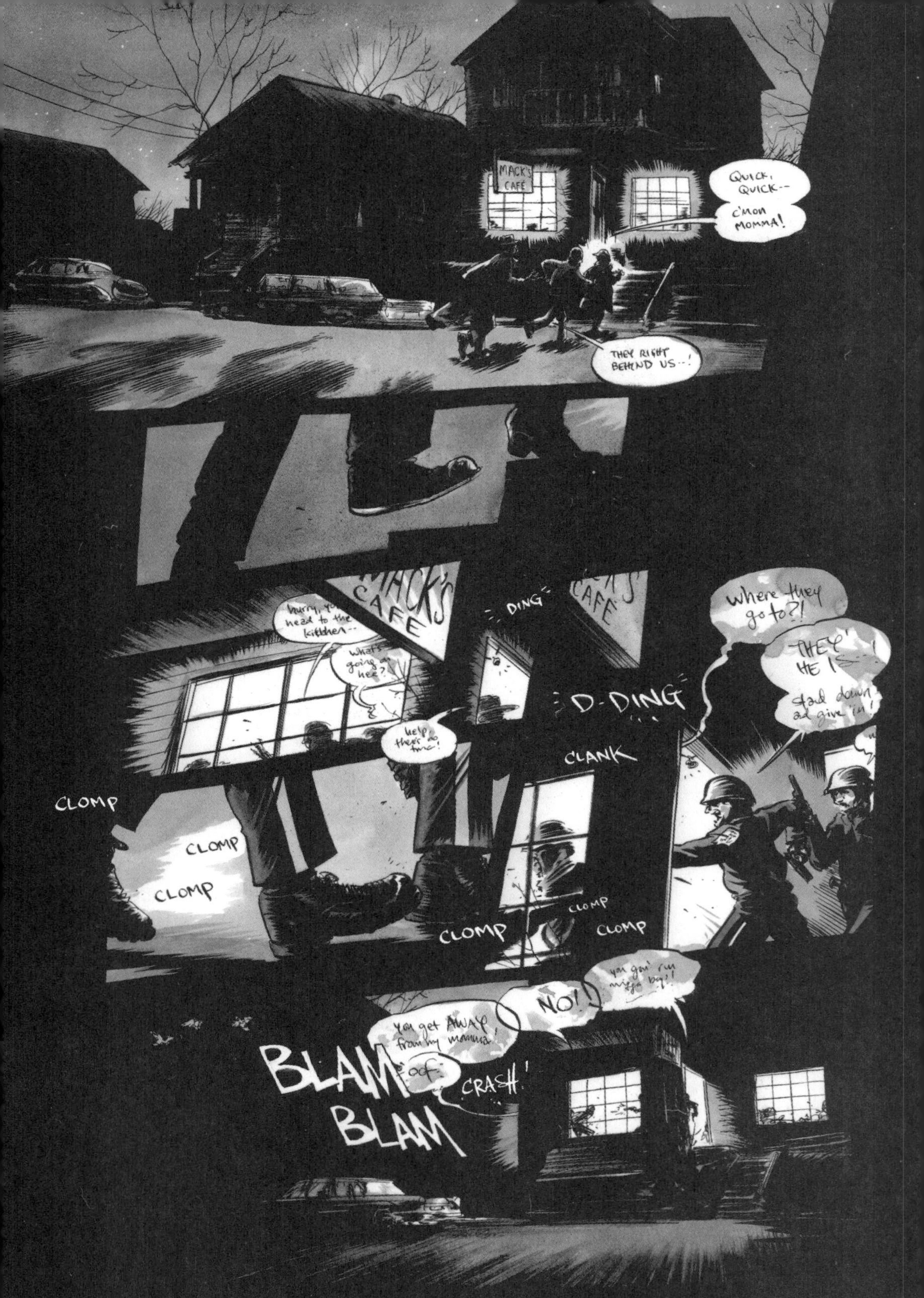

MACK'S CAFÉ
QUICK, QUICK--
C'MON MOMMA!
THEY RIGHT BEHIND US--!
MACK'S CAFE
what's going on here?
help, there's no time!
CLOMP
CLOMP
CLOMP
DING
D-DING
CLANK
CLOMP
CLOMP
CLOMP
where they go to?!
THEY' HE IS--!
NO!
You get AWAY from my mama!
oof
CRASH!
BLAM
BLAM

JIMMIE LEE JACKSON WAS A 26-YEAR-OLD ARMY VETERAN.

ANOTHER HALF HOUR PASSED BEFORE LOCAL POLICE TOOK HIM TO THE COUNTY INFIRMARY.

I RECEIVED WORD THE NEXT DAY THAT
JIMMIE LEE JACKSON WAS CRITICALLY
WOUNDED, BUT STILL **ALIVE.**

HIS SHOOTING WEIGHED HEAVILY ON US ALL--

IF JIMMIE LEE JACKSON DIED, NO ONE COULD SAY **WHAT** WOULD HAPPEN.

TWO DAYS LATER-- MY BIRTHDAY-- I WAS ON MY WAY TO GEORGIA
TO HELP WITH SNCC VOTER REGISTRATION EFFORTS THERE.

--WE HAVE BREAKING NEWS TO REPORT-- PLEASE STAND BY--

WE HAVE RECEIVED REPORTS THAT MALCOLM X HAS BEEN **ASSASSINATED** BY A GROUP OF ARMED GUNMEN IN NEW YORK CITY.

REPEAT--

WE HAVE RECEIVED REPORTS THAT MALCOLM X HAS BEEN ASSASSINATED BY A GROUP OF ARMED GUNMEN IN NEW YORK CITY. MALCOLM X POWER 1965

I HAD MY DIFFERENCES WITH MALCOLM,

BUT AFTER SEEING HIM IN AFRICA, I WAS FILLED WITH GRIEF OVER WHAT **COULD HAVE BEEN** FOR HIM.

HERE--AT THIS FINAL HOUR, IN THIS QUIET PLACE-- HARLEM HAS COME TO BID FAREWELL TO ONE OF ITS **BRIGHTEST** HOPES--

EXTINGUISHED NOW, AND GONE FROM US FOREVER.

THE ACTOR AND ACTIVIST **OSSIE DAVIS** DELIVERED HIS EULOGY.

LAST YEAR, FROM AFRICA, HE WROTE THESE WORDS TO A FRIEND:

"My journey is almost ended, and I have a much broader scope than when I started out, which I believe will add new life and dimension to our struggle for **freedom**, honor, and **dignity** in the states.

"I am writing these things so that you will know for a FACT the tremendous **sympathy** and **support** we have among the African states for our human rights struggle.

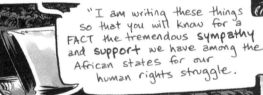

"The main thing is that we keep a **united** front, wherein our most valuable time and energy will not be **wasted** fighting each other."

HOWEVER WE MAY HAVE **DIFFERED** WITH HIM-- OR WITH EACH OTHER **ABOUT** HIM AND HIS VALUE AS A MAN--

Let his going from us only serve to bring us **together**,

now.

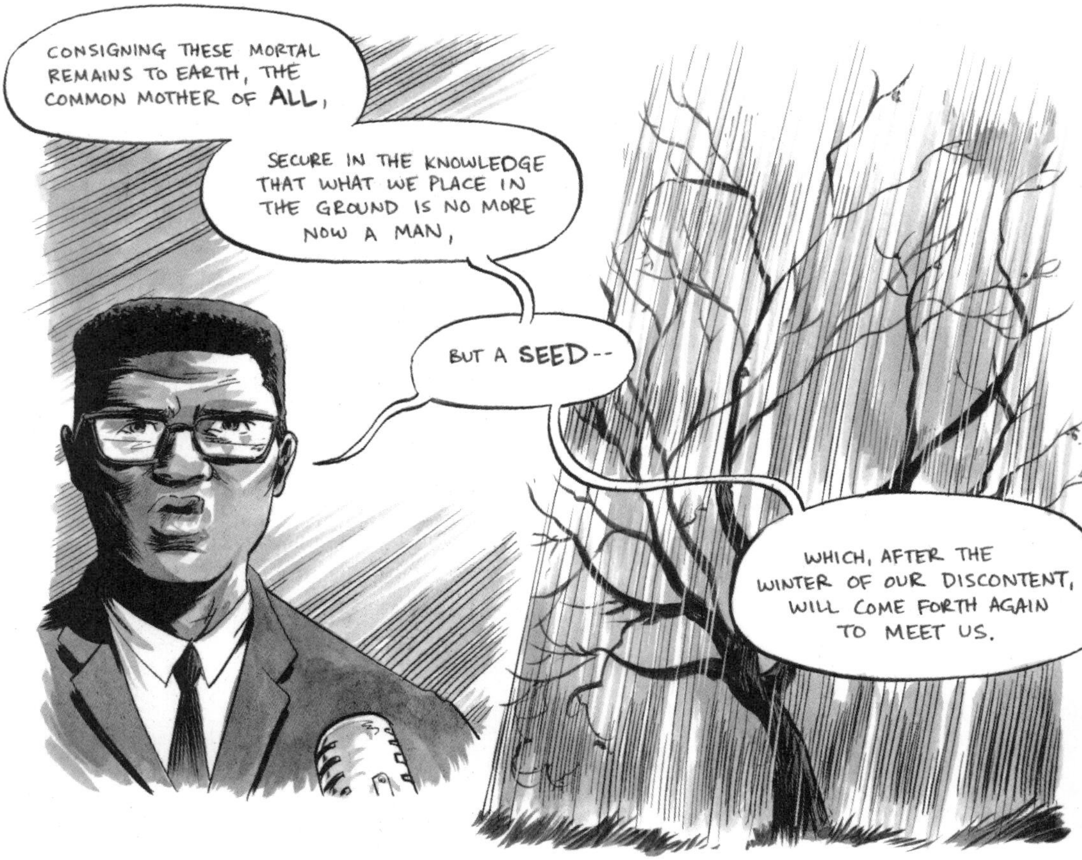
CONSIGNING THESE MORTAL REMAINS TO EARTH, THE COMMON MOTHER OF **ALL**,
SECURE IN THE KNOWLEDGE THAT WHAT WE PLACE IN THE GROUND IS NO MORE NOW A MAN,
BUT A **SEED**--
WHICH, AFTER THE WINTER OF OUR DISCONTENT, WILL COME FORTH AGAIN TO MEET US.

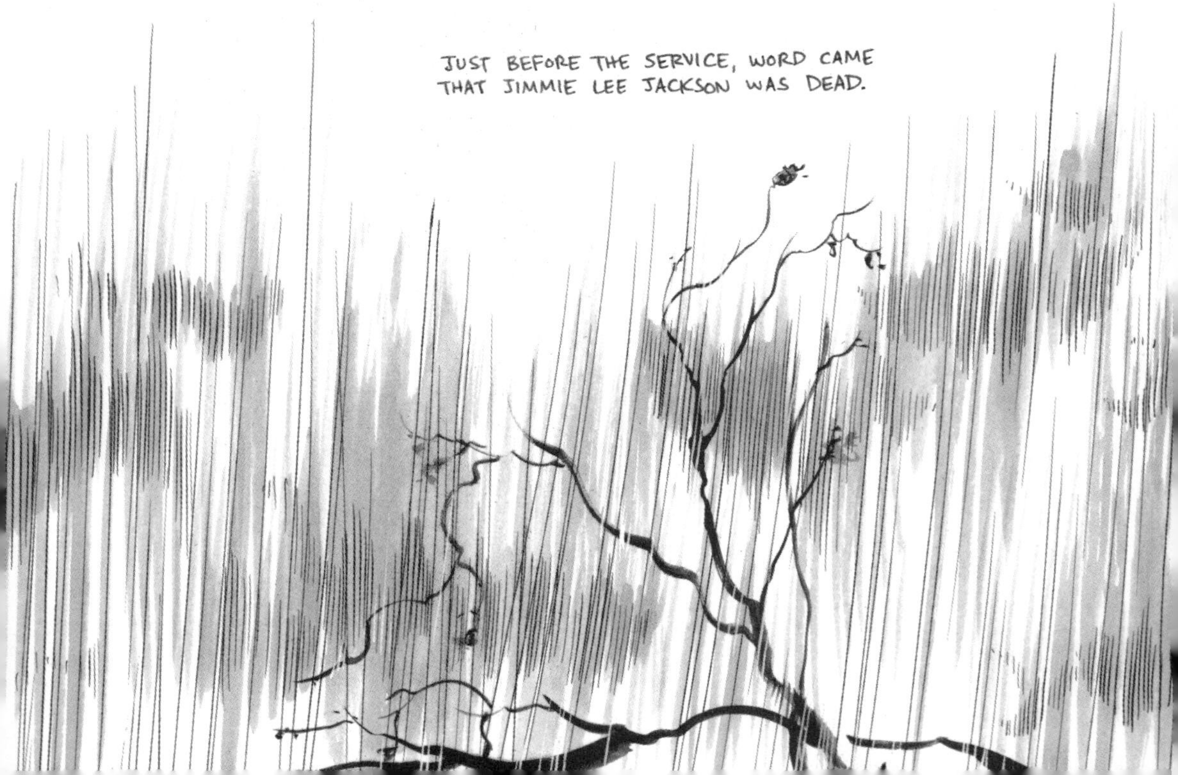
JUST BEFORE THE SERVICE, WORD CAME THAT JIMMIE LEE JACKSON WAS DEAD.

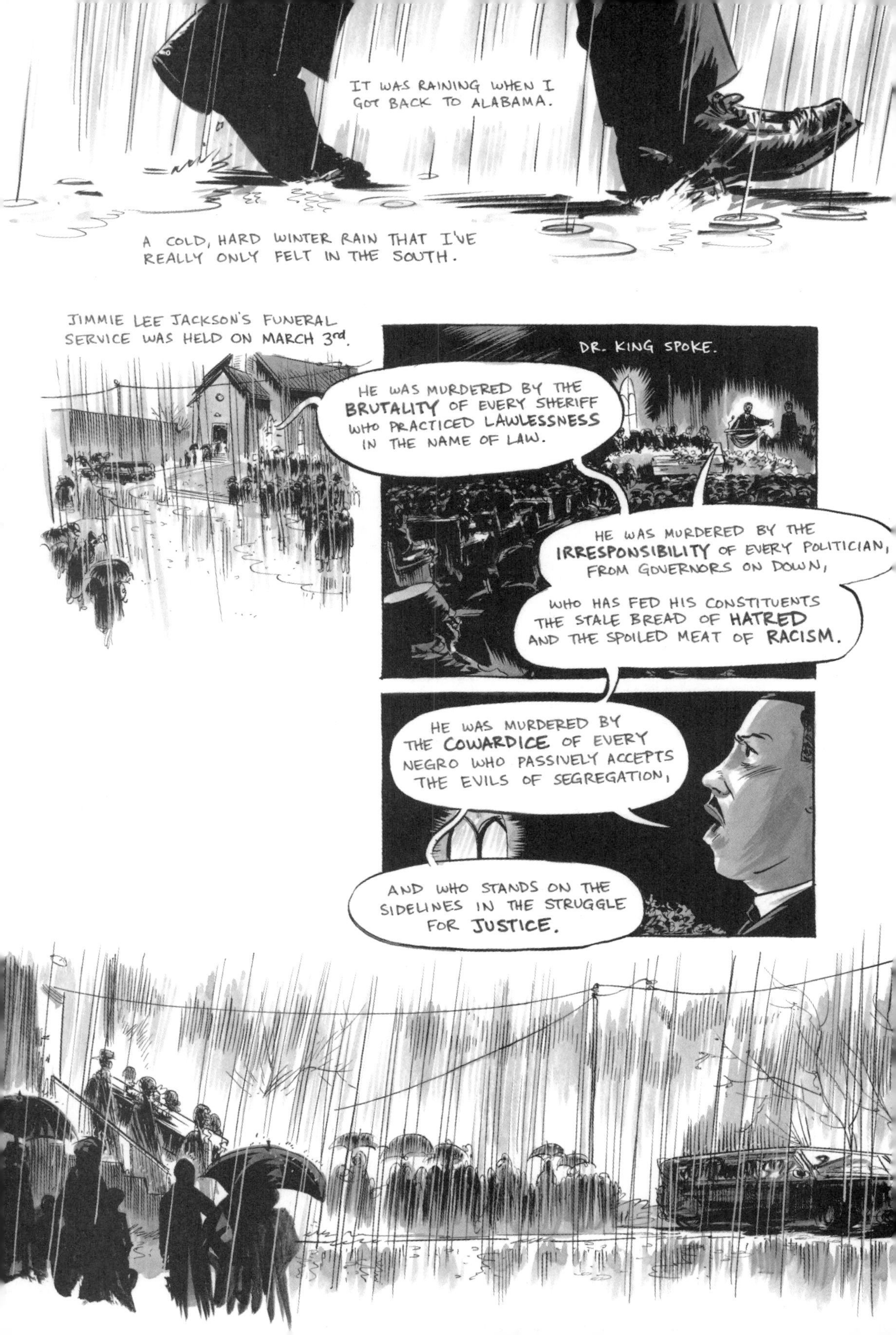
IT WAS RAINING WHEN I GOT BACK TO ALABAMA.
A COLD, HARD WINTER RAIN THAT I'VE REALLY ONLY FELT IN THE SOUTH.
JIMMIE LEE JACKSON'S FUNERAL SERVICE WAS HELD ON MARCH 3rd.
DR. KING SPOKE.
HE WAS MURDERED BY THE BRUTALITY OF EVERY SHERIFF WHO PRACTICED LAWLESSNESS IN THE NAME OF LAW.
HE WAS MURDERED BY THE IRRESPONSIBILITY OF EVERY POLITICIAN, FROM GOVERNORS ON DOWN,
WHO HAS FED HIS CONSTITUENTS THE STALE BREAD OF HATRED AND THE SPOILED MEAT OF RACISM.
HE WAS MURDERED BY THE COWARDICE OF EVERY NEGRO WHO PASSIVELY ACCEPTS THE EVILS OF SEGREGATION,
AND WHO STANDS ON THE SIDELINES IN THE STRUGGLE FOR JUSTICE.

SOMEWHERE ALONG THE WAY,

BEVEL SUGGESTED WE TAKE HIS CASKET ALL THE WAY TO **MONTGOMERY** AND LAY IT ON THE **CAPITOL STEPS.**

GEORGE WALLACE COULD **NOT** IGNORE THAT, AND NEITHER COULD THE STATE OF ALABAMA.

WE BURIED JIMMIE LEE JACKSON THAT DAY,

BUT THE IDEA FOR THE SELMA-TO-MONTGOMERY MARCH WAS **BORN.**

WE HELD PLANNING MEETINGS AND DISCUSSIONS FOR THE NEXT **FOUR DAYS.**

MANY SNCC MEMBERS WERE **AGAINST** THE IDEA OF MARCHING FROM SELMA TO MONTGOMERY,

ESPECIALLY JIM FORMAN.

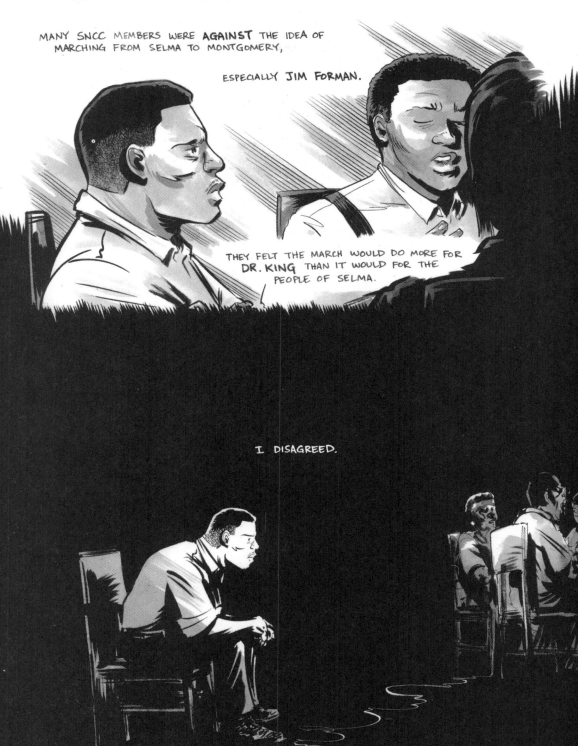

THEY FELT THE MARCH WOULD DO MORE FOR **DR. KING** THAN IT WOULD FOR THE PEOPLE OF SELMA.

I DISAGREED.

IT WAS ONE OF THE MOST DIFFICULT
DECISIONS I HAD EVER DEALT WITH
SINCE BECOMING CHAIRMAN.

THE PEOPLE OF SELMA WERE **HURTING**.

THEY **NEEDED** TO MARCH.

BUT I WAS ALONE IN MY BELIEF
AMONG MY SNCC COLLEAGUES.

WHEN BEVEL FORMALLY ANNOUNCED THAT
DR. KING WOULD BE LEADING A MARCH FROM
SELMA TO MONTGOMERY ON **SUNDAY,**
MARCH 7TH, JIM FORMAN DRAFTED A
LETTER FROM **SNCC** TO DR. KING--

CARRYING MY SIGNATURE
AT THE BOTTOM.

AS CHAIRMAN, I HAD A RESPONSIBILITY AND
AN OBLIGATION TO REPRESENT SNCC'S DECISIONS.

" WE STRONGLY BELIEVE THAT
THE OBJECTIVES OF THE MARCH
DO NOT JUSTIFY THE **DANGERS**.

CONSEQUENTLY, THE STUDENT
NONVIOLENT COORDINATING COMMITTEE
WILL ONLY LIVE UP TO THOSE
MINIMAL COMMITMENTS...

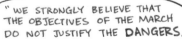

SNCC WOULD HAVE NOTHING
TO DO WITH THIS MARCH--

TO PROVIDE RADIOS AND
CARS, DOCTORS AND NURSES,
AND **NOTHING** BEYOND **THAT**."

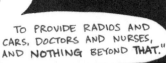

BUT IT WAS A SNCC
LETTER, **NOT** A JOHN
LEWIS LETTER.

MARCH 6, 1965--

FRAZIER'S CAFÉ SOCIETY, ATLANTA GA.

I RETURNED TO ATLANTA, WHERE I MET WITH SEVERAL OF MY SNCC COLLEAGUES IN ONE LAST ATTEMPT TO CONVINCE THEM THAT WE **SHOULD** PARTICIPATE IN THE MARCH.

BUT AFTER SEVERAL HOURS OF DISCUSSION WITH MOST OF THE SNCC EXECUTIVE COMMITTEE, IT BECAME CLEAR I WAS THE **ONLY** PERSON ARGUING FOR US TO PARTICIPATE.

I'M A NATIVE ALABAMIAN-- I **GREW UP** THERE.

I FEEL A DEEP KINSHIP WITH THE PEOPLE THERE ON A LOT OF LEVELS.

YOU KNOW, I'VE BEEN TO SELMA MANY, **MANY** TIMES. I'VE BEEN ARRESTED THERE.

I'VE BEEN **JAILED** THERE.

IF THESE PEOPLE WANT TO MARCH, I'M GOING TO MARCH **WITH THEM.**

YOU DECIDE WHAT **YOU** WANT TO DO,

BUT **I'M** GOING TO MARCH.

AND THAT WAS **THAT.**

IT WAS DECIDED THAT, IF I WERE TO PARTICIPATE IN THE MARCH FROM SELMA TO MONTGOMERY,

I WOULD **NOT** REPRESENT SNCC--

I WOULD MARCH SIMPLY AS **MYSELF**.

SOMETIME AFTER MIDNIGHT WE TOOK OFF FOR SELMA, FOUR HOURS' DRIVE AWAY.

WE ARRIVED AT THE FREEDOM HOUSE AT DAWN, THEN SLEPT FOR A FEW HOURS.

♫ Better get you ready, oh yes... ♫

IT WAS CLOSE TO NOON WHEN WE WOKE UP.

♫ They're comin' through Alabama, oh yes... ♫

♫ hmm mm... m... o... ♫

♪ You can take my freedom, oh yes... ♪

♪ but you cannot take my dignity... ♪

I FIGURED I MIGHT BE ARRESTED,

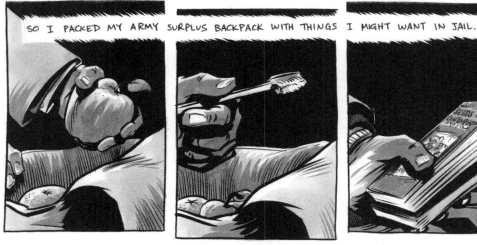

SO I PACKED MY ARMY SURPLUS BACKPACK WITH THINGS I MIGHT WANT IN JAIL.

IT WAS TIME TO GO.

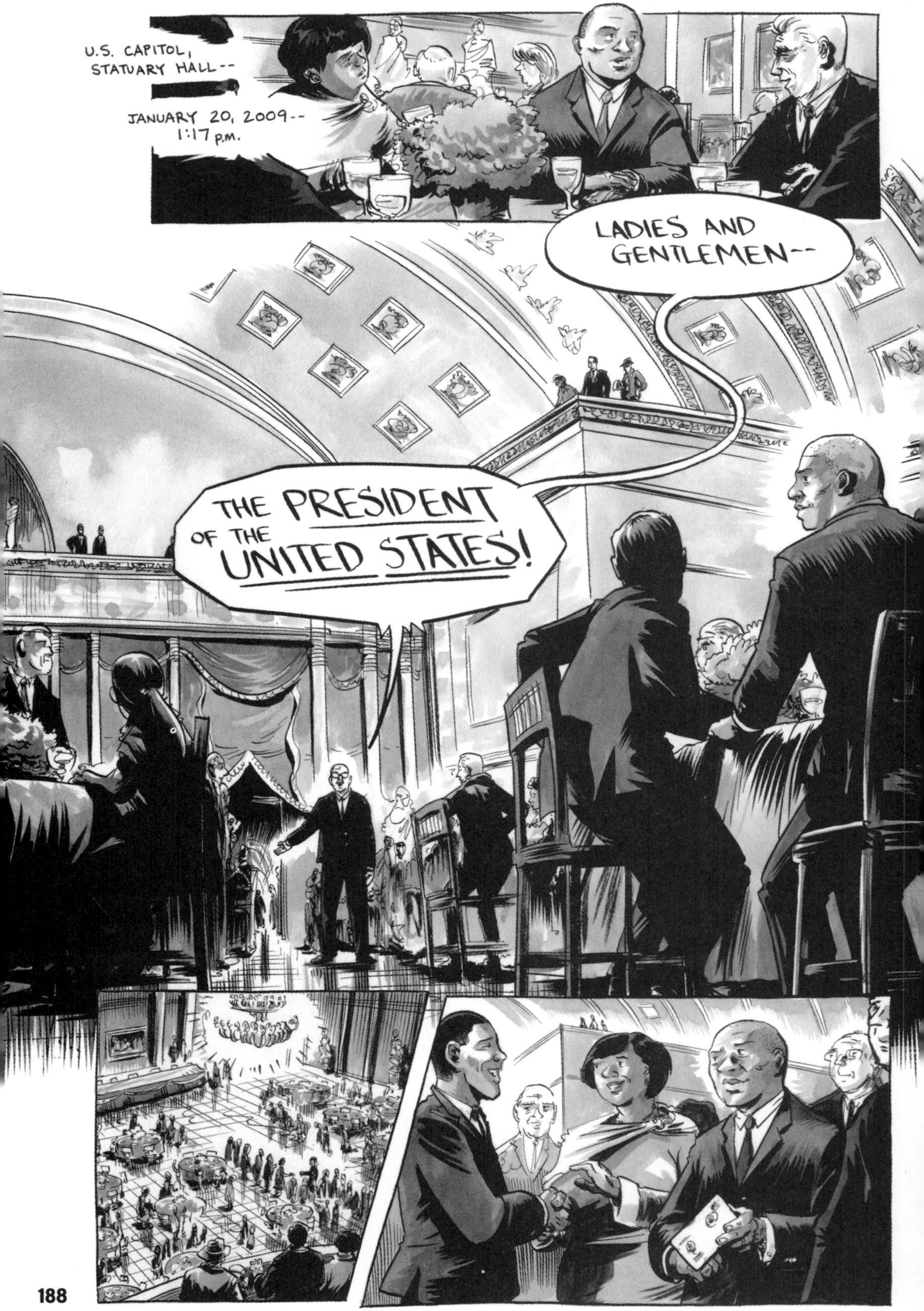
U.S. CAPITOL, STATUARY HALL--
JANUARY 20, 2009-- 1:17 p.m.
LADIES AND GENTLEMEN--
THE PRESIDENT OF THE UNITED STATES!

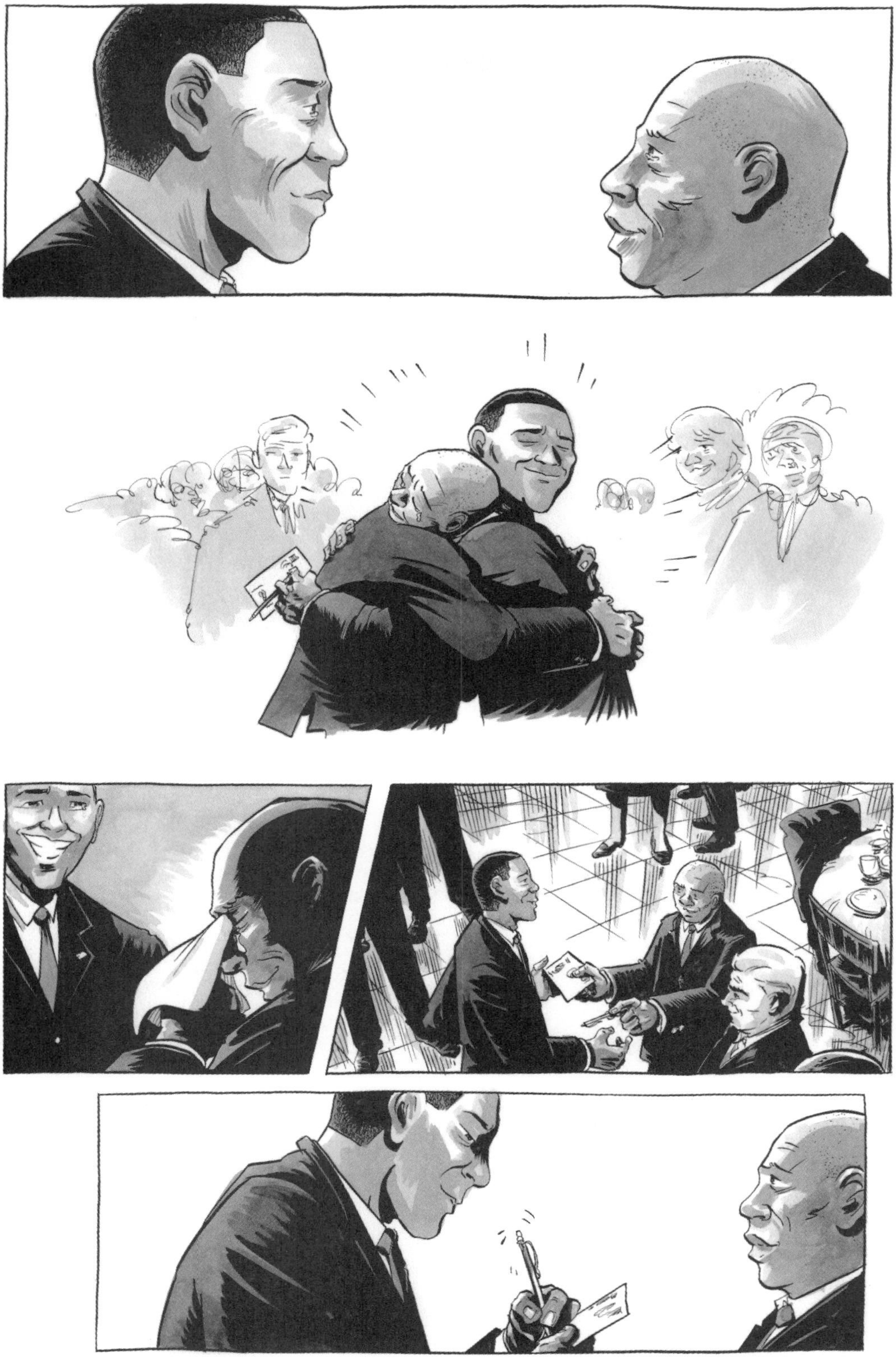

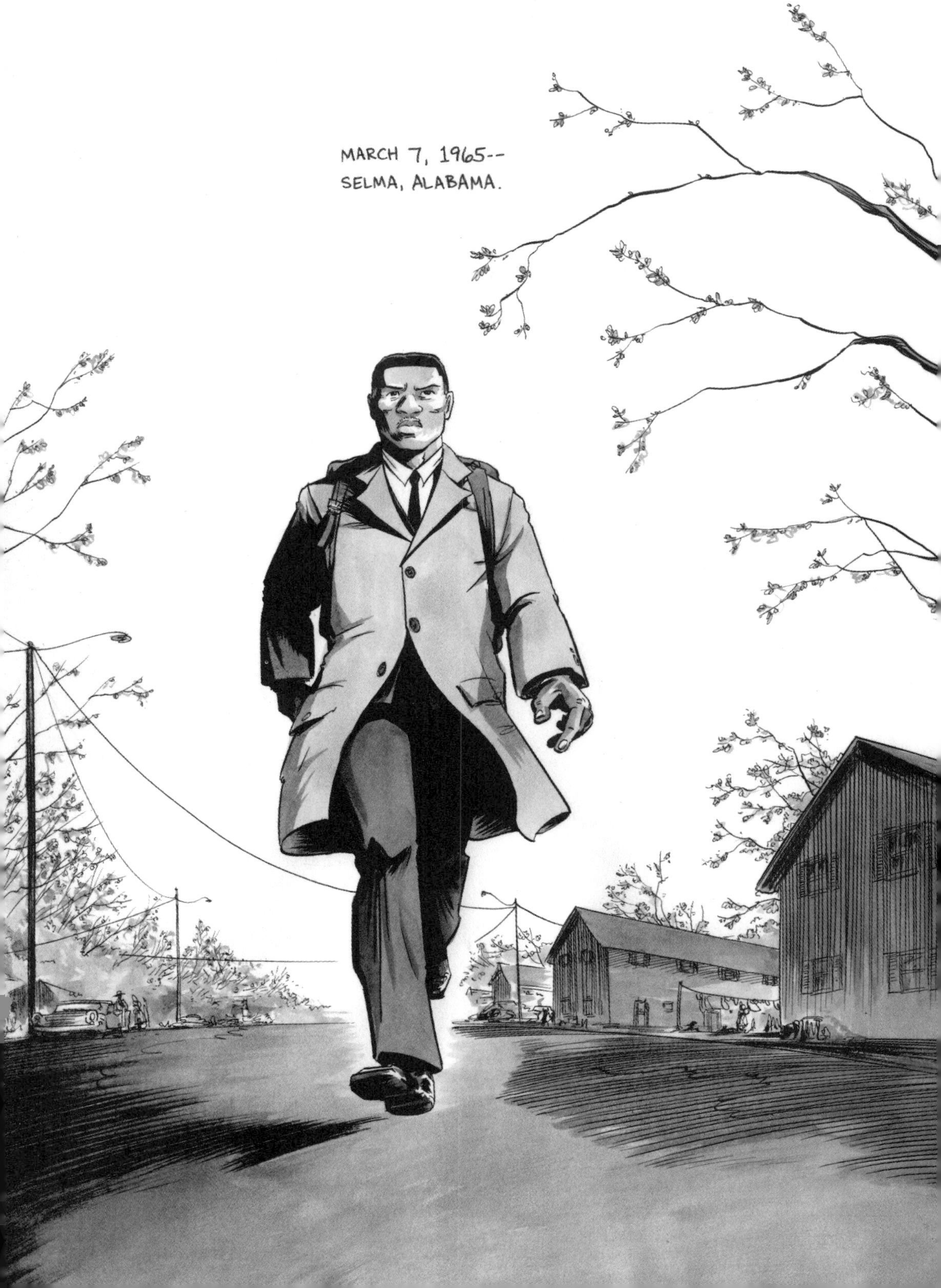
MARCH 7, 1965--
SELMA, ALABAMA.

Maintain eye contact, Ray--

You've gotta connect with your attacker's humanity!

got it.

do not let them shake your faith-- you gotta have love for them!

Bevel,

JOHN--

KING'S NOT COMING.

ANDY YOUNG HAD BEEN SENT BY DR. KING TO TELL US THAT THE MARCH WOULD HAVE TO **WAIT** A DAY--

HE'D MISSED TOO MANY PREACHING COMMITMENTS AT HIS CHURCH IN ATLANTA, WHERE HIS FATHER WAS ILL AND NEEDED HIM TO TAKE HIS PLACE IN THE PULPIT.

BUT THE PEOPLE WERE **HERE**, AND THEY WERE **READY**.

THERE WAS NO WAY TO TURN THEM BACK NOW.

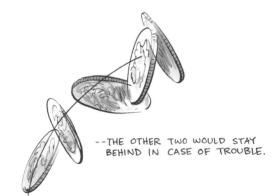

SEEING THAT THE MARCH COULD NOT BE STOPPED, ANDY CALLED DR. KING IN ATLANTA. DR. KING TOLD ANDY TO CHOOSE AMONG THEM-- **ANDY, HOSEA,** OR **BEVEL**-- TO JOIN ME AS CO-LEADER OF THE MARCH.

ONE WOULD MARCH--

--THE OTHER TWO WOULD STAY BEHIND IN CASE OF TROUBLE.

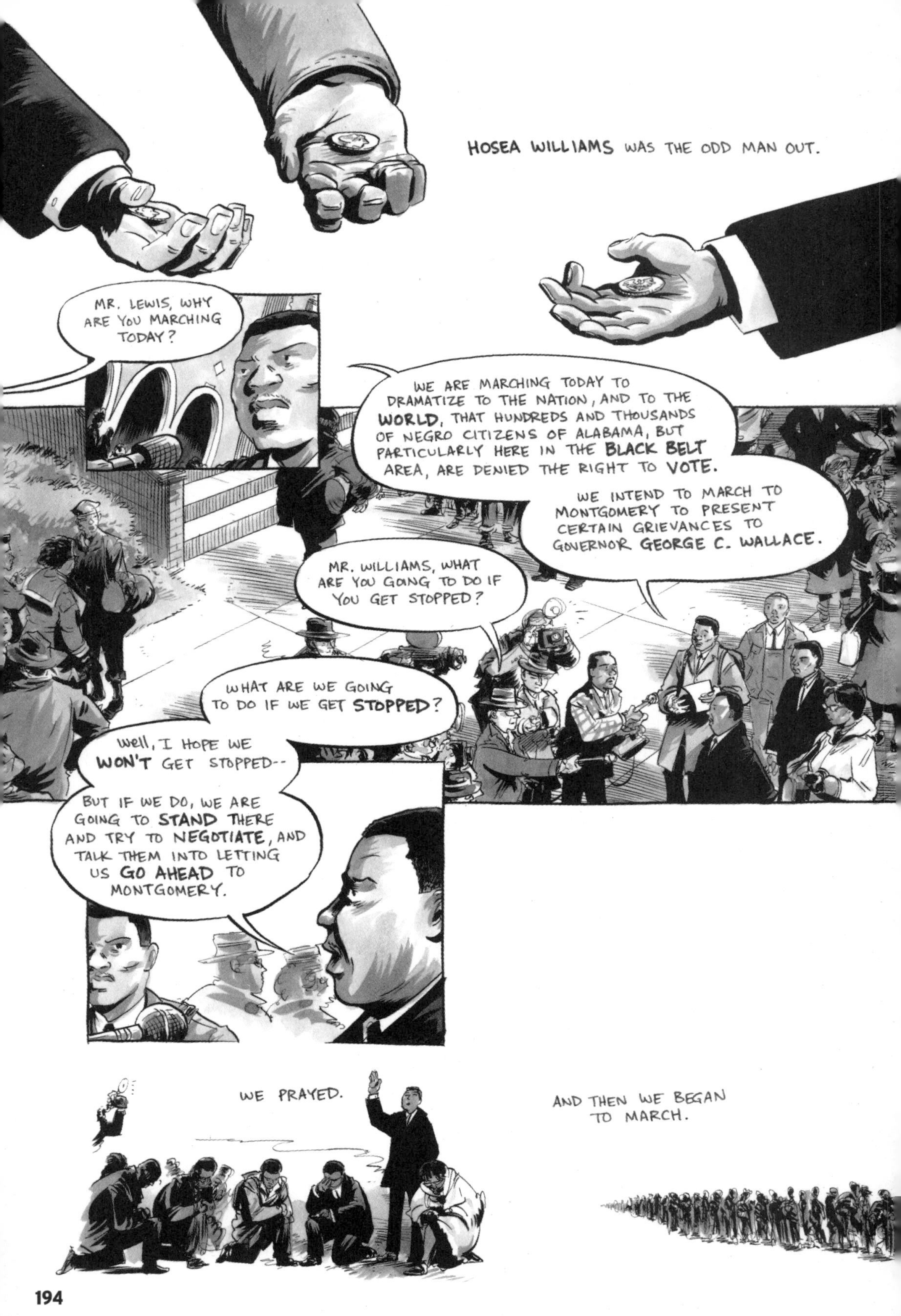

HOSEA WILLIAMS WAS THE ODD MAN OUT.
MR. LEWIS, WHY ARE YOU MARCHING TODAY?
WE ARE MARCHING TODAY TO DRAMATIZE TO THE NATION, AND TO THE WORLD, THAT HUNDREDS AND THOUSANDS OF NEGRO CITIZENS OF ALABAMA, BUT PARTICULARLY HERE IN THE BLACK BELT AREA, ARE DENIED THE RIGHT TO VOTE.
WE INTEND TO MARCH TO MONTGOMERY TO PRESENT CERTAIN GRIEVANCES TO GOVERNOR GEORGE C. WALLACE.
MR. WILLIAMS, WHAT ARE YOU GOING TO DO IF YOU GET STOPPED?
WHAT ARE WE GOING TO DO IF WE GET STOPPED?
WELL, I HOPE WE WON'T GET STOPPED--
BUT IF WE DO, WE ARE GOING TO STAND THERE AND TRY TO NEGOTIATE, AND TALK THEM INTO LETTING US GO AHEAD TO MONTGOMERY.
WE PRAYED.
AND THEN WE BEGAN TO MARCH.

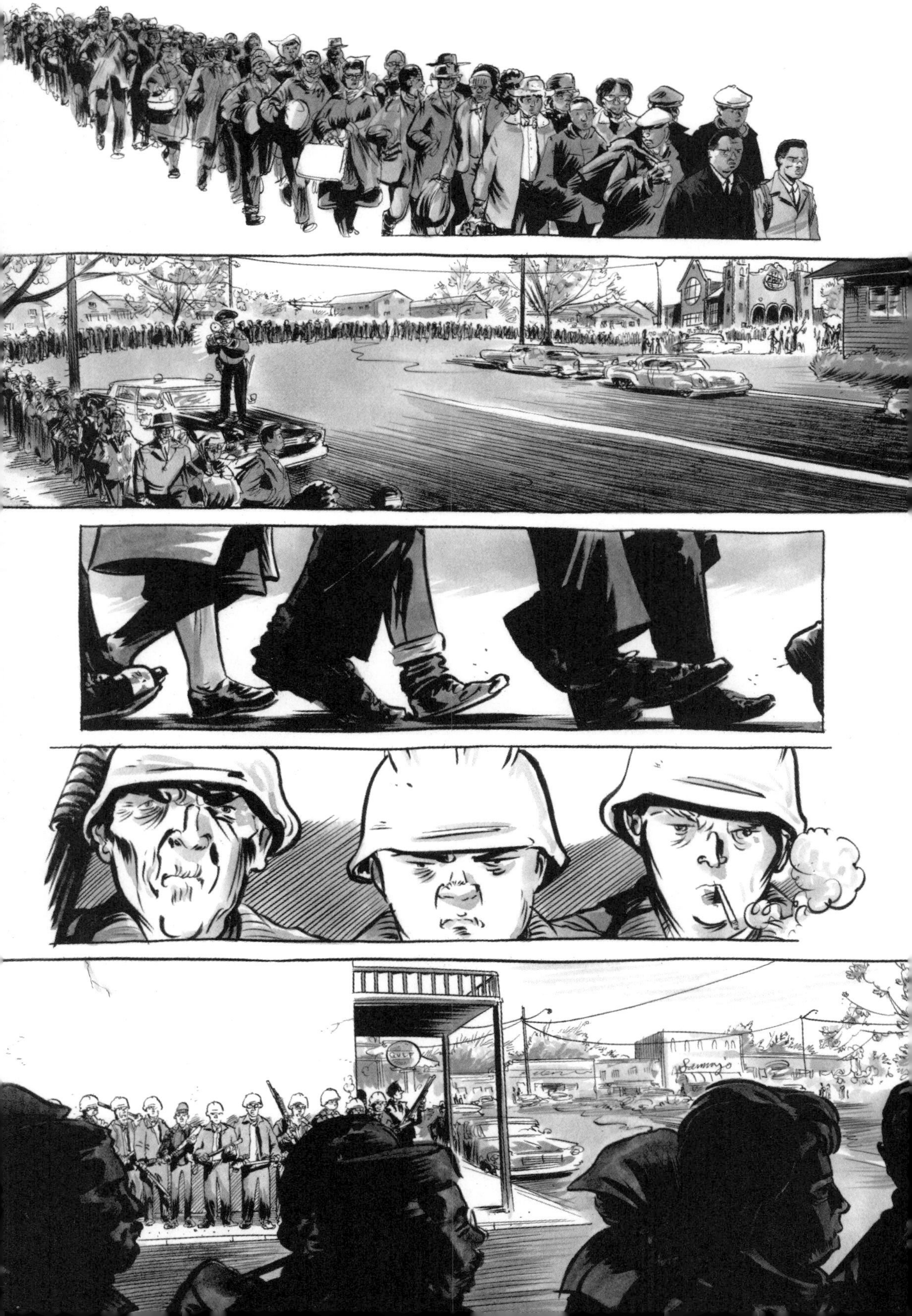

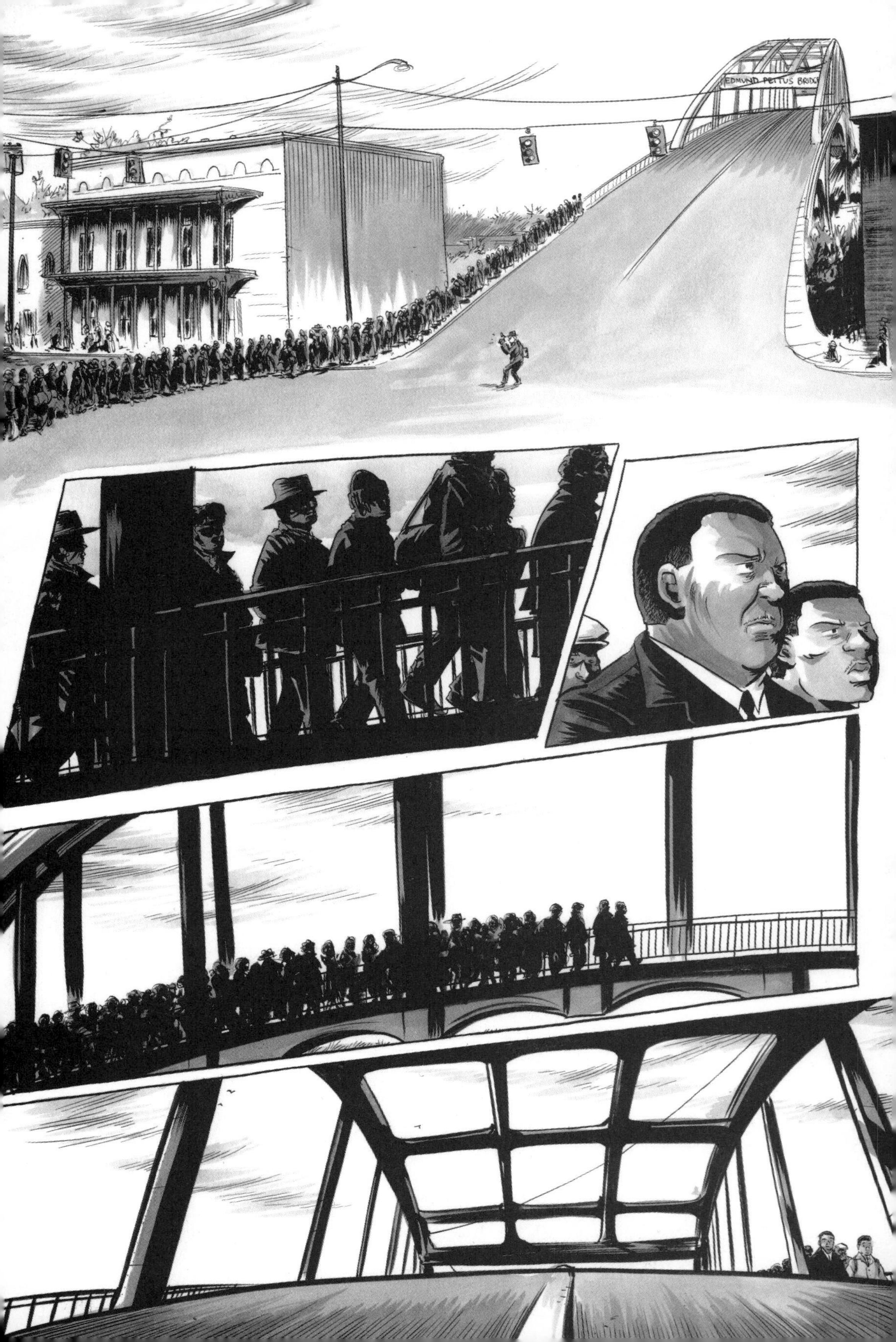
EDMUND PETTUS BRIDG

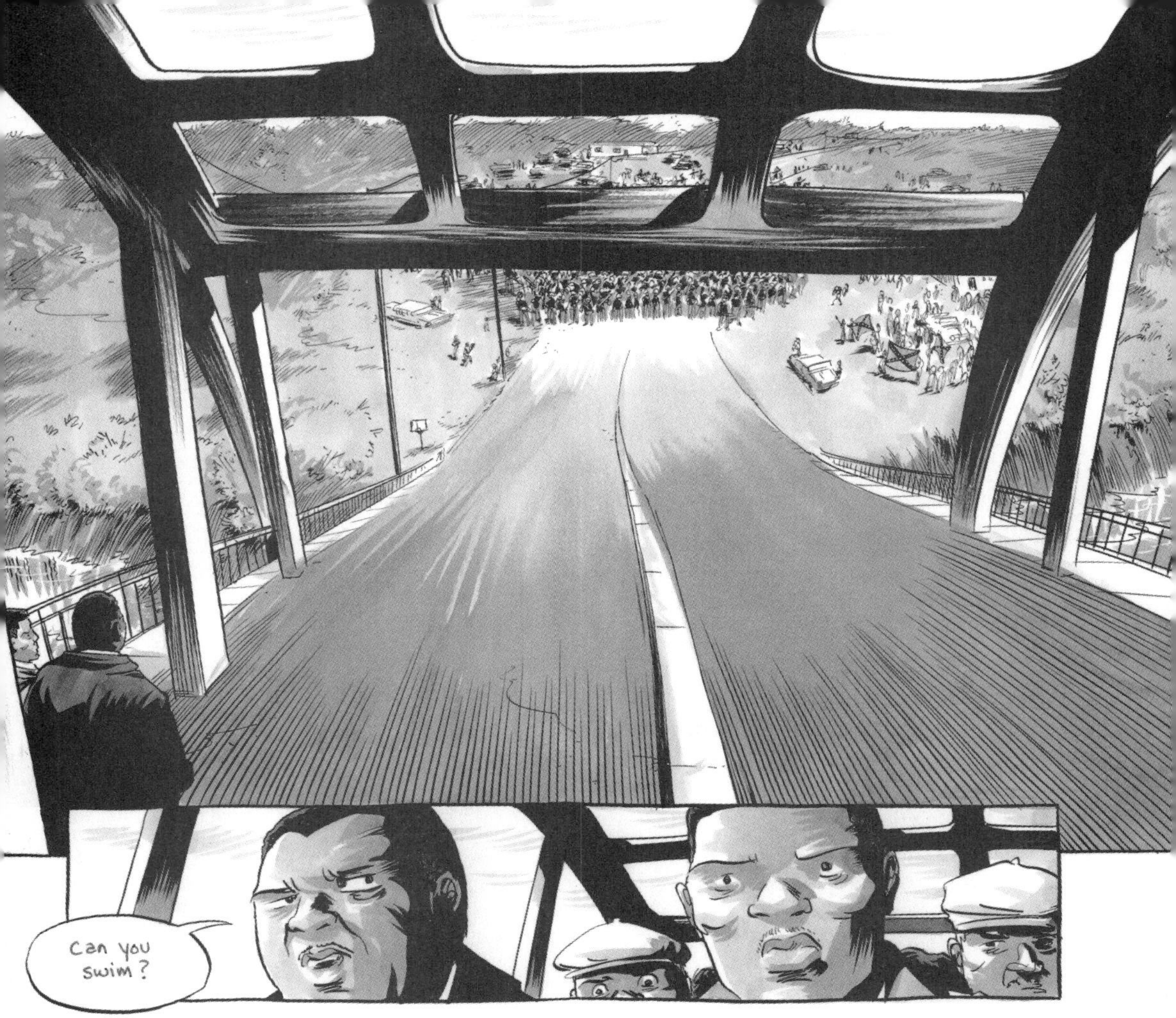

Can you swim?
no.
Well, neither can I.
But we might have to.

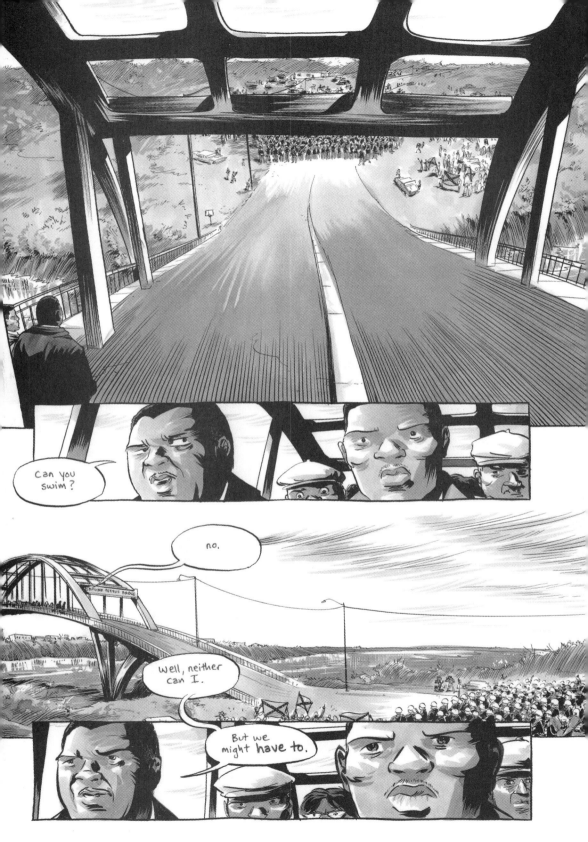

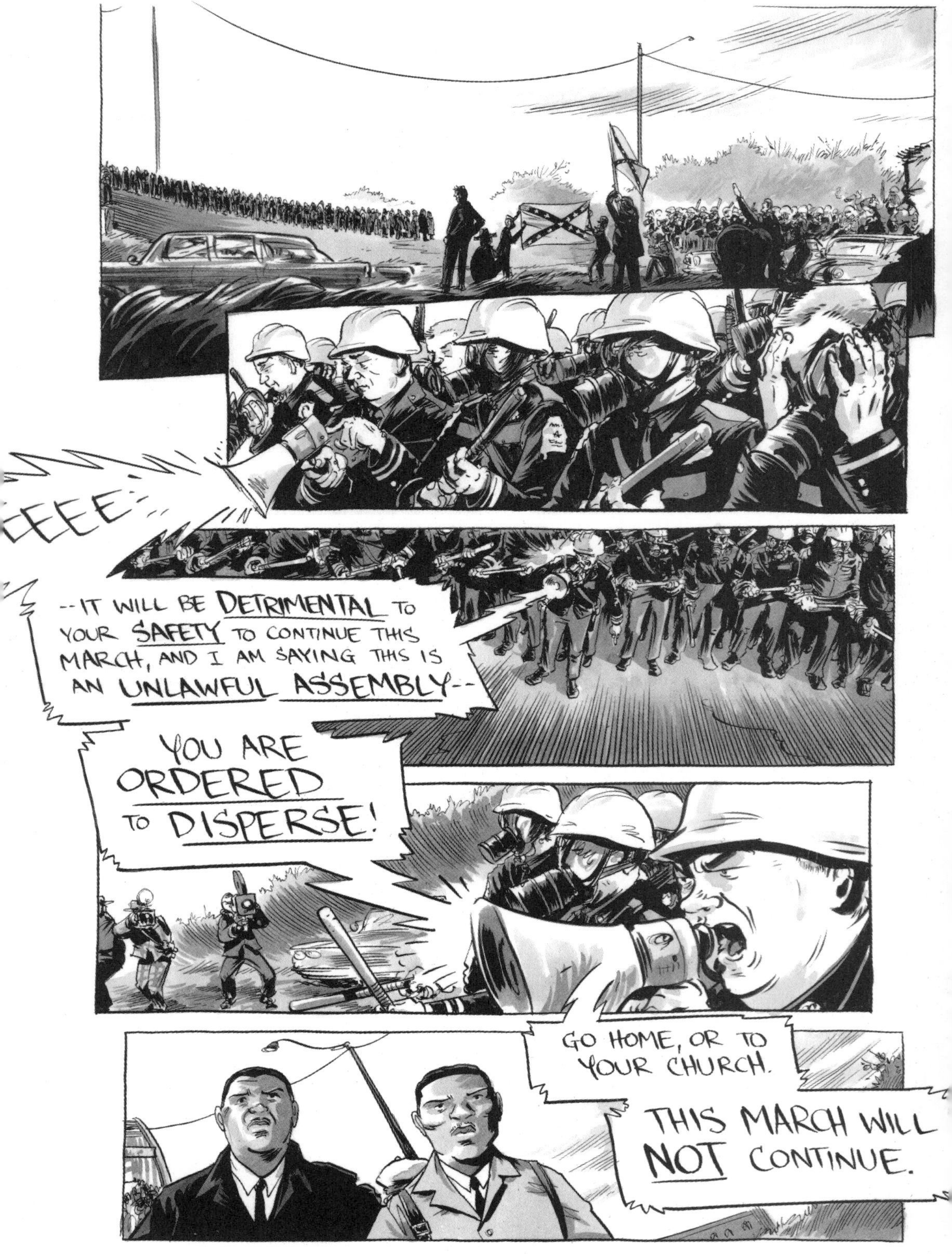
EEEE
--IT WILL BE DETRIMENTAL TO YOUR SAFETY TO CONTINUE THIS MARCH, AND I AM SAYING THIS IS AN UNLAWFUL ASSEMBLY--
YOU ARE ORDERED TO DISPERSE!
GO HOME, OR TO YOUR CHURCH.
THIS MARCH WILL NOT CONTINUE.

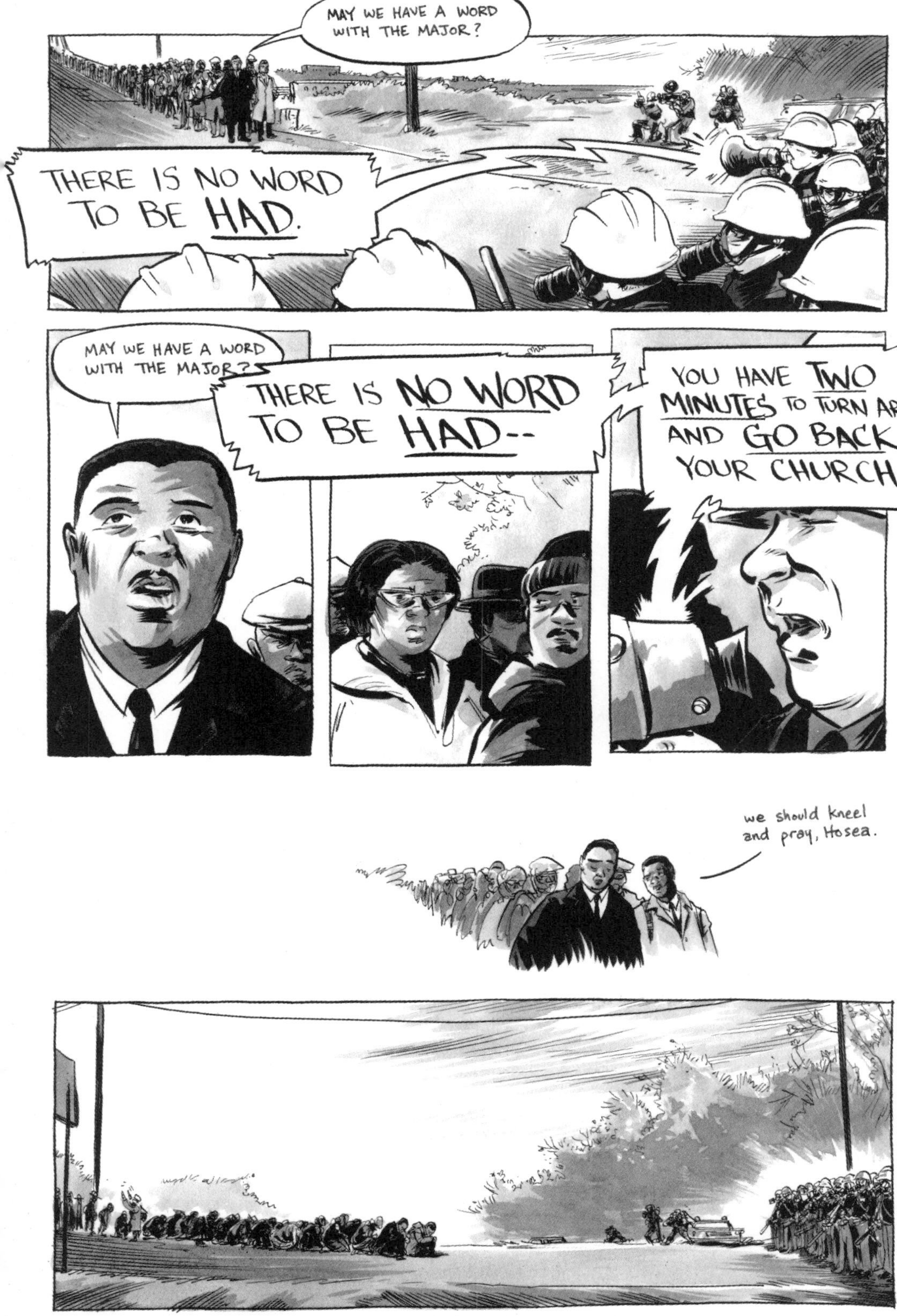
MAY WE HAVE A WORD WITH THE MAJOR?
THERE IS NO WORD TO BE HAD.
MAY WE HAVE A WORD WITH THE MAJOR?
THERE IS NO WORD TO BE HAD--
YOU HAVE TWO MINUTES TO TURN AROUND AND GO BACK TO YOUR CHURCH.
we should kneel and pray, Hosea.

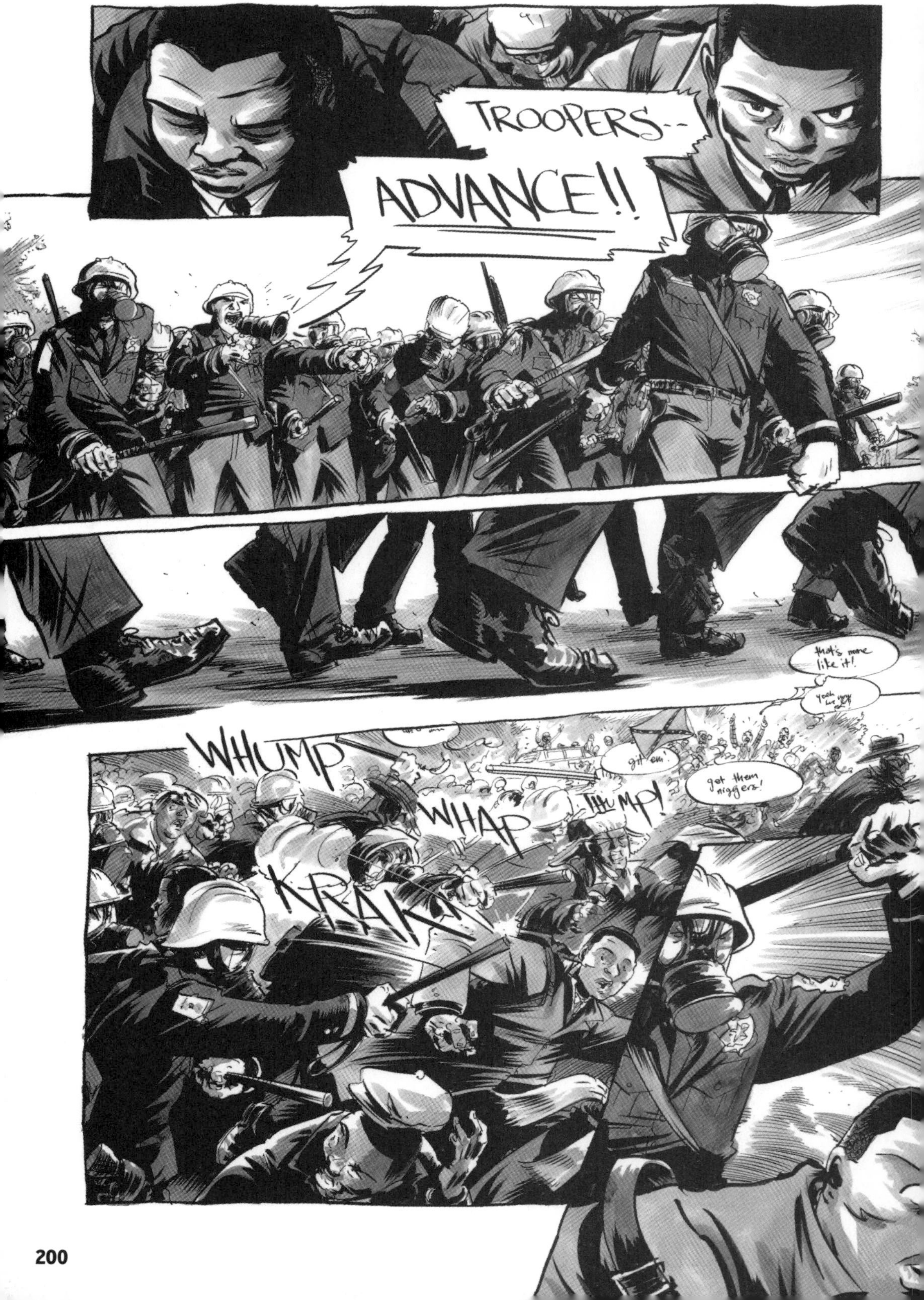
TROOPERS--
ADVANCE!!
that's more like it!
WHUMP
git 'em!
got them niggers!
WHAP
THUMP!
KRAK!

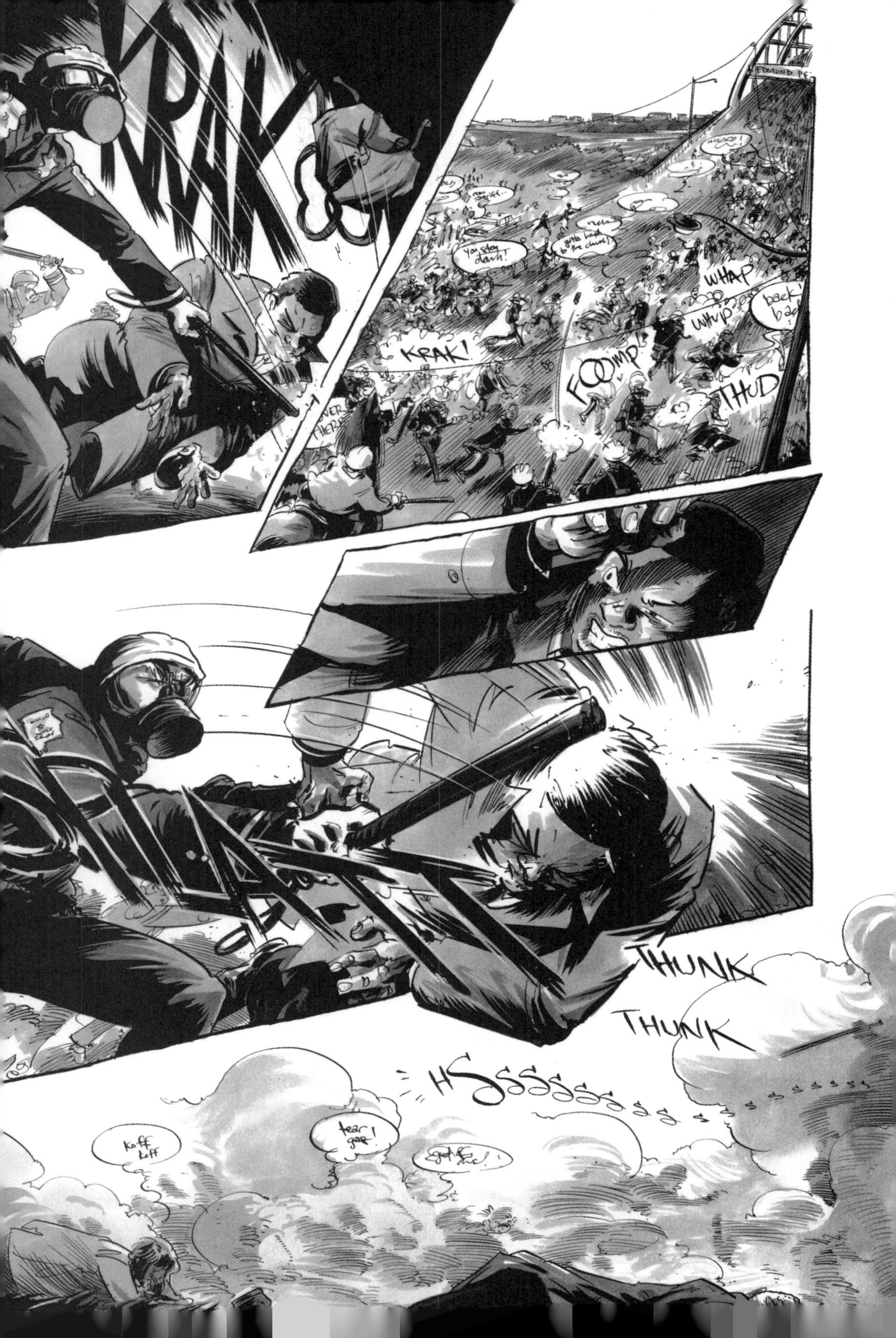
KRAK
You stay down!
gotta head to the church!
WHAP
whip
KRAK!
OVER THERE!
FOOMP!
THUD
THUNK
THUNK
HSSSSSSSS
koff koff
tear gas!

I THOUGHT I SAW DEATH.

I THOUGHT I WAS GOING TO DIE.

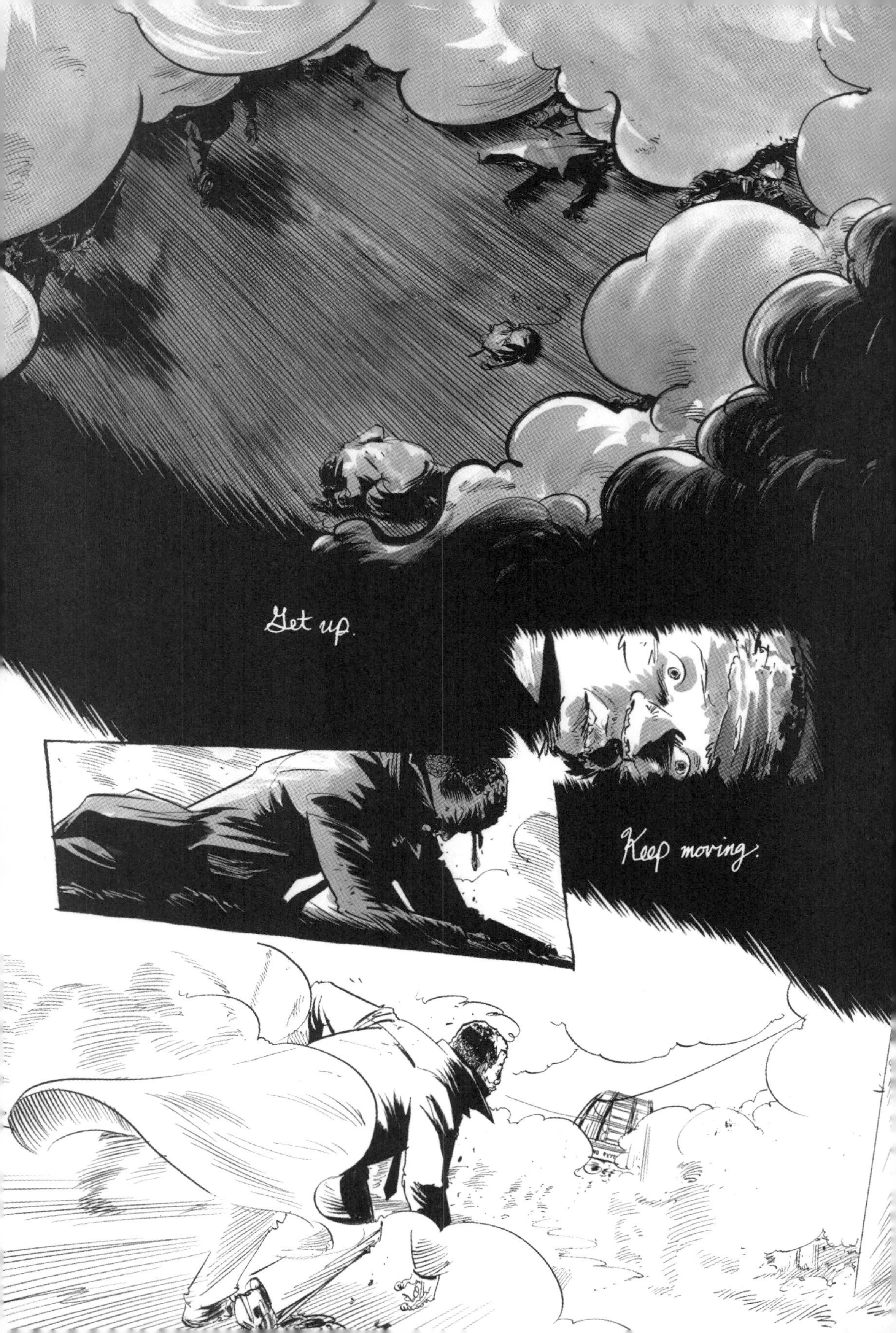
Get up.
Keep moving.

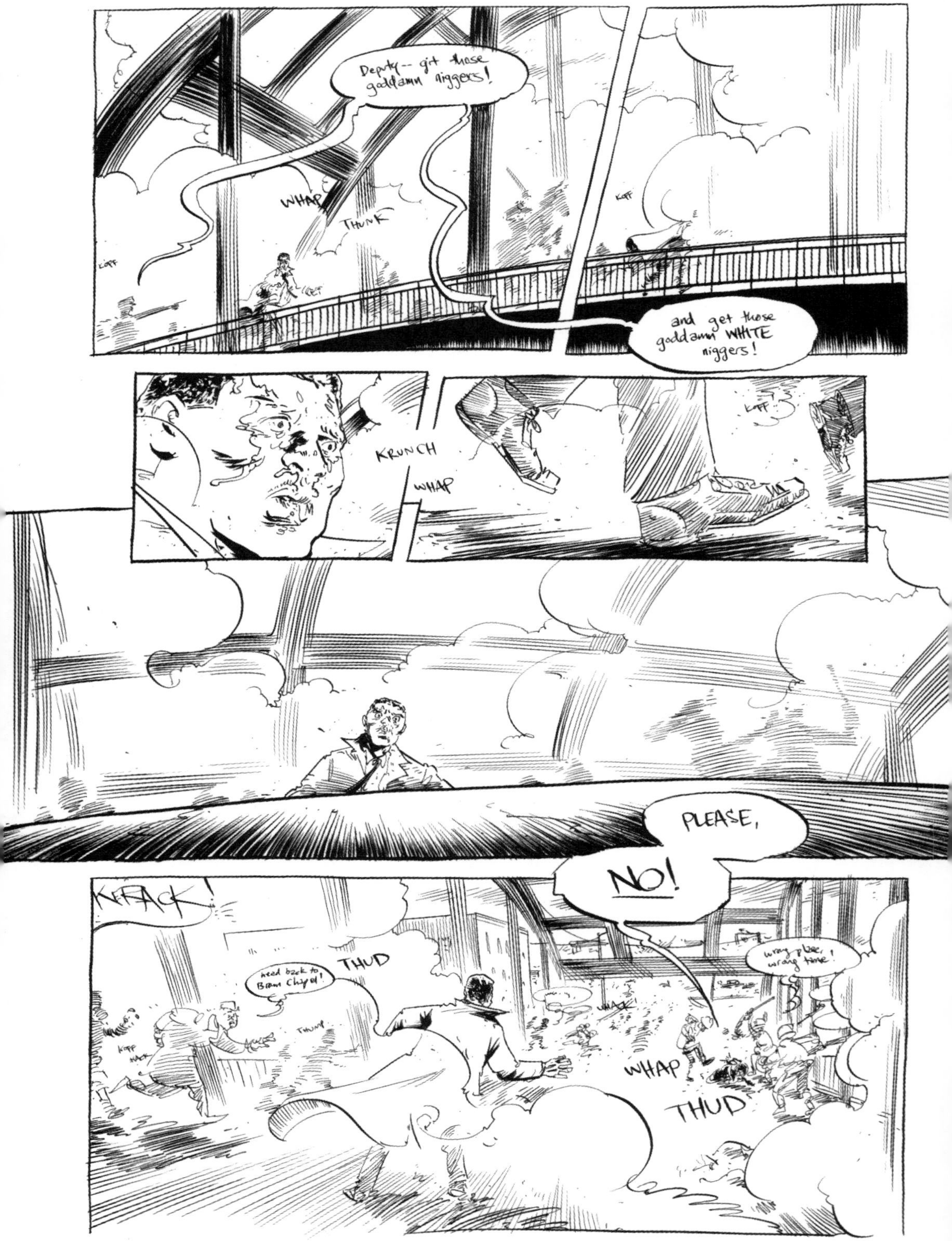
Deputy-- git those goddamn niggers!
WHAP
THUNK
KOFF
KOFF
and get those goddamn WHITE niggers!
KRUNCH
WHAP
KOFF
PLEASE,
NO!
KRACK!
THUD
Head back to Brown Chapel!
THUMP
KOFF
HACK
WHACK
wrong place, wrong time!
WHAP
THUD

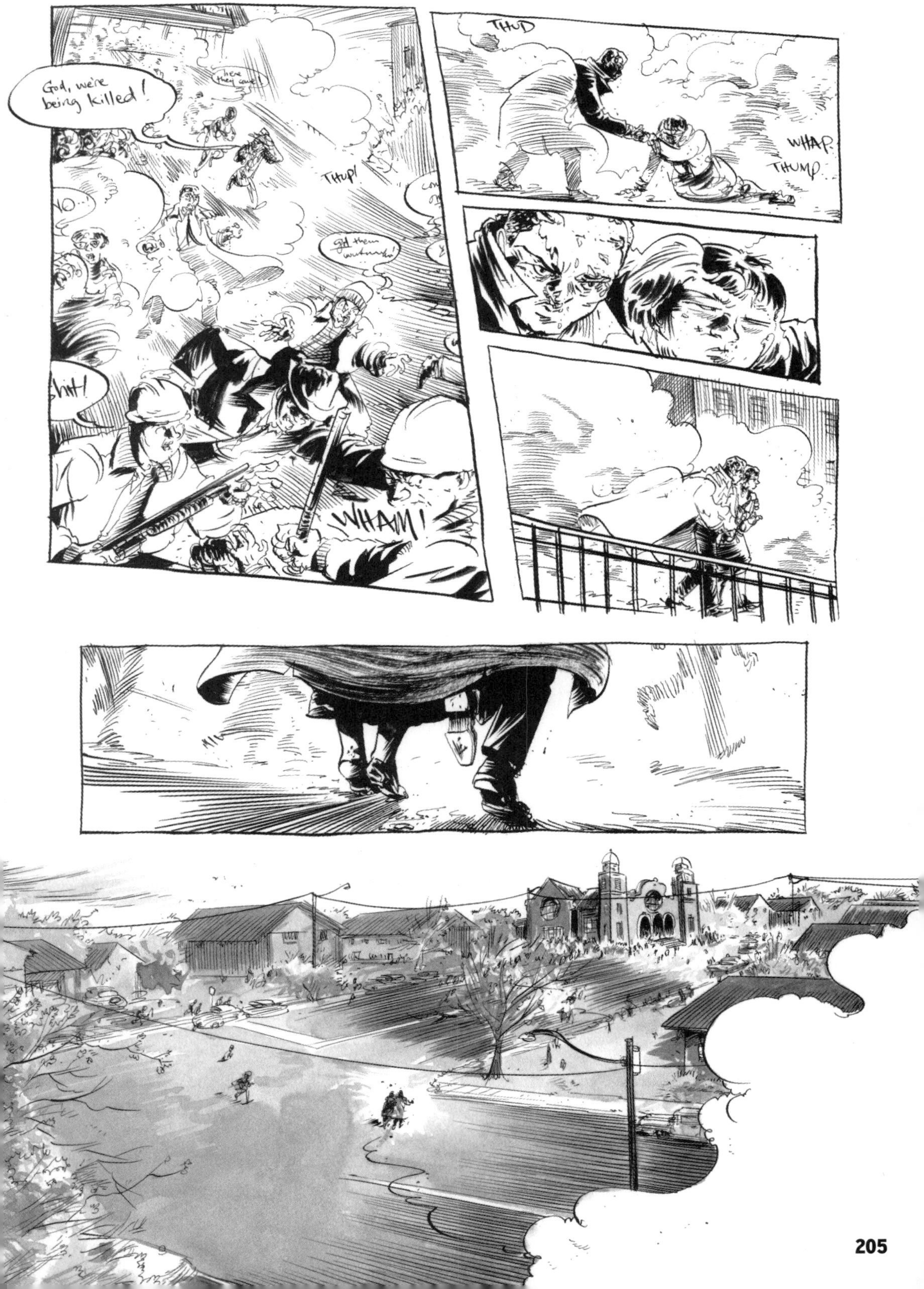
God, we're being killed!
here they come!
NO..!
THUP!
WHAM!
THUD
WHAP
THUMP

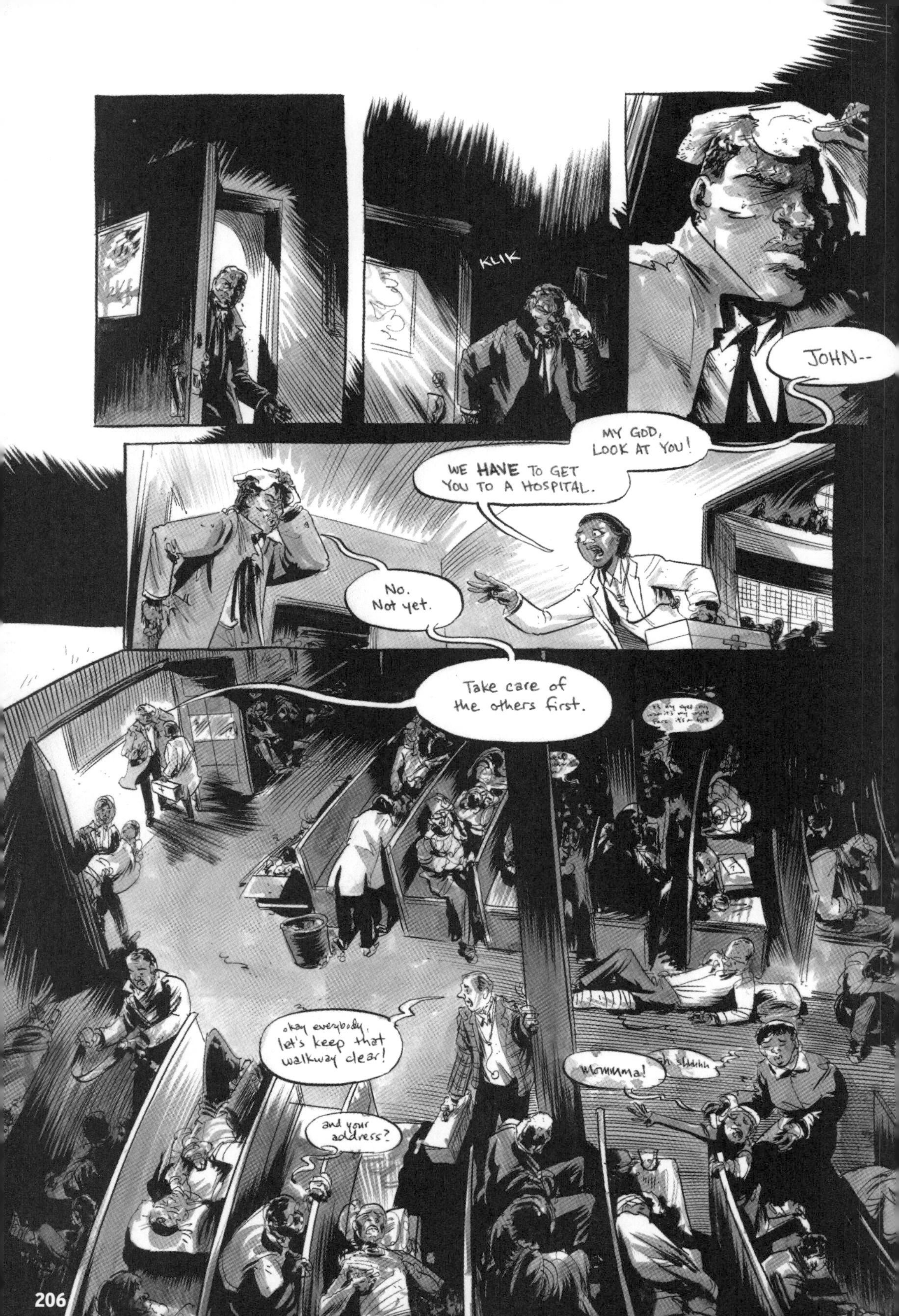
KLIK
JOHN--
MY GOD, LOOK AT YOU!
WE HAVE TO GET YOU TO A HOSPITAL.
No. Not yet.
Take care of the others first.
okay everybody, let's keep that walkway clear!
Mommma!
sh shhhh
and your address?

SOON, BROWN CHAPEL WAS FILLED FOR AN IMPROMPTU MASS MEETING.

HOSEA SPOKE FIRST, TRYING TO CALM EVERYONE'S SHAKEN NERVES.

THEN IT WAS MY TURN.

MY HEAD WAS THROBBING.

I DIDN'T HAVE ANY PREPARED REMARKS.

I JUST SPOKE FROM MY **GUT**.

I DON'T KNOW HOW PRESIDENT JOHNSON CAN SEND TROOPS TO VIETNAM.

I DON'T SEE HOW HE CAN SEND TROOPS TO THE CONGO.

I DON'T SEE HOW WE CAN SEND TROOPS TO **AFRICA**, AND HE CAN'T SEND TROOPS TO **SELMA**, ALABAMA.

amen--!

speak it.

Make it plain!

NEXT TIME WE MARCH, WE MAY HAVE TO KEEP **GOING** WHEN WE GET TO MONTGOMERY--

WE MAY HAVE TO GO ON TO **WASHINGTON**.

AFTER I SAID MY PIECE, I FINALLY AGREED TO GO TO THE HOSPITAL.

NOK!

NOK!

NOK!

THE BOY FROM TROY!

JOHN LEWIS-- HOW YOU FEELING, JOHN?

DR. KING AND RALPH ABERNATHY CAME TO VISIT--

THEY TOLD ME THAT JUST PAST 9:30 THE NIGHT BEFORE, **ABC** CUT INTO ITS SUNDAY MOVIE-- STANLEY KRAMER'S JUDGMENT AT NUREMBERG-- WITH A SPECIAL BULLETIN.

NEWS ANCHOR FRANK REYNOLDS CAME ON-SCREEN TO TELL VIEWERS ABOUT THE DAY'S MARCH, AND THE BRUTAL **VIOLENCE** THAT ACCOMPANIED IT.

ABC THEN SHOWED FIFTEEN MINUTES OF FILM FOOTAGE OF THE ATTACK.

SOMETHING ABOUT THAT DAY TOUCHED A NERVE DEEPER THAN **ANYTHING** THAT HAD COME BEFORE.

--git those goddamn niggers!

And get those goddamn **WHITE** niggers!

PEOPLE JUST COULDN'T BELIEVE THIS WAS HAPPENING IN AMERICA.

MARCH 7, 1965 IN SELMA, ALABAMA QUICKLY BECAME KNOWN AS

BLOODY SUNDAY.

THE RESPONSE FROM ACROSS THE NATION WAS **IMMEDIATE**.

DR. KING TOLD ME THAT THEY'D FILED A REQUEST FOR A FEDERAL INJUNCTION TO **STOP** ALABAMA FROM INTERFERING WITH THE MARCH.

The Washington Post

Marines in Viet-Nam Will Shoot Back If Attacked, But Say

Tear Gas, Clubs Halt 600 in Selma March

HE ALSO PUT OUT A CALL FOR **RELIGIOUS LEADERS** TO COME TO SELMA AND MARCH WITH US. HUNDREDS OF MINISTERS, PRIESTS, AND RABBIS WERE ALREADY ON THEIR WAY.

KLIK

NOK
NOK

THEN JOHN DOAR FROM THE JUSTICE DEPARTMENT CAME BY TO TAKE A STATEMENT FROM ME.

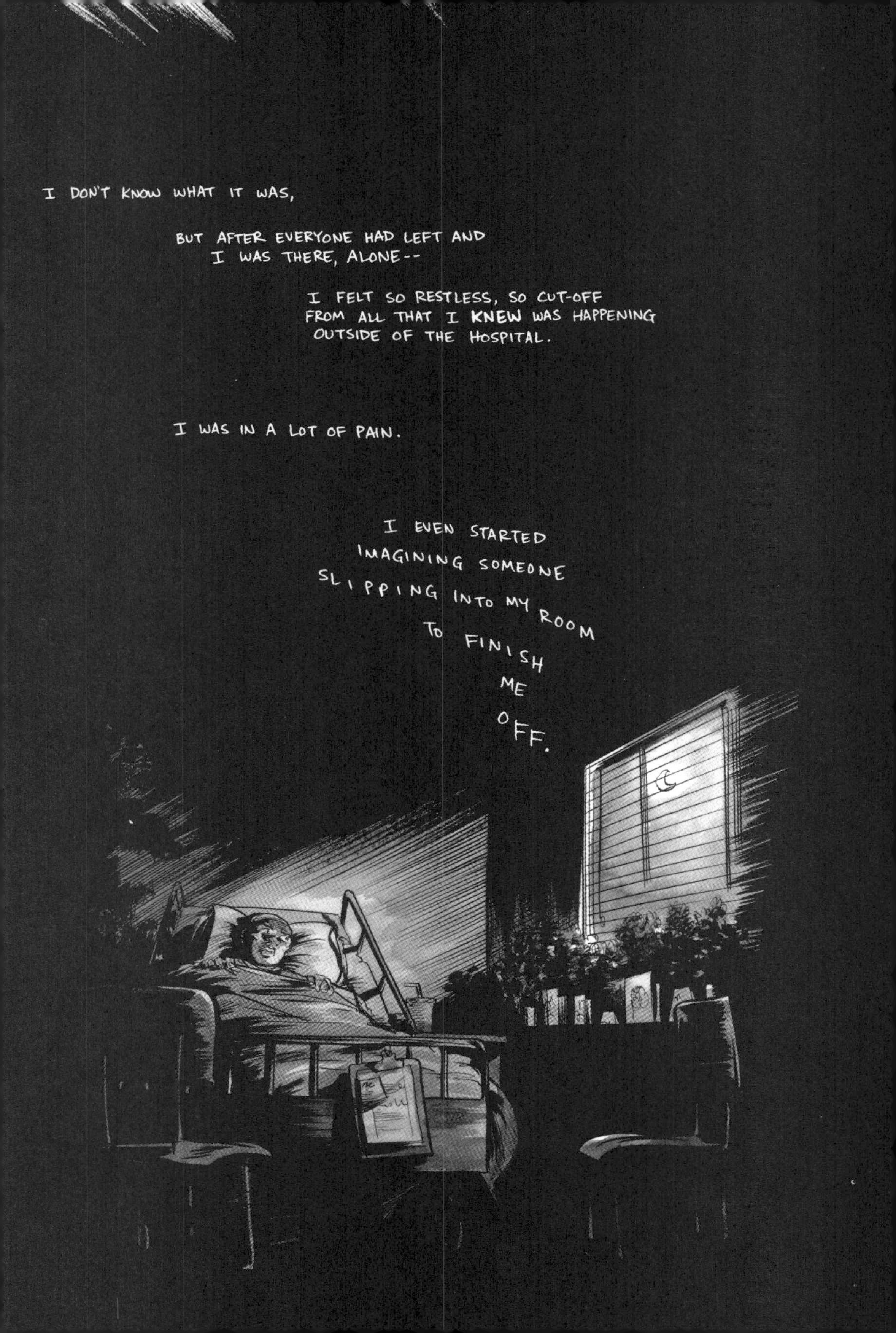
I DON'T KNOW WHAT IT WAS,
BUT AFTER EVERYONE HAD LEFT AND I WAS THERE, ALONE--
I FELT SO RESTLESS, SO CUT-OFF FROM ALL THAT I **KNEW** WAS HAPPENING OUTSIDE OF THE HOSPITAL.
I WAS IN A LOT OF PAIN.
I EVEN STARTED IMAGINING SOMEONE SLIPPING INTO MY ROOM TO FINISH ME OFF.

MARCH 9, 1965.

WHILE I WAS IN THE HOSPITAL AND SNCC AND SCLC WORKED ON THE COURTS, MORE THAN 2,000 PEOPLE ASSEMBLED IN SELMA FOR A SECOND MARCH.

THAT IS YOUR BRIDGE--

YOU GOT THE RIGHT TO MARCH ON IT!

BUT THERE WERE RUMORS ALL MORNING THAT THIS MARCH MIGHT NOT BE ALLOWED TO PROCEED--

THAT DIDN'T SIT WELL WITH WILLIE RICKS, A SNCC ORGANIZER FROM TENNESSEE.

IF SHERIFF CLARK SAYS "DON'T MARCH," WHAT'RE Y'ALL GONNA DO?

WE'RE GONNA MARCH!

IF GEORGE WALLACE SAYS "DON'T MARCH," WHAT'RE Y'ALL GONNA DO?

WE'RE GONNA MARCH!

IF JUDGE JOHNSON SAYS "DON'T MARCH," WHAT'RE Y'ALL GONNA DO?

WE'RE GONNA MARCH!

IF JUDGE HARE SAYS "DON'T MARCH," WHAT'RE Y'ALL GONNA DO?

WE'RE GONNA MARCH!

IF YOUR MOMMA SAYS "DON'T MARCH," WHAT'RE YOU GONNA DO?

WE'RE GONNA MARCH!

IF THE NAACP SAYS "DON'T MARCH," WHAT'RE Y'ALL GONNA DO?

WE'RE GONNA MARCH!

IF MARTIN LUTHER KING SAYS "DON'T MARCH," WHAT'RE Y'ALL GONNA DO--?

WORRIED THAT THINGS MIGHT GET OUT OF HAND, ANDY YOUNG HURRIED TO RESTORE ORDER BEFORE DR. KING BEGAN THE MARCH.

FINALLY, THEY SET OUT.

IF YOU **CAN'T** BE NONVIOLENT, **DON'T** GET IN HERE.

IF YOU CAN'T ACCEPT BLOWS WITHOUT RETALIATING, **DON'T** GET IN THE LINE.

HALT!

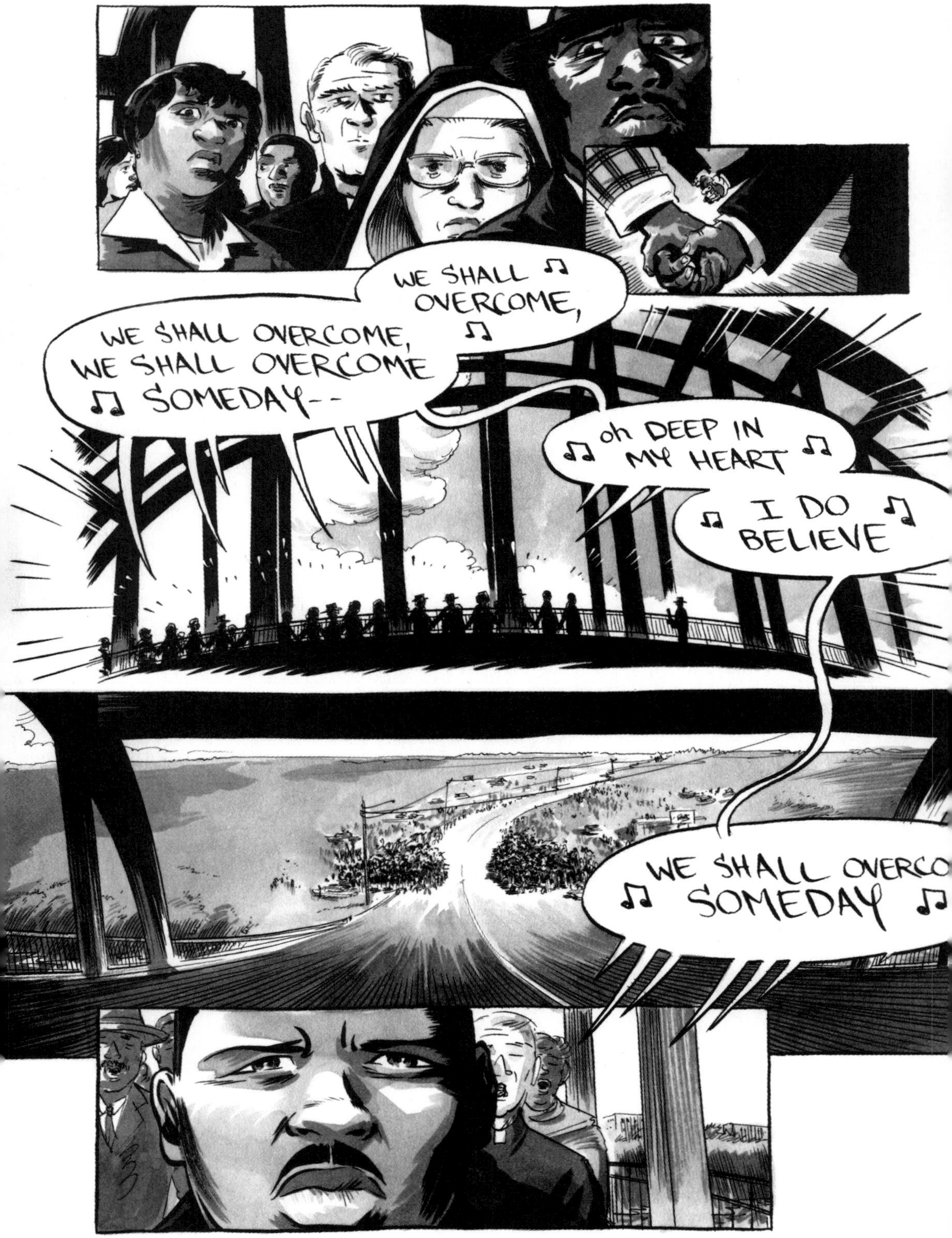
WE SHALL ♫ OVERCOME, ♫
WE SHALL OVERCOME, WE SHALL OVERCOME ♫ SOMEDAY--
♫ oh DEEP IN MY HEART ♫
♫ I DO BELIEVE ♫
♫ WE SHALL OVERCO SOMEDAY ♫

THE COURT HAD **NOT** GRANTED OUR REQUEST FOR AN INJUNCTION AGAINST ALABAMA--

IN FACT, IT HAD ISSUED AN ORDER AGAINST US-- PROHIBITING **ANY** MARCH FROM SELMA TO MONTGOMERY UNTIL A HEARING LATER THAT WEEK.

WE WILL GO BACK TO THE CHURCH NOW.

BUT THERE WAS TOO MUCH AT STAKE TO **CANCEL**--

--SO DR. KING HAD MADE AN AGREEMENT WITH FEDERAL OFFICIALS TO MARCH ONLY **TO** THE BRIDGE, AS A STATEMENT--AND THEN **TURN BACK** TO AWAIT THE HEARING.

US BRIDGE

BUT DR. KING DIDN'T TELL **ANY** OF THE MARCHERS BEFOREHAND.

IT BECAME KNOWN AS "TURNAROUND TUESDAY."

I WAS STILL IN THE HOSPITAL, BUT I LATER HEARD THAT JIM FORMAN EXPLODED, DENOUNCING DR. KING'S "TRICKERY", AND SAYING THAT THIS WAS THE LAST STRAW.

IT'S TIME FOR SNCC TO DO SOMETHING ON OUR **OWN**.

SNCC DECIDED TO GO AHEAD TO MONTGOMERY FOR A **STUDENT SIEGE** ON THE STATE CAPITOL, AS DIANE AND BEVEL HAD SUGGESTED OVER A YEAR EARLIER.

I WAS RELEASED FROM THE HOSPITAL THAT TUESDAY NIGHT.

I WAS STILL IN A LOT OF PAIN-- MY HEAD WAS **POUNDING.**

I HAD NO PROBLEM WITH WHAT DR. KING DID. I THOUGHT IT WAS IN KEEPING WITH THE SPIRIT OF THE MOVEMENT.

THERE COMES A TIME WHEN YOU MUST RETREAT, AND COME BACK TO FIGHT ANOTHER DAY.

FEDERAL DISTRICT JUDGE FRANK JOHNSON HAD ISSUED THE RULING-- THE **SAME** JUDGE THAT HAD ISSUED AN INJUNCTION TO HELP US GET OUT OF MONTGOMERY DURING THE **FREEDOM RIDE.**

I KNEW HE WOULD BE **FAIR** AND MOST LIKELY GIVE US WHAT WE WERE ASKING FOR, IF WE SHOWED RESPECT FOR HIS RULES.

BUT MOST OF MY COLLEAGUES IN **SNCC** DISAGREED WITH ME. THEY WERE SICK OF RULES AND PROCEDURES.

MORE AND MORE, THEY WERE BECOMING SICK OF **ME.**

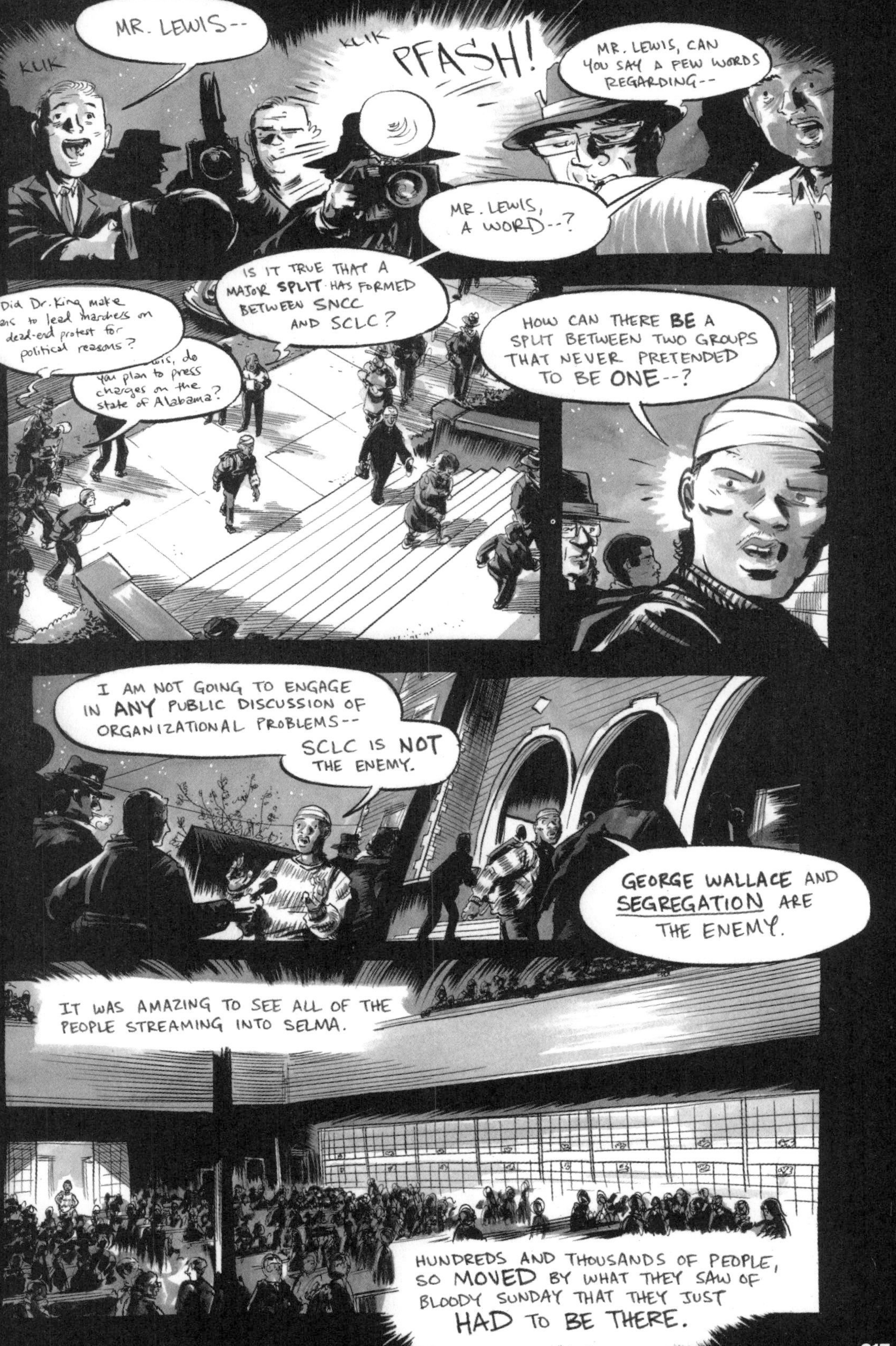

MR. LEWIS--
KLIK
KLIK
PFASH!
MR. LEWIS, CAN YOU SAY A FEW WORDS REGARDING--
MR. LEWIS, A WORD--?
Did Dr. King make plans to lead marches on a dead-end protest for political reasons?
IS IT TRUE THAT A MAJOR SPLIT HAS FORMED BETWEEN SNCC AND SCLC?
wis, do you plan to press charges on the state of Alabama?
HOW CAN THERE BE A SPLIT BETWEEN TWO GROUPS THAT NEVER PRETENDED TO BE ONE--?
I AM NOT GOING TO ENGAGE IN ANY PUBLIC DISCUSSION OF ORGANIZATIONAL PROBLEMS--
SCLC IS NOT THE ENEMY.
GEORGE WALLACE AND SEGREGATION ARE THE ENEMY.
IT WAS AMAZING TO SEE ALL OF THE PEOPLE STREAMING INTO SELMA.
HUNDREDS AND THOUSANDS OF PEOPLE, SO MOVED BY WHAT THEY SAW OF BLOODY SUNDAY THAT THEY JUST HAD TO BE THERE.

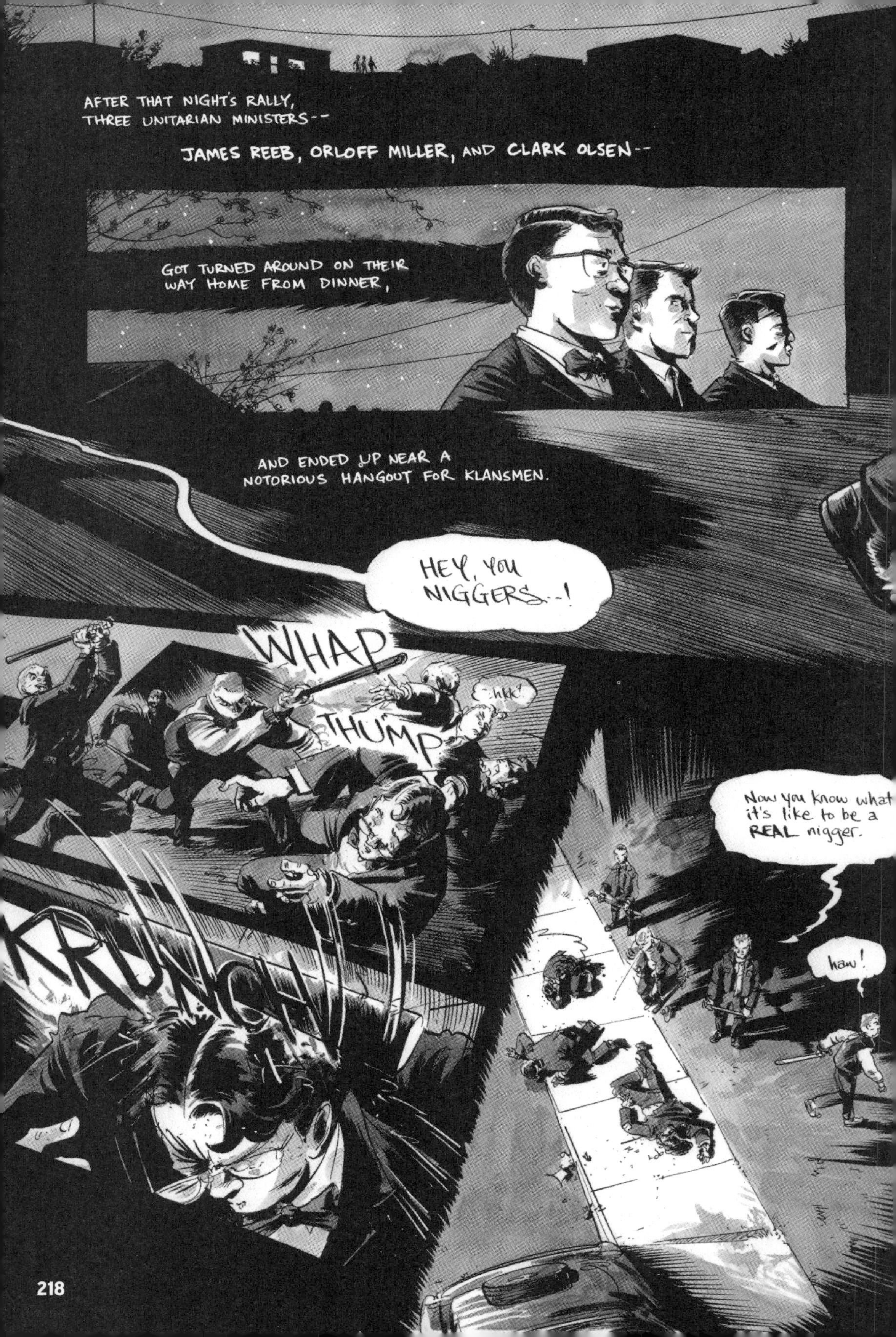
AFTER THAT NIGHT'S RALLY, THREE UNITARIAN MINISTERS--
JAMES REEB, ORLOFF MILLER, AND CLARK OLSEN--
GOT TURNED AROUND ON THEIR WAY HOME FROM DINNER,
AND ENDED UP NEAR A NOTORIOUS HANGOUT FOR KLANSMEN.
HEY, YOU NIGGERS--!
WHAP
-hkk!
THUMP
KRUNCH
Now you know what it's like to be a **REAL** nigger.
haw!

JAMES REEB TOOK THE WORST OF IT, AND IT DIDN'T LOOK LIKE HE WOULD SURVIVE.

NEWS OF HIS BRUTAL ASSAULT DOMINATED HEADLINES AS I WENT TO MONTGOMERY, APPEARING AT JUDGE JOHNSON'S HEARING, WHICH DR. KING HAD AGREED TO WAIT FOR--

--SCLC'S REQUEST FOR AN INJUNCTION TO BLOCK STATE INTERFERENCE, AND ALLOW A SELMA-TO-MONTGOMERY MARCH.

WHERE WERE YOU HIT, MR. LEWIS?

I WAS HIT ON MY HEAD, RIGHT HERE.

AND WHAT WERE YOU HIT WITH?

I WAS HIT WITH A BILLY CLUB--AND I SAW THE STATE TROOPER WHO HIT ME.

HOW MANY TIMES WERE YOU HIT?

I WAS HIT TWICE--

ONCE WHEN I WAS LYING DOWN AND WAS ATTEMPTING TO GET UP.

DO WE UNDERSTAND YOU SAY YOU WERE HIT--

AND THEN ATTEMPTED TO GET UP, AND WERE HIT AGAIN?

RIGHT.

WORD CAME A SHORT TIME LATER THAT REV. JAMES REEB HAD DIED.

THE HEARINGS WENT ON FOR SEVERAL DAYS, AND MORE THAN A DOZEN WITNESSES WERE CALLED--

-- INCLUDING **FBI AGENTS** WHO WITNESSED THE ATTACK, AND EVEN **COLONEL AL LINGO** OF THE ALABAMA STATE TROOPERS.

THOUGH LINGO DIDN'T COME OUT AND **SAY** IT THAT DAY, IT WAS EASY TO INFER THAT THE STATE TROOPERS' ORDERS HAD COME DIRECTLY FROM **GEORGE WALLACE**

WHEN THE HEARINGS RECESSED FOR THE WEEKEND, I FLEW TO NEW YORK CITY TO TAKE PART IN A SYMPATHY RALLY--

-- NEARLY **30,000** PEOPLE PARTICIPATED IN THE MARCH THERE, AND THEY TOOK PLACE IN OTHER CITIES ALL OVER THE COUNTRY.

MORE THAN **15,000** PEOPLE TURNED OUT IN WASHINGTON, D.C. TO HEAR **FANNIE LOU HAMER**.

IT'S TIME <u>NOW</u> TO STOP BEGGING THEM FOR WHAT SHOULD HAVE BEEN DONE <u>100 YEARS AGO</u>!

WE HAVE <u>STOOD UP</u> ON OUR FEET, AND GOD KNOWS WE'RE **ON OUR <u>WAY</u>**!

ACROSS THE STREET, GEORGE WALLACE MET WITH PRESIDENT JOHNSON IN AN ATTEMPT TO CONVINCE HIM TO **STOP** THE SELMA MARCH.

UNFORTUNATELY FOR WALLACE, HIS PLEAS **BACKFIRED**.

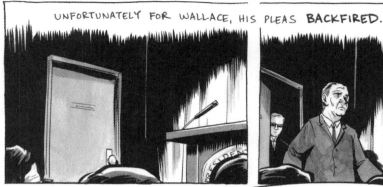

THE EVENTS OF LAST SUNDAY CANNOT AND **WILL NOT** BE REPEATED, BUT THE DEMONSTRATIONS IN SELMA HAVE A MUCH **LARGER** MEANING--

THEY ARE A PROTEST AGAINST A **DEEP** AND VERY **UNJUST** FLAW IN AMERICAN DEMOCRACY <u>ITSELF</u>.

NINETY-FIVE YEARS AGO, OUR CONSTITUTION WAS **AMENDED** TO REQUIRE THAT NO AMERICAN BE DENIED THE **RIGHT TO VOTE** BECAUSE OF RACE OR COLOR.

ALMOST A CENTURY LATER, MANY AMERICANS ARE **KEPT** FROM VOTING, SIMPLY BECAUSE THEY ARE NEGROES.

THEREFORE--

THIS MONDAY, I WILL SEND TO THE CONGRESS A REQUEST FOR **LEGISLATION** TO **CARRY OUT** THIS AMENDMENT OF THE CONSTITUTION.

221

WHEREVER THERE IS DISCRIMINATION, THIS LAW WILL STRIKE DOWN **ALL** **RESTRICTIONS** USED TO DENY PEOPLE THE RIGHT TO VOTE...

IF STATE OFFICIALS **REFUSE** TO COOPERATE, THEN CITIZENS WILL BE REGISTERED BY **FEDERAL** OFFICIALS.

=PLOK=

MONDAY EVENING, DR. KING AND I RETURNED TO SELMA TO WATCH THE PRESIDENT'S SPEECH IN THE HOME OF DR. JACKSON, THE TOWN DENTIST.

I SPEAK TONIGHT FOR THE DIGNITY OF **MAN** AND THE **DESTINY** OF DEMOCRACY.

AT TIMES, HISTORY AND FATE **MEET** AT A **SINGLE** TIME, IN A **SINGLE** PLACE, TO SHAPE A <u>TURNING POINT</u> IN MAN'S UNENDING SEARCH FOR FREEDOM.

SO IT WAS AT <u>LEXINGTON</u> AND <u>CONCORD</u>. SO IT WAS A CENTURY AGO AT **APPOMATTOX**--

SO IT WAS LAST WEEK IN <u>SELMA</u>, <u>ALABAMA</u>.

THERE, LONG-SUFFERING MEN AND WOMEN PEACEFUL PROTESTED THE DENIAL OF THEIR RIGHTS AS AMERICANS. MANY OF TH WERE BRUTALLY ASSAULT

ONE GOOD MAN-- A MAN OF GOD-- WAS <u>KILLED.</u>

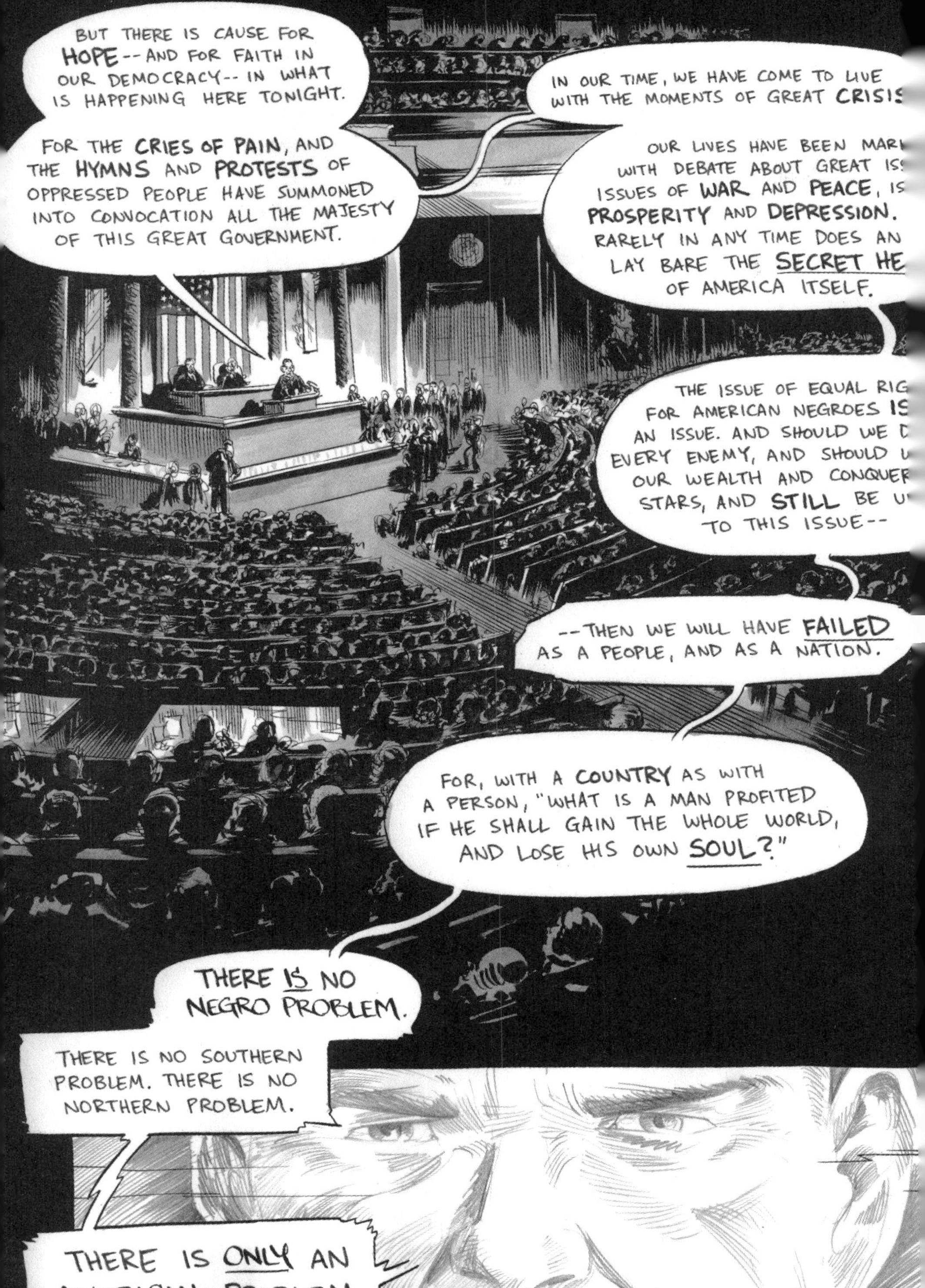

BUT THERE IS CAUSE FOR HOPE--AND FOR FAITH IN OUR DEMOCRACY--IN WHAT IS HAPPENING HERE TONIGHT.
FOR THE CRIES OF PAIN, AND THE HYMNS AND PROTESTS OF OPPRESSED PEOPLE HAVE SUMMONED INTO CONVOCATION ALL THE MAJESTY OF THIS GREAT GOVERNMENT.
IN OUR TIME, WE HAVE COME TO LIVE WITH THE MOMENTS OF GREAT CRISIS
OUR LIVES HAVE BEEN MAR WITH DEBATE ABOUT GREAT IS ISSUES OF WAR AND PEACE, IS PROSPERITY AND DEPRESSION. RARELY IN ANY TIME DOES AN LAY BARE THE SECRET HE OF AMERICA ITSELF.
THE ISSUE OF EQUAL RIG FOR AMERICAN NEGROES IS AN ISSUE. AND SHOULD WE EVERY ENEMY, AND SHOULD OUR WEALTH AND CONQUER STARS, AND STILL BE TO THIS ISSUE--
--THEN WE WILL HAVE FAILED AS A PEOPLE, AND AS A NATION.
FOR, WITH A COUNTRY AS WITH A PERSON, "WHAT IS A MAN PROFITED IF HE SHALL GAIN THE WHOLE WORLD, AND LOSE HIS OWN SOUL?"
THERE IS NO NEGRO PROBLEM.
THERE IS NO SOUTHERN PROBLEM. THERE IS NO NORTHERN PROBLEM.
THERE IS ONLY AN AMERICAN PROBLEM.

BUT EVEN IF WE PASS THIS BILL, THE BATTLE WILL NOT BE OVER. WHAT HAPPENED IN SELMA IS PART OF A FAR LARGER MOVEMENT, WHICH REACHES INTO EVERY SECTION AND STATE OF AMERICA.

IT IS THE EFFORT OF AMERICAN NEGROES TO SECURE FOR THEMSELVES THE FULL BLESSINGS OF AMERICAN LIFE.

LIVE FROM U.S. CAPITOL

THEIR CAUSE MUST BE OUR CAUSE, TOO.

BECAUSE IT'S NOT JUST NEGROES, BUT REALLY IT'S ALL OF US, WHO MUST OVERCOME THE CRIPPLING LEGACY OF BIGOTRY AND INJUSTICE --

AND WE SHALL OVERCOME.

IT WAS ONE OF THE MOST MOVING SPEECHES I HAVE EVER HEARD AN AMERICAN PRESIDENT GIVE ON CIVIL RIGHTS.

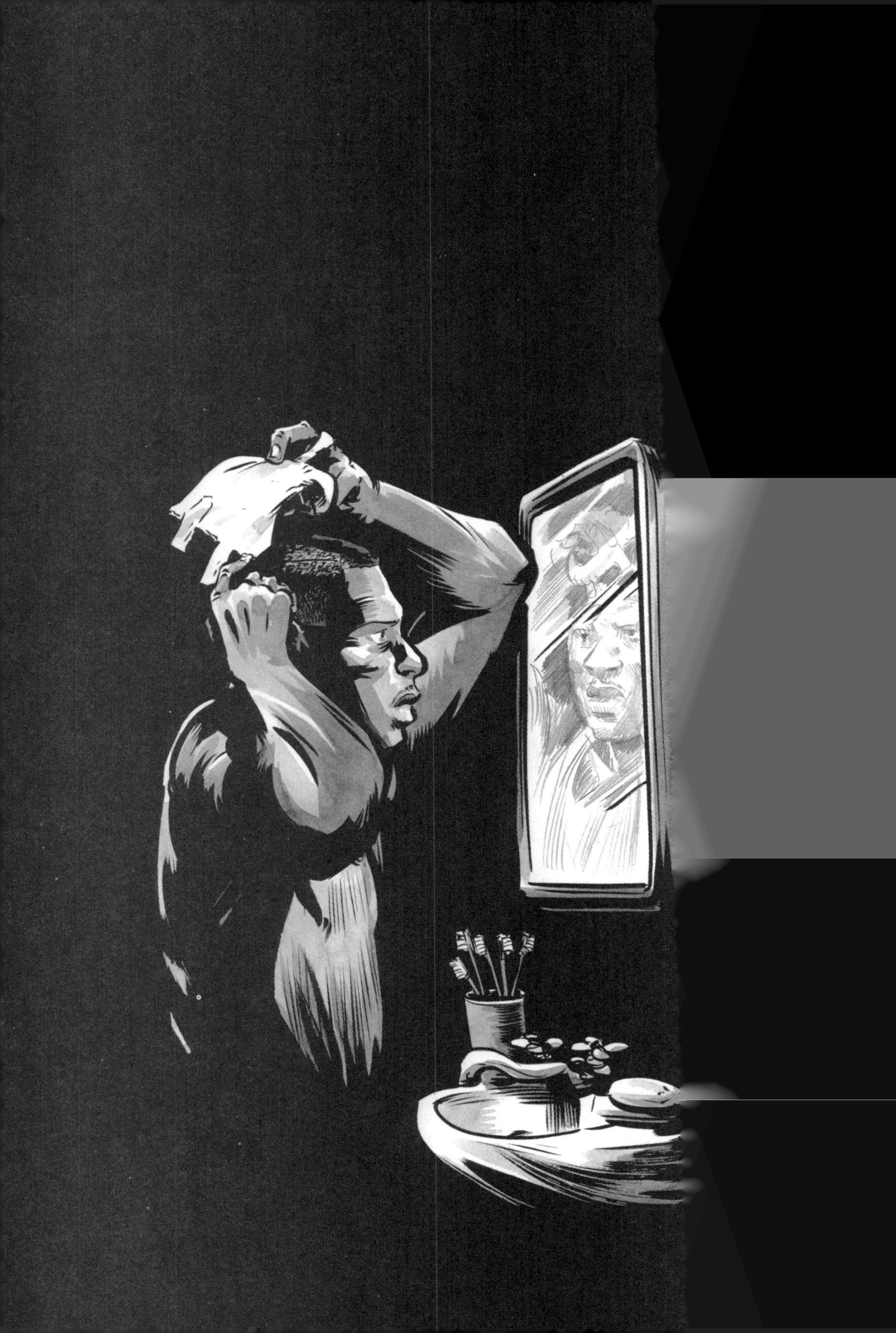

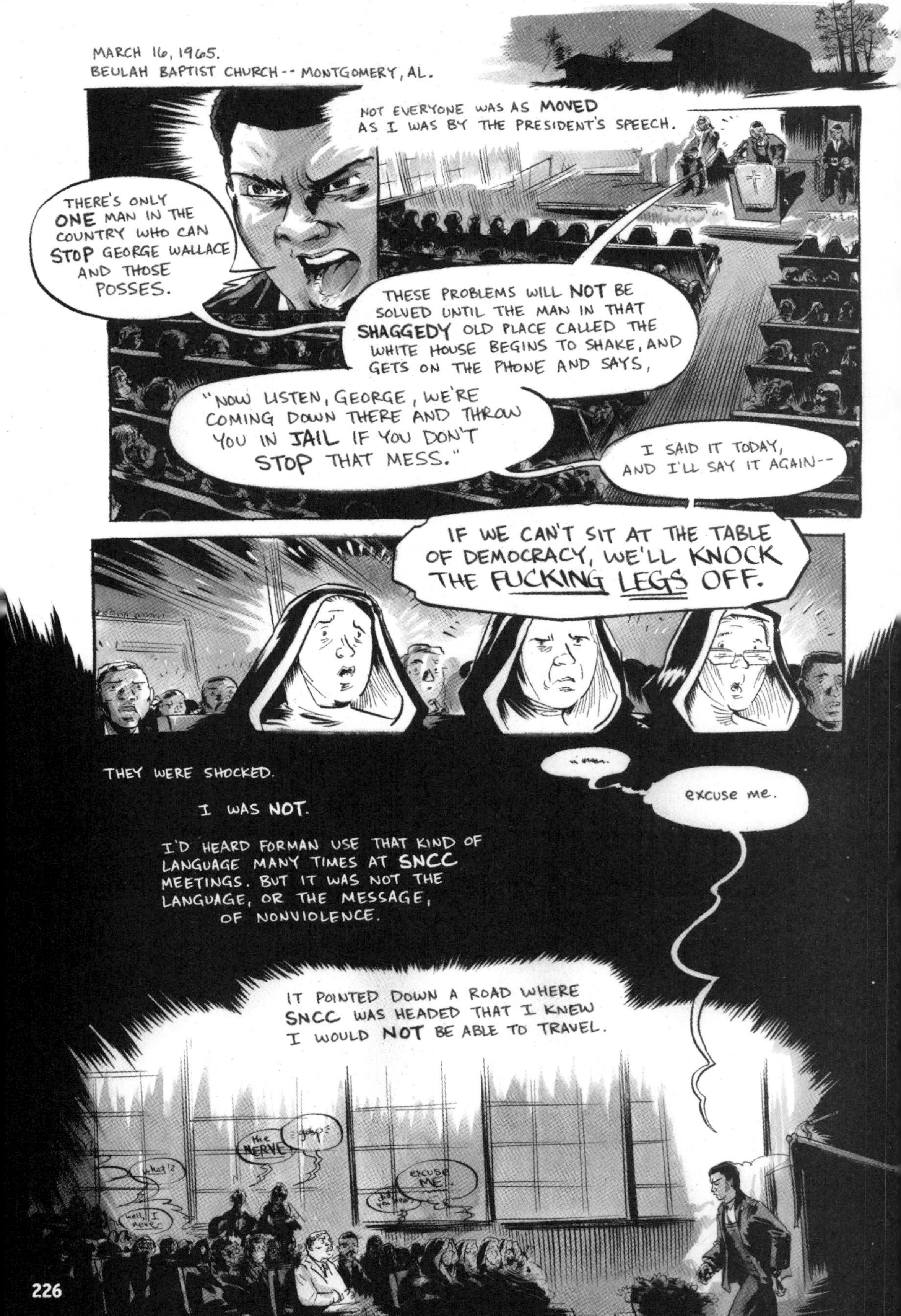
MARCH 16, 1965.
BEULAH BAPTIST CHURCH -- MONTGOMERY, AL.
NOT EVERYONE WAS AS MOVED AS I WAS BY THE PRESIDENT'S SPEECH.
THERE'S ONLY ONE MAN IN THE COUNTRY WHO CAN STOP GEORGE WALLACE AND THOSE POSSES.
THESE PROBLEMS WILL NOT BE SOLVED UNTIL THE MAN IN THAT SHAGGEDY OLD PLACE CALLED THE WHITE HOUSE BEGINS TO SHAKE, AND GETS ON THE PHONE AND SAYS,
"NOW LISTEN, GEORGE, WE'RE COMING DOWN THERE AND THROW YOU IN JAIL IF YOU DON'T STOP THAT MESS."
I SAID IT TODAY, AND I'LL SAY IT AGAIN--
IF WE CAN'T SIT AT THE TABLE OF DEMOCRACY, WE'LL KNOCK THE FUCKING LEGS OFF.
THEY WERE SHOCKED.
I WAS NOT.
I'D HEARD FORMAN USE THAT KIND OF LANGUAGE MANY TIMES AT SNCC MEETINGS. BUT IT WAS NOT THE LANGUAGE, OR THE MESSAGE, OF NONVIOLENCE.
excuse me.
IT POINTED DOWN A ROAD WHERE SNCC WAS HEADED THAT I KNEW I WOULD NOT BE ABLE TO TRAVEL.
the NERVE
gasp
what!?
well, I never
excuse ME.

unbelievable

well i dunno he's got a point--

I feel him--

hey, can we just pipe down?

i mean we've come this far--

let's just stand--

if you don't like it--

okay, then see you later--

now--

I'M NOT SATISFIED AS LONG AS THE NEGRO SEES LIFE AS A LONG AND EMPTY CORRIDOR WITH A "NO EXIT" SIGN AT THE END--

THE CUP OF ENDURANCE HAS RUN OVER.

enough is enough man I'm tired

ha!

de Lawd!

DR. KING--!

THE JUDGE HAS ISSUED HIS RULING--

THE INJUNCTION HAS BEEN GRANTED!

THE MARCH FROM SELMA TO MONTGOMERY WILL BE ALLOWED.

THE MARCH WAS SET:

MARCH 21ST, EXACTLY TWO WEEKS AFTER BLOODY SUNDAY.

227

MARCH 21ST--
SELMA, ALABAMA.

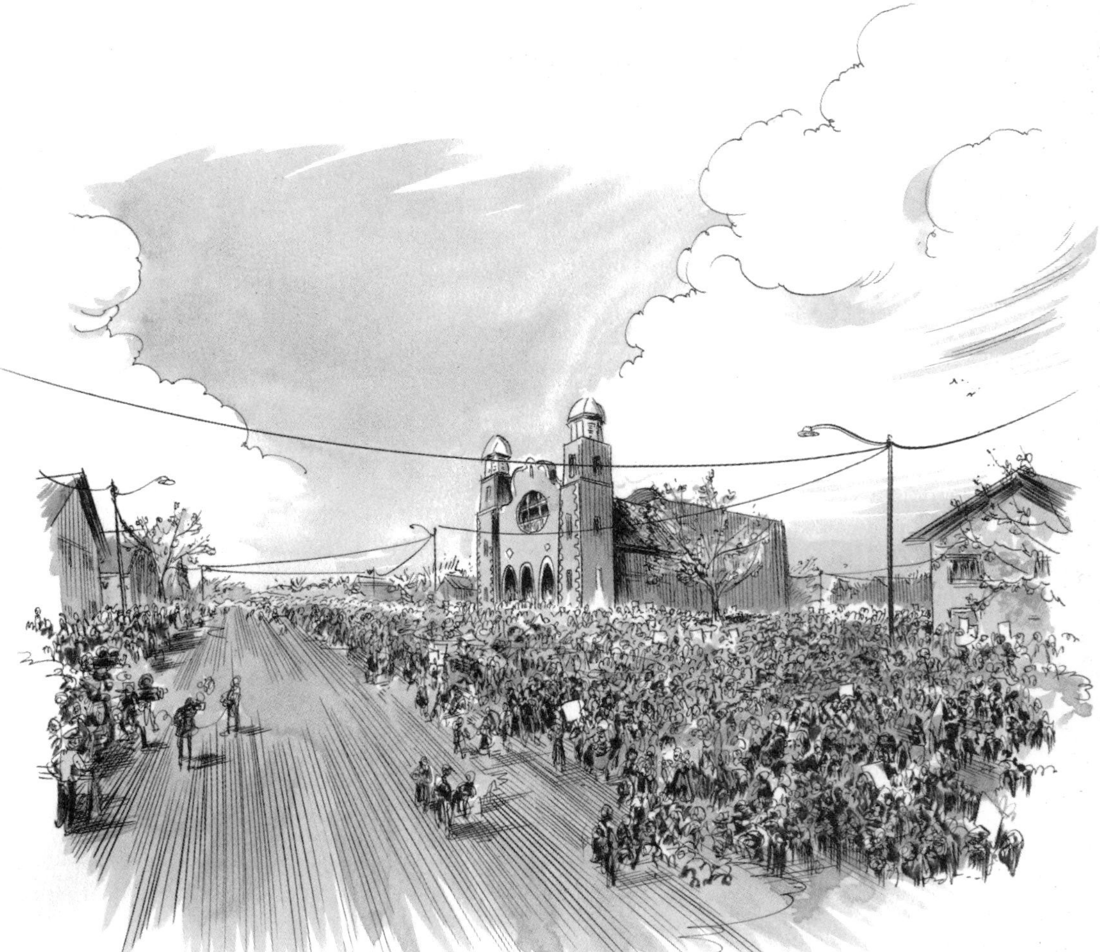

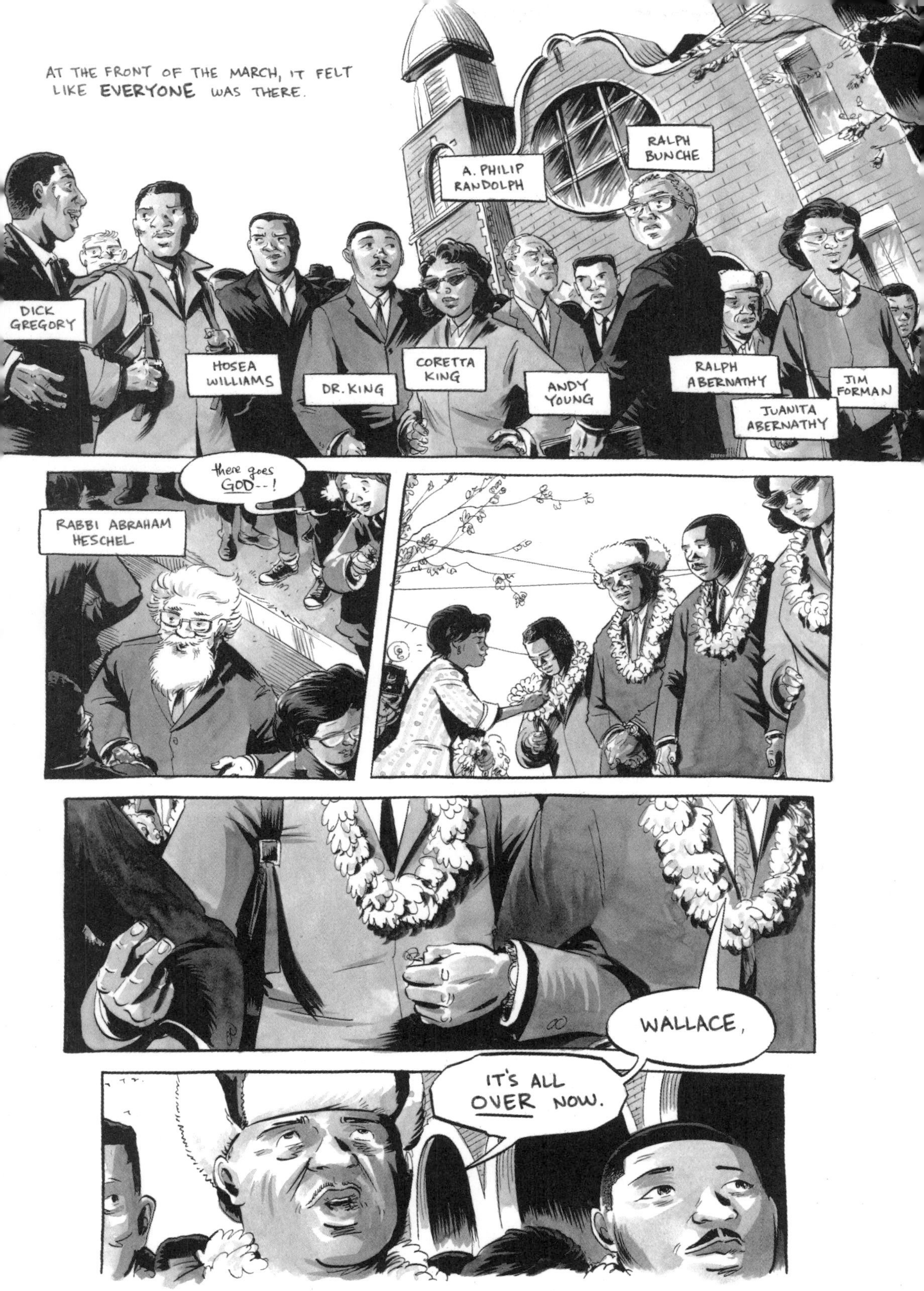
AT THE FRONT OF THE MARCH, IT FELT LIKE EVERYONE WAS THERE.
A. PHILIP RANDOLPH
RALPH BUNCHE
DICK GREGORY
HOSEA WILLIAMS
DR. KING
CORETTA KING
ANDY YOUNG
RALPH ABERNATHY
JUANITA ABERNATHY
JIM FORMAN
there goes GOD--!
RABBI ABRAHAM HESCHEL
WALLACE,
IT'S ALL OVER NOW.

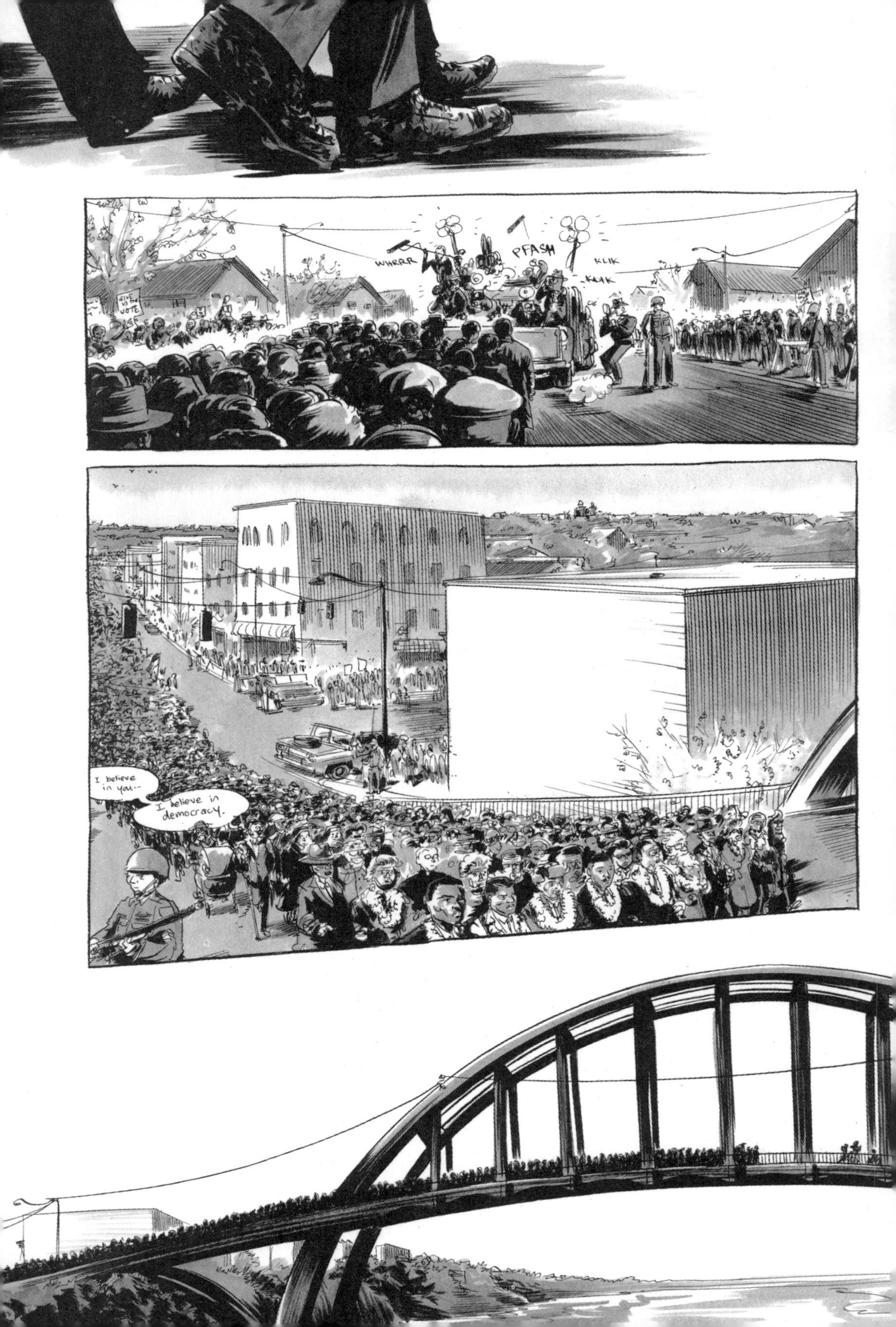
GIVE US THE VOTE
WHRRR
PFASH
KLIK
KLIK
I believe in you--
I believe in democracy.

WE COVERED SEVEN MILES THE FIRST DAY.

THAT NIGHT, THE MARCHERS MADE THE MOST OF THEIR EVENING TOGETHER. I WOULD WALK THE ENTIRE 54-MILE ROUTE, BUT I HAD TO SPEND EACH NIGHT BACK IN SELMA, WITH A DOCTOR NEARBY IN CASE SOMETHING WENT WRONG WITH MY HEAD.

WE COVERED 16 MILES THE NEXT DAY.

IT WAS A MARVEL OF ORGANIZING, KEEPING EVERYONE TOGETHER, PROPERLY FED, AND SAFE.

PICK 'EM UP AND LAY 'EM DOWN, ♫

ON TUESDAY, THE WEATHER WAS MISERABLE BUT NO ONE COMPLAINED.

NO ONE FELL BACK.

WE COVERED ELEVEN MILES THAT DAY.

ALL THE WAY FROM SELMA TOWN ♫

SOMETIMES WHEN WE'D STOP TO REGROUP, REPORTERS WOULD ASK ME HOW I WAS FEELING OR WHAT I THOUGHT OF SOME PARTICULAR RESPONSE TO THE MARCH.

JOHN-- WHAT DO YOU THINK OF THE RESOLUTION PASSED BY THE ALABAMA STATE LEGISLATURE, ACCUSING THE MARCHERS OF "FORNICATION" IN THEIR TENTS?

ALL THESE SEGREGATIONISTS CAN THINK OF IS FORNICATION-- AND THAT IS WHY WE HAVE SO MANY DIFFERENT SHADES OF NEGROES.

WE COVERED **16** MORE MILES THE NEXT DAY,

MAKING CAMP JUST A FEW MILES FROM THE STATE CAPITOL.

AS NIGHT FELL,

THE SCENE TURNED INTO A CELEBRATION-- A **FESTIVAL**.

HARRY BELAFONTE ORGANIZED A CONCERT WITH DOZENS OF CELEBRITIES AND ENTERTAINERS--

NINA SIMONE, TONY BENNETT, SAMMY DAVIS JR., BILLY ECKSTINE, LEONARD BERNSTEIN, JOAN BAEZ, AND PETER, PAUL, AND MARY. IT WAS A SPECTACLE--

A SALUTE TO **SELMA**.

MARCH 25th
MONTGOMERY, ALABAMA

THIS IS A **REVOLUTION**--

...A REVOLUTION THAT WON'T FIRE A **SHOT**!

WE COME TO LOVE THE **HELL** OUT OF THE STATE OF ALABAMA!

FOR THE FINAL RALLY, RALPH ABERNATHY MANAGED THE PLATFORM.

WE WILL NOW HAVE MRS. AMELIA BOYNTON READ TO YOU A PETITION--

MRS. BOYNTON FROM SELMA, ALABAMA!

PETITION:

TO THE HONORABLE **GEORGE D. WALLACE**-- AGENT OF GOD, CITIZEN OF THE UNITED STATES, AND GOVERNOR OF THE STATE OF ALABAMA...

WE HAVE COME TO REPRESENT THE NEGRO CITIZENS OF ALABAMA AS FREEDOM-LOVING PEOPLE FROM **ALL OVER** THE UNITED STATES, AND THE **WORLD**. WE HAVE COME **NOT ONLY** FIVE DAYS AND FIFTY MILES--

BUT WE HAVE COME FROM **THREE CENTURIES** OF TROUBLE AND HARDSHIP...

WE **MUST** HAVE THE RIGHT TO **VOTE**.

WE **MUST** HAVE EQUAL PROTECTION UNDER THE LAW, AND AN END TO POLICE BRUTALITY.

WHEN IT WAS MY TURN TO SPEAK, I LET IT **ALL** OUT-- **FIVE YEARS** OF BEATINGS AND ARRESTS BUBBLING OUT OF MY SOUL.

MY FELLOW FREEDOM FIGHTERS--

AS A NATIVE OF TROY, ALABAMA, JUST FIFTY MILES FROM HERE, I'M HAPPY TO BE ABLE TO STAND HERE AND SHARE THIS **GREAT MOMENT** IN **HISTORY.**

WE ARE INVOLVED IN A **NONVIOLENT WAR**--

WE **ARE** INVOLVED IN A **NONVIOLENT REVOLUTION.**

WE DON'T **HAVE GUNS.**

WE DON'T HAVE MISSILES. WE DON'T HAVE TEAR GAS.

THE ONLY THING WE HAVE IS OUR **BODIES**--

-- OUR **TIRED FEET.**

THE **SAME** FEET THAT BROUGHT US FROM SELMA TO MONTGOMERY IN OUR WEARY BODIES--

WILL TAKE US TO **VICTORY** RIGHT HERE IN THE STATE OF ALABAMA!

THE **FIRST LADY** OF THE **MOVEMENT**-- WHO, IN NINETEEN HUNDRED AND FIFTY-FIVE, ON DECEMBER THE FIRST, WOULD NOT GET UP WHEN EVERYBODY ELSE WAS GETTING UP TO GIVE HER SEAT TO A WHITE MAN--

MRS. ROSA **PARKS!**

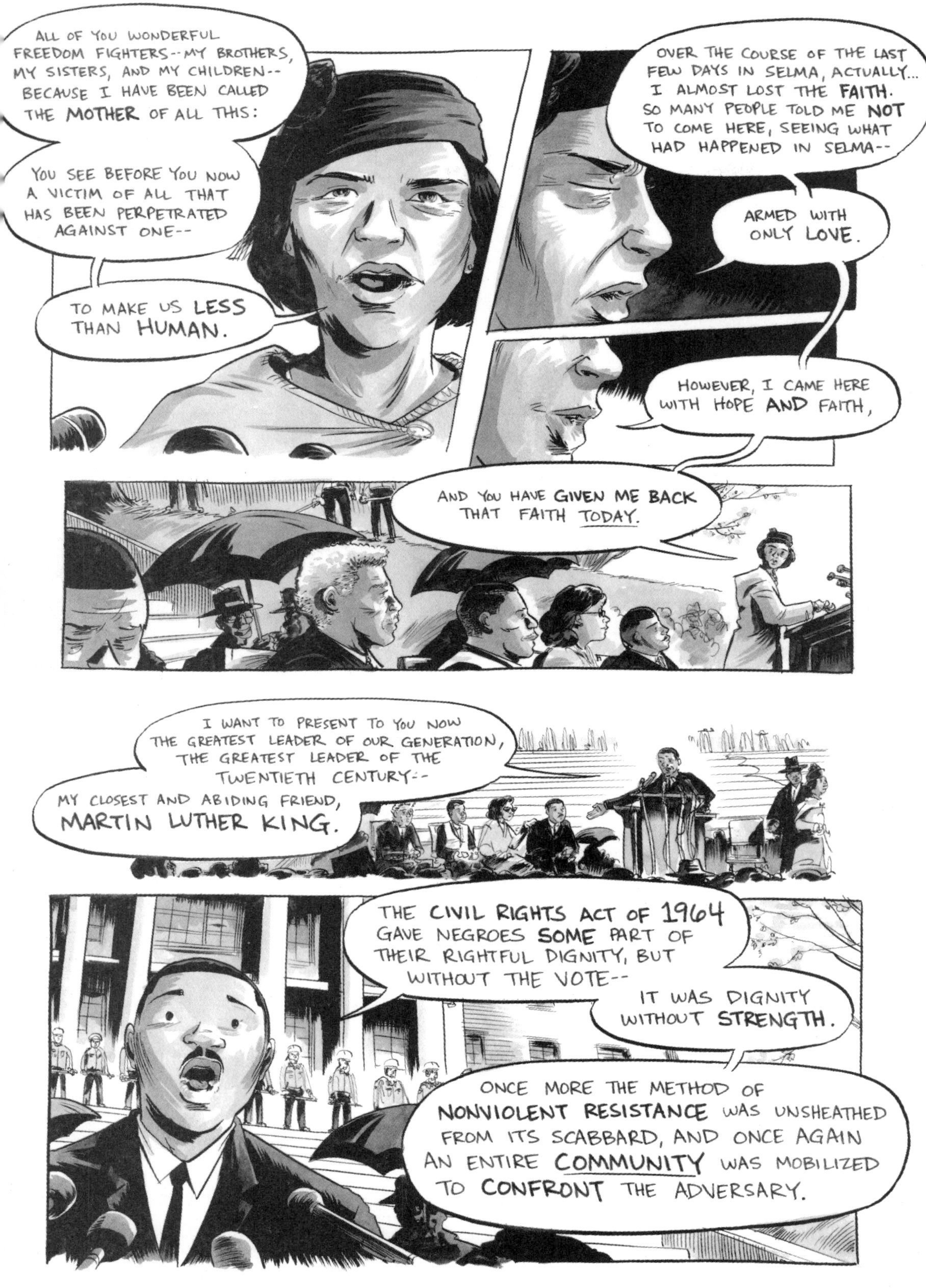
ALL OF YOU WONDERFUL FREEDOM FIGHTERS--MY BROTHERS, MY SISTERS, AND MY CHILDREN--BECAUSE I HAVE BEEN CALLED THE MOTHER OF ALL THIS:
YOU SEE BEFORE YOU NOW A VICTIM OF ALL THAT HAS BEEN PERPETRATED AGAINST ONE--
TO MAKE US LESS THAN HUMAN.
OVER THE COURSE OF THE LAST FEW DAYS IN SELMA, ACTUALLY... I ALMOST LOST THE FAITH. SO MANY PEOPLE TOLD ME NOT TO COME HERE, SEEING WHAT HAD HAPPENED IN SELMA--
ARMED WITH ONLY LOVE.
HOWEVER, I CAME HERE WITH HOPE AND FAITH,
AND YOU HAVE GIVEN ME BACK THAT FAITH TODAY.
I WANT TO PRESENT TO YOU NOW THE GREATEST LEADER OF OUR GENERATION, THE GREATEST LEADER OF THE TWENTIETH CENTURY--
MY CLOSEST AND ABIDING FRIEND, MARTIN LUTHER KING.
THE CIVIL RIGHTS ACT OF 1964 GAVE NEGROES SOME PART OF THEIR RIGHTFUL DIGNITY, BUT WITHOUT THE VOTE--
IT WAS DIGNITY WITHOUT STRENGTH.
ONCE MORE THE METHOD OF NONVIOLENT RESISTANCE WAS UNSHEATHED FROM ITS SCABBARD, AND ONCE AGAIN AN ENTIRE COMMUNITY WAS MOBILIZED TO CONFRONT THE ADVERSARY.

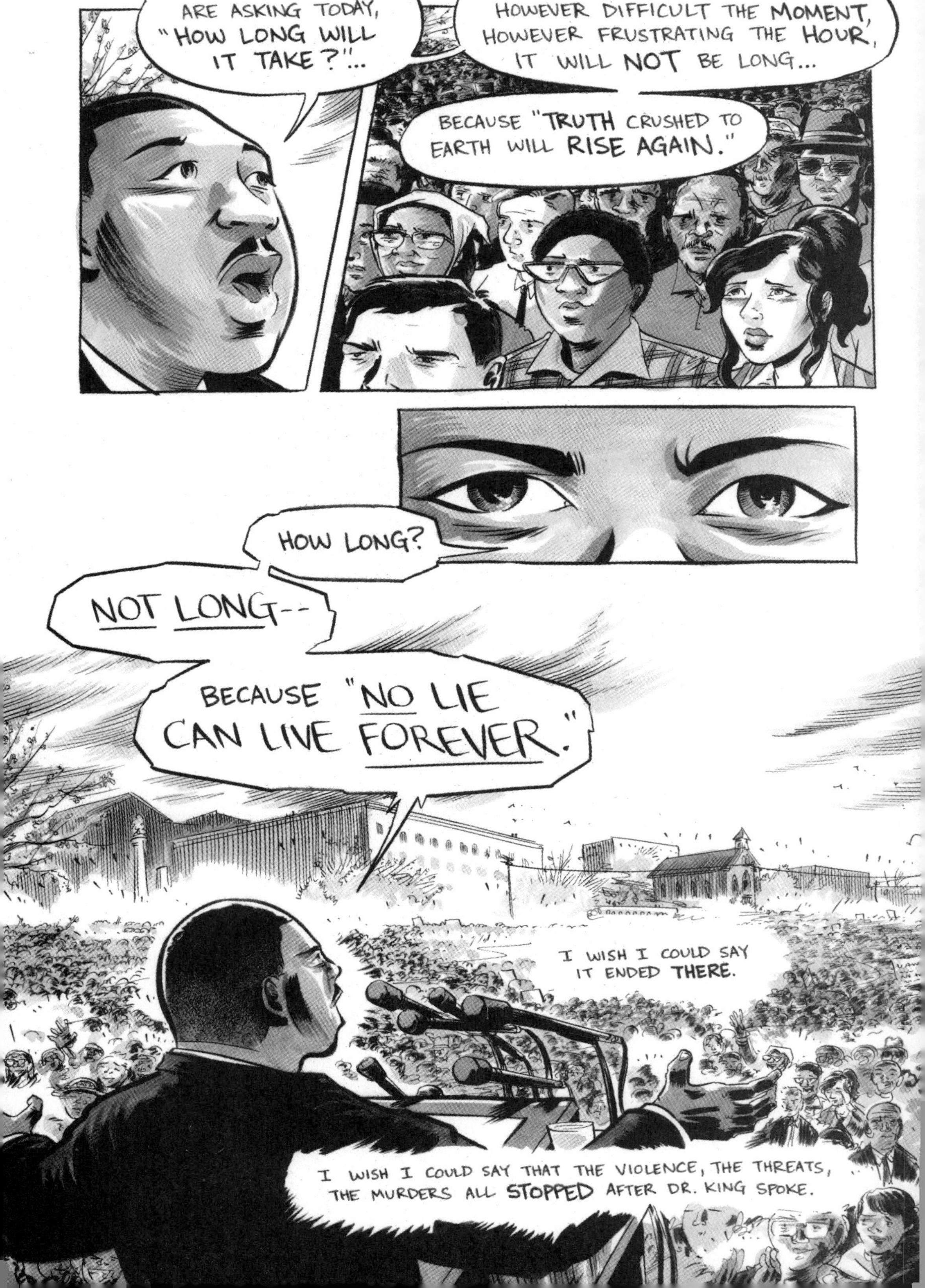
I KNOW YOU ARE ASKING TODAY, "HOW LONG WILL IT TAKE?"...
I COME TO SAY TO YOU THIS AFTERNOON: HOWEVER DIFFICULT THE MOMENT, HOWEVER FRUSTRATING THE HOUR, IT WILL NOT BE LONG...
BECAUSE "TRUTH CRUSHED TO EARTH WILL RISE AGAIN."
HOW LONG?
NOT LONG--
BECAUSE "NO LIE CAN LIVE FOREVER."
I WISH I COULD SAY IT ENDED THERE.
I WISH I COULD SAY THAT THE VIOLENCE, THE THREATS, THE MURDERS ALL STOPPED AFTER DR. KING SPOKE.

VIOLA LIUZZO WAS A 39-YEAR-OLD MOTHER FROM DETROIT
WHO HAD COME TO ALABAMA AFTER BLOODY SUNDAY.

AFTER THE RALLY AT THE CAPITOL, SHE AND LEROY MOTON,
A 19-YEAR-OLD ACTIVIST FROM DALLAS COUNTY, BEGAN
SHUTTLING VOLUNTEERS BACK TO SELMA.

ON THEIR WAY BACK TO MONTGOMERY TO PICK
UP ANOTHER CARLOAD OF VOLUNTEERS, THEY
REALIZED THEY WERE BEING FOLLOWED.

THE PURSUERS PULLED UP ALONGSIDE LIUZZO'S DRIVER-SIDE WINDOW

AND FIRED A SINGLE SHOT INTO HER HEAD,
KILLING HER.

FOUR AND A HALF MONTHS AFTER THAT DAY,
ON **AUGUST 6th,**

AFTER A LONG JOURNEY THROUGH BOTH
HOUSES OF CONGRESS,

THE **1965 VOTING RIGHTS ACT** WAS
SIGNED INTO LAW BY PRESIDENT LYNDON JOHNSON.

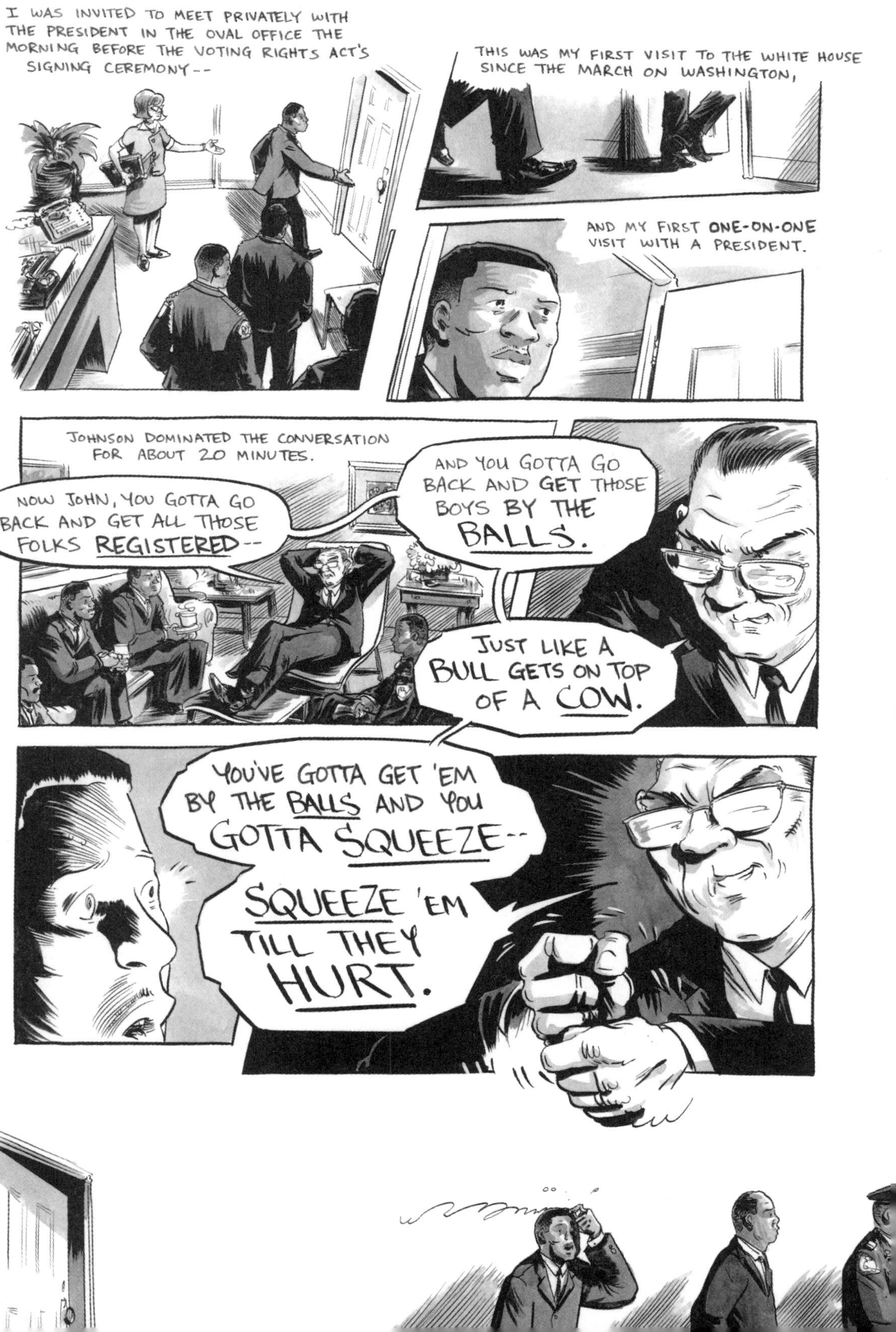
I WAS INVITED TO MEET PRIVATELY WITH THE PRESIDENT IN THE OVAL OFFICE THE MORNING BEFORE THE VOTING RIGHTS ACT'S SIGNING CEREMONY--
THIS WAS MY FIRST VISIT TO THE WHITE HOUSE SINCE THE MARCH ON WASHINGTON,
AND MY FIRST ONE-ON-ONE VISIT WITH A PRESIDENT.
JOHNSON DOMINATED THE CONVERSATION FOR ABOUT 20 MINUTES.
NOW JOHN, YOU GOTTA GO BACK AND GET ALL THOSE FOLKS REGISTERED--
AND YOU GOTTA GO BACK AND GET THOSE BOYS BY THE BALLS.
JUST LIKE A BULL GETS ON TOP OF A COW.
YOU'VE GOTTA GET 'EM BY THE BALLS AND YOU GOTTA SQUEEZE--
SQUEEZE 'EM TILL THEY HURT.

AT THE SIGNING CEREMONY THAT AFTERNOON IN THE CAPITOL-- IN THE SHADOW OF ABRAHAM LINCOLN-- I FELT DIFFERENT. I WAS DEEPLY MOVED, YES--

BUT I FELT SOMETHING CHANGE, SOMETHING SHIFT.

TODAY IS A TRIUMPH FOR FREEDOM AS HUGE AS ANY VICTORY THAT HAS EVER BEEN WON ON ANY BATTLEFIELD...

TODAY, THE NEGRO STORY AND THE AMERICAN STORY FUSE AND BIND.

THIS LAW COVERS MANY PAGES. BUT THE HEART OF THE LAW IS PLAIN--

WHEREVER, BY CLEAR AND OBJECTIVE STANDARDS, STATES AND COUNTIES ARE USING REGULATIONS, OR LAWS, OR TESTS TO DENY THE RIGHT TO VOTE, THEN THEY WILL BE STRUCK DOWN.

IF IT IS CLEAR THAT STATE OFFICIALS STILL INTEND TO DISCRIMINATE, THEN FEDERAL EXAMINERS WILL BE SENT IN TO REGISTER ALL ELIGIBLE VOTERS...

IF ANY COUNTY IN THIS NATION DOES NOT WANT FEDERAL INTERVENTION, IT NEED ONLY OPEN ITS POLLING PLACES TO ALL OF ITS PEOPLE.

THE VOTE IS THE MOST POWERFUL INSTRUMENT EVER DEVISED BY MAN FOR BREAKING DOWN INJUSTICE AND DESTROYING THE TERRIBLE WALLS WHICH IMPRISON MEN BECAUSE THEY ARE DIFFERENT FROM OTHER MEN.

TODAY, WHAT IS PERHAPS THE LAST OF THE LEGAL BARRIERS IS TUMBLING.

THERE WILL BE MANY ACTIONS, AND MANY DIFFICULTIES, BEFORE THE RIGHTS WOVEN INTO LAW ARE ALSO WOVEN INTO THE FABRIC OF OUR NATION--

BUT THE STRUGGLE FOR EQUALITY MUST NOW MOVE TOWARD A DIFFERENT BATTLEFIELD.

THAT DAY WAS THE END OF A VERY LONG ROAD.

c'mon around here.

IT WAS THE LAST DAY OF THE MOVEMENT AS I KNEW IT.

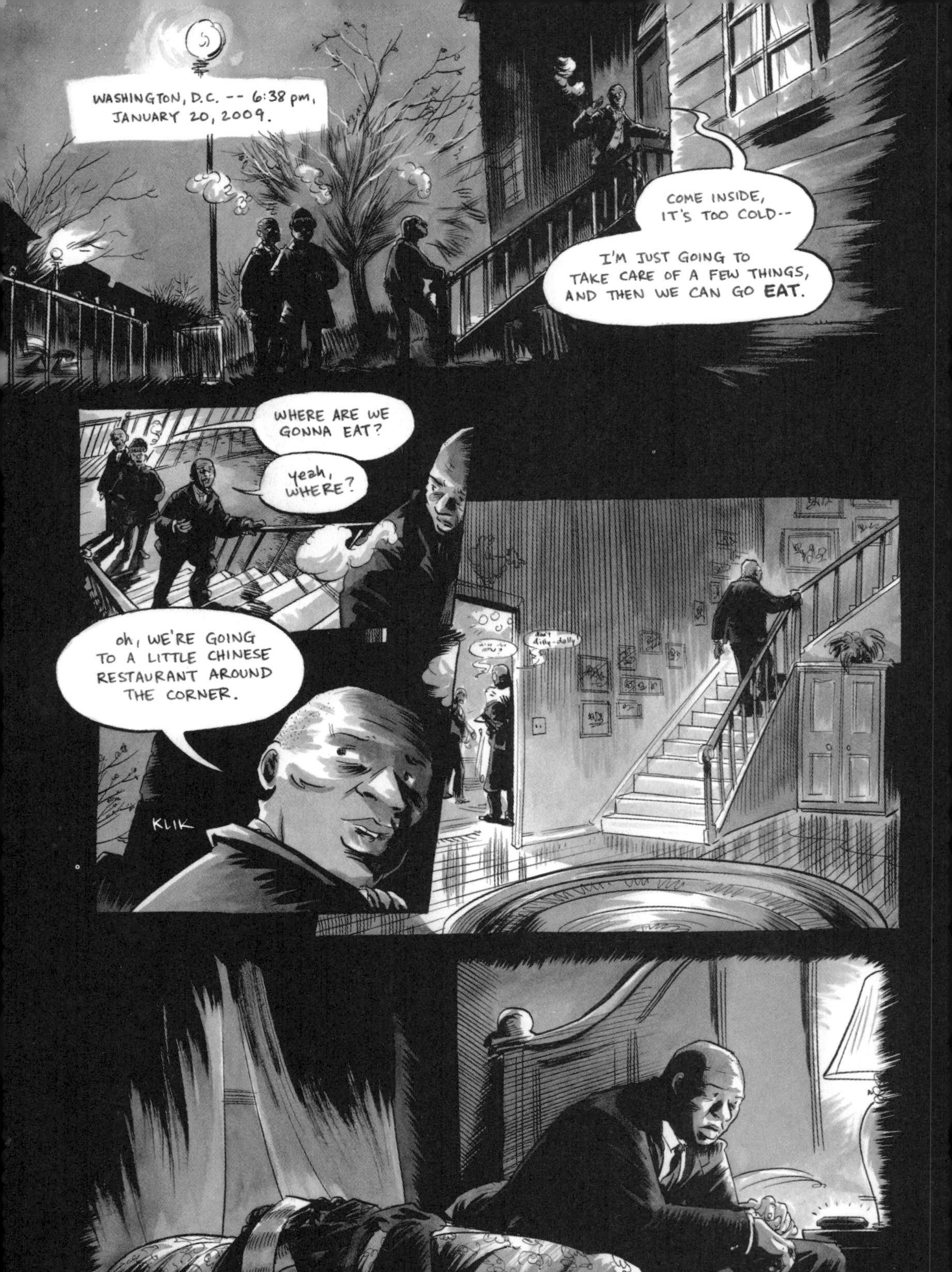
WASHINGTON, D.C. -- 6:38 pm, JANUARY 20, 2009.
COME INSIDE, IT'S TOO COLD--
I'M JUST GOING TO TAKE CARE OF A FEW THINGS, AND THEN WE CAN GO **EAT**.
WHERE ARE WE GONNA EAT?
yeah, WHERE?
oh, WE'RE GOING TO A LITTLE CHINESE RESTAURANT AROUND THE CORNER.
KLIK
don't dilly-dally

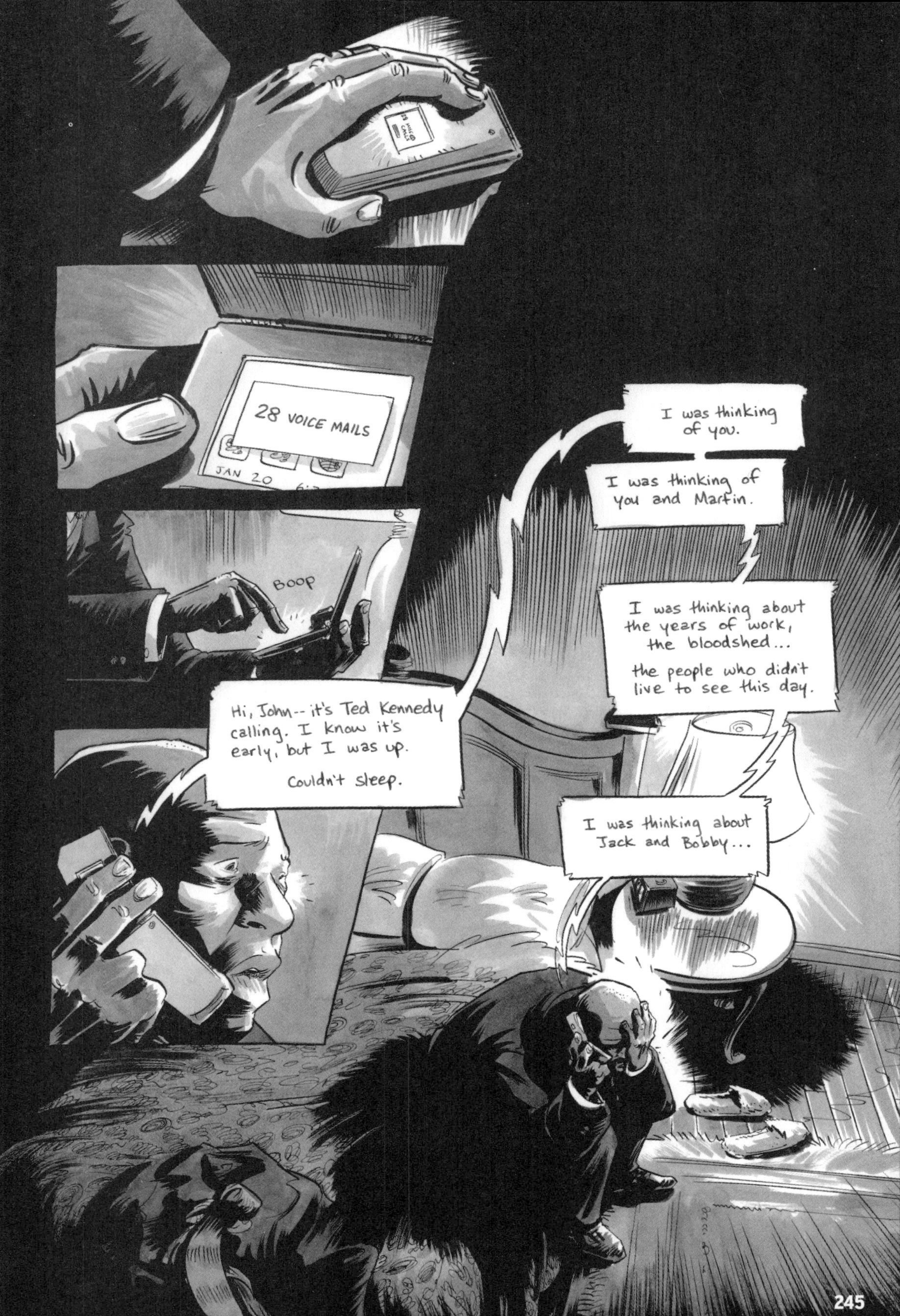

28 VOICE MAILS
JAN 20
BOOP
Hi, John-- it's Ted Kennedy calling. I know it's early, but I was up.
Couldn't sleep.
I was thinking of you.
I was thinking of you and Martin.
I was thinking about the years of work, the bloodshed...
the people who didn't live to see this day.
I was thinking about Jack and Bobby...

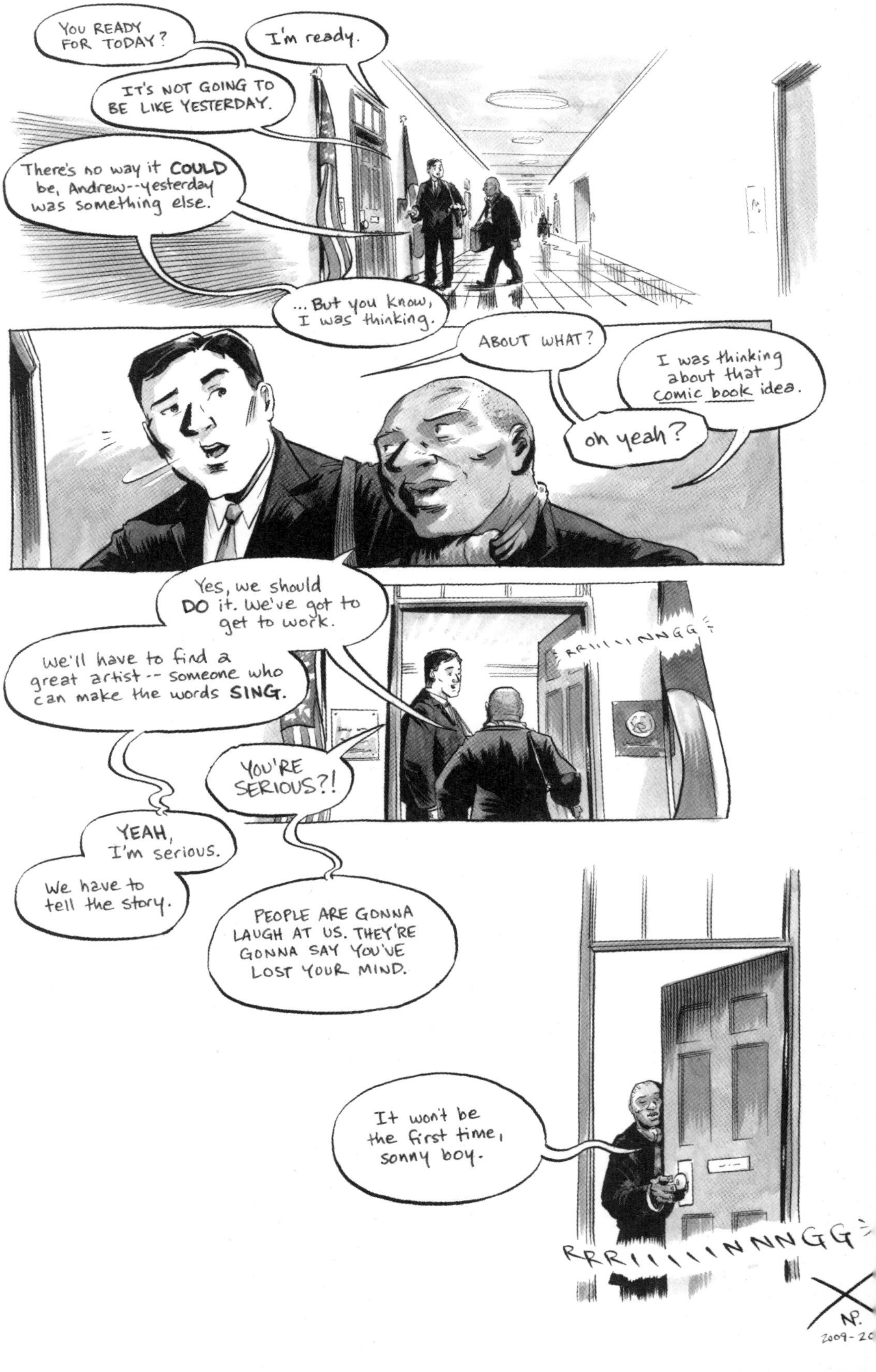
You READY FOR TODAY?
I'm ready.
IT'S NOT GOING TO BE LIKE YESTERDAY.
There's no way it COULD be, Andrew--yesterday was something else.
...But you know, I was thinking.
ABOUT WHAT?
I was thinking about that comic book idea.
oh yeah?
Yes, we should DO it. We've got to get to work.
RRIIIIINNGG
We'll have to find a great artist -- someone who can make the words SING.
YOU'RE SERIOUS?!
YEAH, I'm serious.
We have to tell the story.
PEOPLE ARE GONNA LAUGH AT US. THEY'RE GONNA SAY YOU'VE LOST YOUR MIND.
It won't be the first time, sonny boy.
RRRIIIIIINNNGG
NP. 2009-20

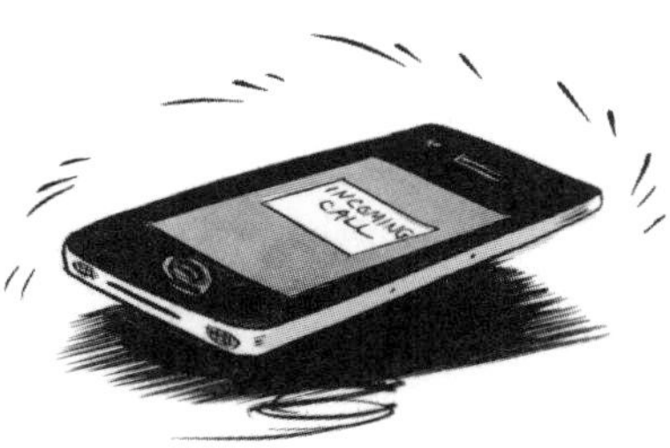
INCOMING CALL

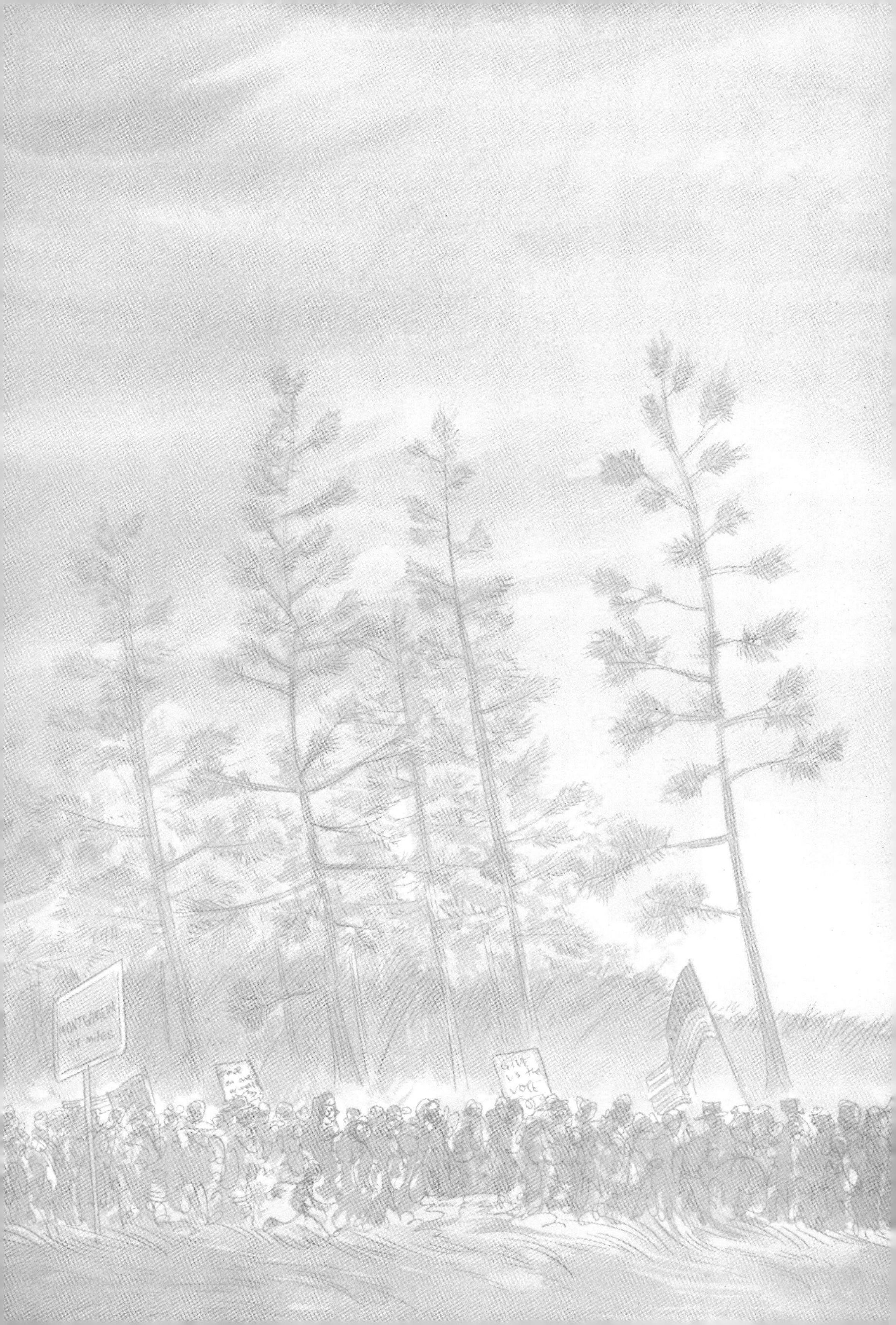
MONTGOMERY
37 miles
GIVE us the VOTE

ACKNOWLEDGMENTS

I am deeply grateful to Andrew Aydin and Nate Powell for their hard work, persistence, and commitment to making it real, making it plain, and telling the whole truth. I am also grateful to Leigh Walton for his work editing this book. And I want to thank IDW and Top Shelf for their openness, their support, and their powerful work.

John Lewis

I will forever be indebted to my mom for the opportunities in my life that her hard work and sacrifice made possible. I am more than grateful to John Lewis, whose trust, faith, and friendship have filled my life with purpose. I am in awe of Nate Powell's talent and grateful to have worked with him. I am deeply appreciative of Sara for her patience and support, Vaughn for his guidance and friendship, and Dom for reminding me to have fun. I wish Jordan could see this. And thank you, Mr. Parker, Mrs. Fuentes, Jacob Gillison, A.D. Frazier, Professor Uchimura, and all of the teachers and mentors that gave me the courage to walk this road.

Andrew Aydin

I'd like to dedicate my work on this book to the memory of Sarah Kirsch (1970–2012), whose compassion, humanity, vision, and talent deeply shaped the direction of my life from my early teenage years; to my wife, Rachel, a true original and cranky do-gooder committed to helping those who need a hand; and to our amazing daughters, Harper and Everly, in hopes of their growing into a world more humane, more considerate, more loving — a world they and their entire generation will inherit. Let's make the world worth it.

Nate Powell

ABOUT THE AUTHORS

JOHN LEWIS is the U.S. Representative for Georgia's fifth congressional district and an American icon widely known for his role in the civil rights movement.

Photo by Eric Etheridge

As a student at American Baptist Theological Seminary in 1959, Lewis organized sit-in demonstrations at segregated lunch counters in Nashville, Tennessee. In 1961, he volunteered to participate in the Freedom Rides, which challenged segregation at interstate bus terminals across the South. He was beaten severely by angry mobs and arrested by police for challenging the injustice of "Jim Crow" segregation in the South.

From 1963 to 1966, Lewis was Chairman of the Student Nonviolent Coordinating Committee (SNCC). As head of SNCC, Lewis became a nationally recognized figure, dubbed one of the "Big Six" leaders of the civil rights movement. At the age of 23, he was an architect of and a keynote speaker at the historic March on Washington in August 1963.

In 1964, John Lewis coordinated SNCC efforts to organize voter registration drives and community action programs during the Mississippi Freedom Summer. The following year, Lewis helped spearhead one of the most seminal moments of the civil rights movement. Together with Hosea Williams, another notable civil rights leader, John Lewis led over 600 peaceful, orderly protesters across the Edmund Pettus Bridge in Selma, Alabama, on March 7, 1965. They intended to march from Selma to Montgomery to demonstrate the need for voting rights in the state. The marchers were attacked by Alabama state troopers in a brutal confrontation that became known as "Bloody Sunday." News broadcasts and photographs revealing the senseless cruelty of the segregated South helped hasten the passage of the Voting Rights Act of 1965.

Despite physical attacks, serious injuries, and more than 40 arrests, John Lewis remained a devoted advocate of the philosophy of nonviolence. After leaving SNCC in 1966, he continued to work for civil rights, first as Associate Director of the Field Foundation, then with the Southern Regional Council, where he became Executive Director of the Voter Education Project (VEP). In 1977, Lewis was appointed by President Jimmy Carter to direct more than 250,000 volunteers of ACTION, the federal volunteer agency.

In 1981, Lewis was elected to the Atlanta City Council. He was elected to the U.S. House of Representatives in November 1986 and has represented Georgia's fifth district there ever since. In 2011 he was awarded the Medal of Freedom by President Barack Obama.

Lewis's 1998 memoir, *Walking with the Wind: A Memoir of the Movement*, won numerous honors, including the Robert F. Kennedy, Lillian Smith, and Anisfield-Wolf Book Awards. His subsequent book, *Across That Bridge: Life Lessons and a Vision for Change*, won the NAACP Image Award.

(From left to right): Nate Powell, Congressman John Lewis, Andrew Aydin.

Photo by Sandi Villarreal

ANDREW AYDIN, an Atlanta native, currently serves as Digital Director & Policy Advisor in the Washington, D.C., office of Rep. John Lewis. After learning that his boss had been inspired as a young man by the 1950s comic book *Martin Luther King & The Montgomery Story*, Aydin conceived the *March* series and collaborated with Rep. Lewis to write it, while also composing a master's thesis on the history and impact of *The Montgomery Story*. Today, he continues to write comics and lecture about the history of comics in the civil rights movement.

Previously, he served as Communications Director and Press Secretary during Rep. Lewis's 2008 and 2010 re-election campaigns, as District Aide to Rep. John Larson (D–CT), and as Special Assistant to Connecticut Lt. Governor Kevin Sullivan. Aydin is a graduate of the Lovett School in Atlanta, Trinity College in Hartford, and Georgetown University in Washington, D.C. Visit www.andrewaydin.com for more information.

NATE POWELL is a *New York Times* best-selling graphic novelist born in Little Rock, Arkansas, in 1978. He began self-publishing at age 14, and graduated from School of Visual Arts in 2000.

His work includes *You Don't Say, Any Empire, Swallow Me Whole, The Silence of Our Friends, The Year of the Beasts*, and Rick Riordan's *The Lost Hero*. Powell's comics have received such honors as the Eisner Award, two Ignatz Awards, four YALSA Great Graphic Novels for Teens selections, and a *Los Angeles Times* Book Prize finalist selection.

In addition to *March*, Powell has spoken about his work at the United Nations and created animated illustrations for SPLC's documentary *Selma: The Bridge to the Ballot*.

Powell is currently writing and drawing his next book, *Cover*, and drawing *Two Dead* with writer Van Jansen. He lives in Bloomington, Indiana. Visit Nate's website at www.seemybrotherdance.org for more information.

PRAISE FOR THE *MARCH* TRILOGY

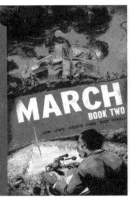

March: Book One	March: Book Two	March: Book Three	March (Trilogy Slipcase Set)
128 pages, $14.95 (US)	192 pages, $19.95 (US)	256 pages, $19.99 (US)	Three Volumes, $49.99 (US)
ISBN: 978-1-60309-300-2	ISBN: 978-1-60309-400-9	ISBN: 978-1-60309-402-3	ISBN: 978-1-60309-395-8

#1 *New York Times* and *Washington Post* Bestseller
Coretta Scott King Book Award—Author Honor
Robert F. Kennedy Book Award—Special Recognition
Street Literature Book Award Medal
ALA Notable Books
YALSA's Top 10 Great Graphic Novels for Teens
YALSA's Outstanding Books for the College Bound
***Reader's Digest*'s Graphic Novels Every Grown-Up Should Read**
Added to New York City Schools curriculum and taught in over 40 states
Selected for college & university reading programs across America

"Congressman John Lewis has been a resounding moral voice in the quest for equality for more than 50 years, and I'm so pleased that he is sharing his memories of the Civil Rights Movement with America's young leaders. In *March*, he brings a whole new generation with him across the Edmund Pettus Bridge, from a past of clenched fists into a future of outstretched hands."
—President Bill Clinton

"With *March*, Congressman John Lewis takes us behind the scenes of some of the most pivotal moments of the Civil Rights Movement. In graphic novel form, his first-hand account makes these historic events both accessible and relevant to an entire new generation of Americans."
— LeVar Burton

"*March* is one of the most important graphic novels ever created—an extraordinary presentation of an extraordinary life, and proof that young people can change the world. I'm stunned by the power of these comics, and grateful that Congressman Lewis's story will enlighten and inspire future generations of readers and leaders."
— Raina Telgemeier

"There is perhaps no more important modern book to be stocked in American school libraries than *March*."
— *The Washington Post*

"Essential reading…*March* is a moving and important achievement…the story of a true American superhero."
—*USA Today*

"Brave acts of civil disobedience…[give] *March* its educational value even as Powell's drawings give Lewis's crisp narration an emotional power."   —*The New York Times*

"Superbly told history."   —*Publishers Weekly* (starred review)

"Powell captures the danger and tension in stunning cinematic spreads, which dramatically complement Lewis's powerful story…The story of the civil rights movement is a triumphant one, but Lewis's account is full of nuance and personal struggle, both of which impart an empowering human element to an often mythologized period of history…this is a must-read."
                                                      — *Booklist* (starred review)

"An astonishingly accomplished graphic memoir that brings to life a vivid portrait of the civil rights era, Lewis's extraordinary history and accomplishments, and the movement he helped lead…Its power, accessibility and artistry destine it for awards, and a well-deserved place at the pinnacle of the comics canon."   —NPR

"*March* provides a potent reminder that the sit-ins, far from being casually assembled, were well-coordinated, disciplined events informed by a rigorous philosophy…Likely to prove inspirational to readers for years to come."   —*Barnes and Noble Review*

"A riveting chronicle of Lewis's extraordinary life…it powerfully illustrates how much perseverance is needed to achieve fundamental social change."   —*O, The Oprah Magazine*

"*March* offers a poignant portrait of an iconic figure that both entertains and edifies, and deserves to be placed alongside other historical graphic memoirs like *Persepolis* and *Maus*."
                                                      —*Entertainment Weekly*

"The civil rights movement can seem to some like a distant memory…John Lewis refreshes our memories in dramatic fashion."   —*The Chicago Tribune*

"When a graphic novel tries to interest young readers in an important topic, it often feels forced. Not so with the exhilarating *March*…Powerful words and pictures."   —*The Boston Globe*

"This memoir puts a human face on a struggle that many students will primarily know from textbooks… Visually stunning, the black-and-white illustrations convey the emotions of this turbulent time…This insider's view of the civil rights movement should be required reading for young and old; not to be missed."   —*School Library Journal* (starred review)

"A powerful tale of courage and principle igniting sweeping social change, told by a strong-minded, uniquely qualified eyewitness…The heroism of those who sat and marched…comes through with vivid, inspiring clarity."   —*Kirkus Reviews* (starred review)

"Lewis's remarkable life has been skillfully translated into graphics…Segregation's insult to personhood comes across here with a visual, visceral punch. This version of Lewis's life story belongs in libraries to teach readers about the heroes of America."
                                                      —*Library Journal* (starred review)

"Powell's drawings in *March* combine the epic sweep of history with the intimate personal details of memoir, and bring Lewis's story to life in a way that feels entirely unfamiliar. *March* is shaping up to be a major work of history and graphic literature."   —*Slate*

"In a new graphic memoir, the civil rights leader shows youth how to get in trouble—good trouble."   —*In These Times*

March: Book Three © 2016 John Lewis and Andrew Aydin.

Written by John Lewis and Andrew Aydin
Art by Nate Powell

Published by Top Shelf Productions
PO Box 1282
Marietta, GA 30061-1282
USA

Editor-in-Chief: Chris Staros

Edited by Leigh Walton
Coloring on Three-Volume Collected Slipcase Edition: José Villarrubia
Designed by Chris Ross and Nate Powell

Visit our online catalog at www.topshelfcomix.com.

Printed in Canada.

2020   2019   2018   2017   2016   3   5   7   9   10   8   6   4   2